SCHOLASTIC

Fountas & Pinnell

Comprehension Clubs

Deep Reading · Deep Thinking · Deep Discussion

Credits: p. 144 (Monitor): © Tanatat/Dreamstime

ISBN-13: 978-0-545-53391-1
ISBN-10: 0-545-53391-0

Table of Contents

Characteristics of Units of Study

Assessment & Forms

Technology

Comprehension Clubs and the Common Core State Standards

Comprehension Clubs Units at a Glance

Research Base & Bibliography

Welcome!

Dear Colleagues in Literacy Teaching:

As teachers, one of our greatest challenges is teaching readers to comprehend texts. We want them to articulate deep understandings and demonstrate their developing proficiency in the classroom and on tests. But in the pursuit of these important goals, we need to bear in mind one guiding principle: books must be worth understanding, talking about, and reading. Children need access to worthy texts, and they must experience and understand them at a deep level.

In the critical years—kindergarten through Grade 5—children need to engage with a rich array of texts. Quality matters. So does quantity. The memorable books children read stay with them and continue to support their learning and enhance their lives. Reading supports thinking and expands intellectual powers. Readers do much more than process words and remember details. Readers grasp the larger ideas, connect texts with other texts, apply what the writer is saying to their own lives and world, fall in love with characters, notice the writer's craft, and evaluate and critique.

We have created *Comprehension Clubs* to support teachers in helping their students become proficient and joyful readers. Teaching for deep comprehension cannot be confined to one lesson or one short period of a day. Our students are engaged in comprehending a wide range of texts all day, every day, and we need to make the most of every opportunity to urge them to deeper levels of understanding.

Our goal is to expand students' understandings and enjoyment of texts through numerous opportunities to think, talk, and write about their thinking related to a variety of literary and informational texts. Such immersion—especially through talk—reflects and extends their thinking about complex, global ideas. When you create powerful, frequent opportunities for talking about texts, you offer your students a profound opportunity to learn vocabulary, enrich background knowledge, and develop literary understandings—the building blocks of comprehension.

Scholastic's *Comprehension Clubs* allows you to teach intentionally through theme sets that combine interactive read-alouds and facilitated book club discussions. You'll notice specific prompts to invite thinking within the text, beyond the text, and about the text. The prompts ensure that your students focus on the diverse books provided and engage in high-level thinking. With your guidance, your students will apply complex thinking—synthesizing, inferring, analyzing, and critiquing—to the comprehending of texts.

We have relished the process of reading and selecting high-quality texts and have organized them by the overarching ideas—topics, themes, and genres—that will help readers think across texts. You will find that the topics and themes in each unit of study support in-depth inquiry and joy in learning about oneself, others, and the world beyond. As students engage with the books—talk about them with each other, extend and refine their thinking through writing in their reader's notebooks, and share their learning through unit projects—they learn to apply these larger concepts to their own world. Every student deserves the intellectual rigor that *Comprehension Clubs* provides.

We know that you will enjoy reading, writing, and talking with your students about this rich collection of literary and informational texts. We are excited to share this exemplary set of resources with you to support the language and literacy achievement of every child you teach.

Sincerely,

Irene and Gay

Why *Comprehension Clubs*?

Because proficient reading is a complex process involving an intricate orchestration of multiple skills, strategies, and conceptual understandings also known as *systems of strategic actions* (Fountas & Pinnell, 2006). Each reader builds a system for processing texts that begins with early reading behaviors and becomes a network of strategic activities for reading increasingly complex texts.

Comprehension Clubs is . . .

* a comprehensive program with six themed units of study per grade, each organized in a spiraled curriculum that includes a collection of books and teaching materials that allow for rich, in-depth, text-based conversation about readings and complex, global ideas.

* a carefully selected library of interactive read-aloud anchor texts supported by topically relevant student book club titles, enabling students to do deep cross-textual analysis, to read widely across topics, and to build deep and sustaining background knowledge on developmentally appropriate topics.

* streaming audio support for every student book club title.

Comprehension Clubs provides . . .

* sufficiently complex texts worthy of being read, analyzed, thought about deeply, and discussed.

* extensive opportunities for all students to engage with texts and to talk and write about texts, in both interactive read-aloud sessions and student- or teacher-led book club sessions.

* texts, both fiction and informational, with a variety of important genres and text types.

* vocabulary support.

* comprehension support.

* information about the supportive and challenging features of given texts.

* assessment opportunities.

* audio support for all self-selected student book club books.

* pacing options.

* teacher and student materials that model and support close reading; deep, text-dependent analysis; and academic discussion.

* options for culminating text-based unit projects that integrate reading, writing, speaking, and listening.

Components

You can purchase *Comprehension Clubs* by **individual theme units** or by **grade-level sets**.

Each Grade-Level Set Includes

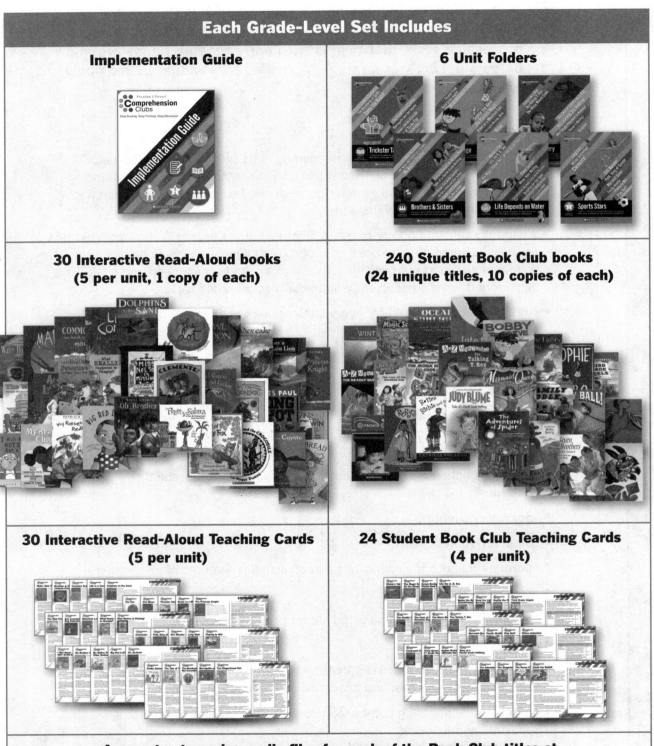

Implementation Guide

6 Unit Folders

30 Interactive Read-Aloud books
(5 per unit, 1 copy of each)

240 Student Book Club books
(24 unique titles, 10 copies of each)

30 Interactive Read-Aloud Teaching Cards
(5 per unit)

24 Student Book Club Teaching Cards
(4 per unit)

**Access to streaming audio files for each of the Book Club titles at
http://www.comprehensionclubs.scholastic.com.**

Each Individual Theme Set Includes

Implementation Guide

1 Unit Folder

5 Interactive Read-Aloud books

40 Student Book Club books
(4 unique titles, 10 copies of each)

5 Interactive Read-Aloud Teaching Cards

4 Student Book Club Teaching Cards

Access to streaming audio files for each of the Book Club titles at
http://www.comprehensionclubs.scholastic.com.

Units of Study Matrix

Each theme–based unit of study is framed around a unifying topic, theme, or genre. The spiraling nature of the curriculum introduces your students to increasingly complex text requiring stronger, more advanced systems of strategic actions.

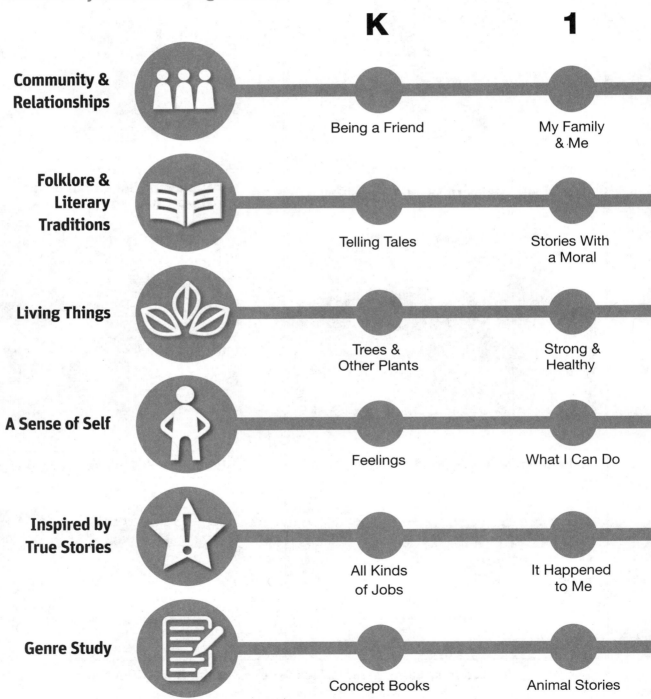

	K	**1**
Community & Relationships	Being a Friend	My Family & Me
Folklore & Literary Traditions	Telling Tales	Stories With a Moral
Living Things	Trees & Other Plants	Strong & Healthy
A Sense of Self	Feelings	What I Can Do
Inspired by True Stories	All Kinds of Jobs	It Happened to Me
Genre Study	Concept Books	Animal Stories

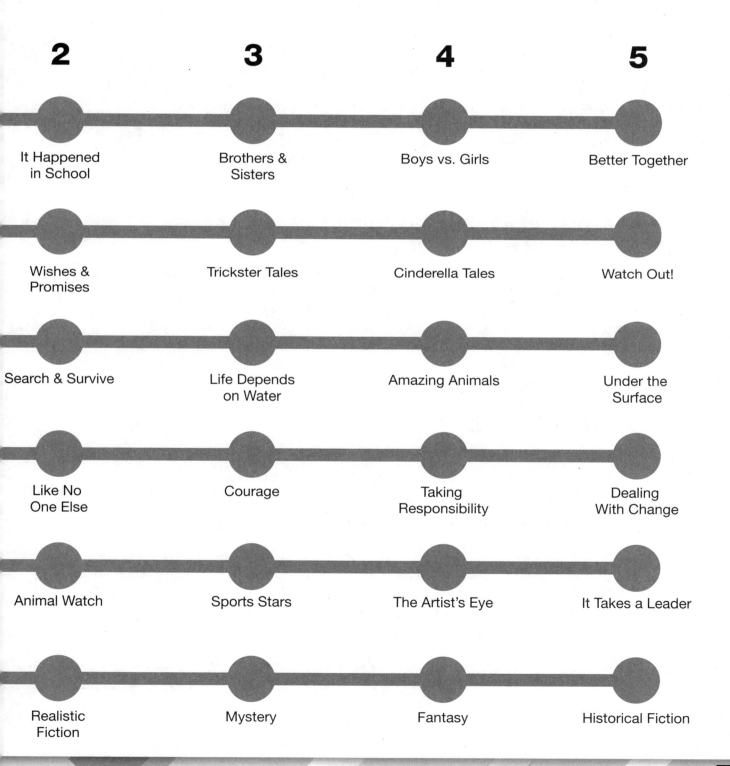

2

It Happened in School

Wishes & Promises

Search & Survive

Like No One Else

Animal Watch

Realistic Fiction

3

Brothers & Sisters

Trickster Tales

Life Depends on Water

Courage

Sports Stars

Mystery

4

Boys vs. Girls

Cinderella Tales

Amazing Animals

Taking Responsibility

The Artist's Eye

Fantasy

5

Better Together

Watch Out!

Under the Surface

Dealing With Change

It Takes a Leader

Historical Fiction

Making the Matrix Work for You

Scholastic's *Comprehension Clubs* is an engaging, age-appropriate collection of fiction and informational books grouped into units of study with teaching support. The books are categorized by theme, topic, and genre. Additionally, each book is tied to a Unit of Study Matrix and showcases a new strategic action; the books reflect an upward spiral of complexity.

Across the year and across the grades, the texts become more sophisticated conceptually and linguistically. The readings offer opportunities for your students to build vocabulary, expand content and themes, extend knowledge of genre and text structure, offer deeper literary connections, and expand reading power for processing increasingly complex text. Further, the matrix brings coherence and provides deeper conceptual thinking that cannot be accomplished by reading any one title alone.

Advantages of an Age-Appropriate Book Collection

Within the supportive talk structure of the interactive read-aloud and student book club (with audio support), student reading levels are not an issue. Indeed, *all* students are supported by the collaborative conversation surrounding the books and ideas, authors, and understandings. All students will be engaged by the high-quality, intriguing texts and will be able to understand the texts to deepen their knowledge. The age-appropriate collection offers many advantages, including those enumerated below.

Comprehension Clubs

- provides experience with a wide variety of texts within each unit of study.
- promotes growth toward grade-level reading proficiency; each book offers a reading challenge.
- makes it easier to select books for whole-class discussion and student book clubs.
- lends itself to flexible grouping.
- provides a way to access and assess students' progress.
- provides an exemplary book collection that can be expanded over time.

Flexibility of Use

In general, what makes a book easy or difficult to understand is complex, relative, and variable from student to student. But again, since your students engage with each book within the supportive context of a read-aloud or a book club discussion, every student can interact with a meaning of the text through the rich conversation that surrounds the book. And the close reading, rereading, and writing that students do help them become confident readers in multiple ways. Supporting students as they take ownership of their own learning tells students that they can learn on their own and build their knowledge and interests as lifelong, avid readers.

Text Variety

Readers benefit from experiencing a variety of texts. Within a varied set, multiple factors make books appealing and accessible to all children. These factors include age appropriateness and conceptual, topical, and thematic curricular goals. Further, a wide range of text characteristics, some more challenging than others, occur within literary and informational texts. Simply said, when working with heterogeneous groups in classroom reading, a broad base of text provides the richest learning opportunities. For this reason, the units of study include both literary and informational texts. Most include one or more examples of the following, as developmentally appropriate:

- sophisticated picture books that provide an opportunity to expand vocabulary, interpret stories, and recognize how illustrations contribute to the understanding of a story. Like a short story, a picture book provides the advanced reader with complex reading material that does not take several days to complete.

- informational books that are generally shorter. These present complex ideas along with some technical language. They challenge students to acquire and discuss ideas and information and to go beyond the text to research topics of interest.

- longer stories, chapter books, and novels. These longer selections provide an opportunity for readers to sustain reading over time, focusing on details and getting to know the characters as they develop.

Building Community

The collaborative nature of both the interactive read-aloud and the student book club discussions helps create a cooperative, productive, literate community in which all students are recognized for their strengths and respected for their ideas.

Further, the scaffolding provided by the streaming audio for each book club title allows students, even struggling readers or English language learners who need extra support, to access the titles and join the discussions with fellow students. All students will be granted access to grade-level thinking, vocabulary, concepts, and ideas, regardless of their reading levels.

And the matrix, with themes spiraled across the grades, ensures that all teachers within a school community will begin to develop a shared language about books and about reading culture.

After all, community begins with communication. The rich text talk that surrounds shared literary experiences evolves into a familiar and inspiring common language about books, authors, and classroom routines. A shared language makes classroom communication more meaningful, inviting, and efficient.

Overarching Unit Goals

Comprehension Clubs' **spiral curriculum revisits the same basic topics at each grade, exploring concepts at a higher level of difficulty and in greater depth. Each unit can stand on its own; however, the impact is even more powerful when students progress through** *Comprehension Clubs***, unit by unit and grade by grade.**

Community & Relationships focuses on writers who show how people negotiate relationships. *As students progress, they explore friendship, family dynamics, school situations, the special rivalry and support between siblings, how misunderstandings and assumptions can complicate relationships between girls and boys, and finally, how people team up to accomplish important goals.*

Folklore & Literary Traditions focuses on classics from a variety of cultural traditions, and key elements of folklore. *As students advance, they gain familiarity with well-known characters, stories that teach lessons, magical wishes and promises, tricksters, variations on Cinderella, the significance of warnings, and how folklore provides a foundation for contemporary fantasy.*

Living Things focuses on how authors of informational texts present facts and persuade readers to share their opinions. *Students build knowledge and vocabulary about life science, spiraling from an exploration of plants, to wellness, to how animals survive in the wild, to the importance of water to life, to a deeper dive into animal behavior, and then returning to a look at the tools and techniques scientists use to learn more about the human body.*

A Sense of Self focuses on how authors explain the significance of emotions and the role feelings play in building confidence, courage, and empathy: qualities necessary for success in life. *Students begin by using their reading to build vocabulary that names and describes feeling and progress to exploring stories that focus on how characters recognize their abilities, build confidence to face their fears, take responsibility for their actions, and deal with change.*

Inspired by True Stories focuses on biographies and real-world situations. *Beginning with an overview of jobs, students go on to read autobiographical stories from favorite authors, and progress to explore how caring for and studying animals changes people's lives. In Grades 3–5, students explore the qualities that allowed people to excel in sports, in the arts, and as leaders.*

Genre Study focuses on analyzing and comparing how authors approach a genre. Students will think deeply about the decisions authors make and consider how this decision-making process may help them craft their own writing. *The six genres highlighted as students progress from grade to grade are concept books, animal stories, realistic fiction, mystery, fantasy, and historical fiction.*

How *Comprehension Clubs* Works in Your Classroom

What follows is a quick, step-by-step overview of the instructional routine for each unit of study. The good news is that the routine will be familiar to you because you are already reading aloud in your classroom and your students are already reading independently. You will need to adjust every step according to the age of your students and their unique needs and interests.

As an example, let's follow one complete unit of study, *Life Depends on Water*, from the Grade 3 "Living Things" theme set.

① Unit Folder

Review the Unit Folder, including the inside flaps and the back cover for a comprehensive overview of the unit, the titles, the learning goals, and the big idea that binds the books together conceptually. You'll also find a quick-read-overview of recurring themes, the literary focus, a note about social and emotional development, and a reading-writing connection.

② The Interactive Read-Alouds

Read aloud interactively to your students each one of your read-aloud titles (typically, one book per day) during your whole-class instructional time. Prepare for the read-aloud using the corresponding teaching card; the book summary, author note, and overview of key understandings will help familiarize you with the book. Suggested Stopping Points to Invite Thinking elicit students' analysis and require students to cite textual evidence as you guide them in mastery of the Key Understandings.

Use the back of the card to **Support, Assess,** and **Scaffold and Extend** the learning for students. Always connect Key Understandings of each title to other titles in the unit. Note similarities and differences, as well as recurring themes, big ideas, genres, and vocabulary reflected across texts.

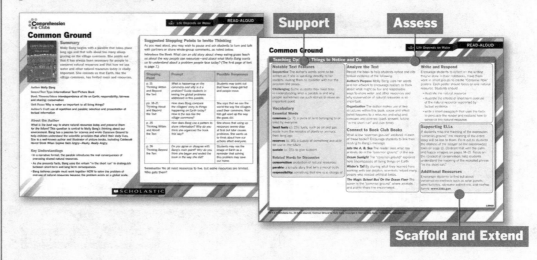

Introduce each of the four Student Book Club books with a very brief booktalk that stems from your knowledge of your students coupled with your analysis of the text on Day 2 of the unit. Prepare by familiarizing yourself with the teaching card and the book. Allow students to choose the title that interests them most, pass out the books, and encourage students to begin reading during their independent reading time in class or at home.

Use streaming audio to support students who will benefit from hearing the text read aloud by accessing the audio versions of the book club books at *http://www.comprehensionclubs.scholastic.com*. Type in the user name "hear" and the password "books" and follow the prompts on the site to find specific audiobooks.

Remind older students to prepare for the club by recording their questions, observations, and ideas, and citing textual evidence in their readers' notebooks. They should capture what they think is most important, what they do not understand, and where they want to make cross-textual connections.

Scaffold younger students to read and think about their books as developmentally appropriate. Suggestions and ideas are provided on the teaching cards.

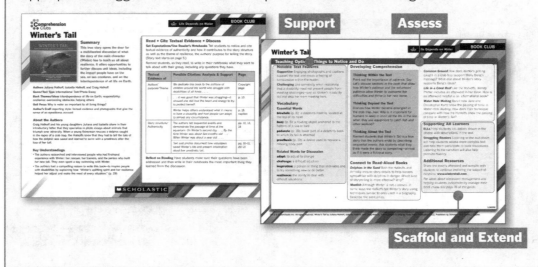

(4) Facilitated Student Book Club Sessions

Meet with each book club, one club at a time; depending on the age of your students and their experience—and the complexity of the book they are discussing—give them 15 to 30 minutes to discuss and probe the book. Use the teaching card to help students notice the Essential Vocabulary words and use suggestions for prompting a rich discussion. As students engage in discussion, encourage them to build on the thinking of their peers and support their own thinking by citing specific evidence from the text. Use the back of the card to **Support**, **Assess**, and **Scaffold and Extend** learning for students. Always connect each title to other titles in the unit, noting key understandings as well as similarities and differences.

(5) Unit Wrap-Up

Connect the book club books to the read-aloud books as you encourage student conversation about the overarching theme and big ideas that all nine books reflect.

What are the essential understandings of the unit of study? Keep in mind your overarching instructional goals: to develop your students' strategic actions—to expand their knowledge of content and themes and deepen their understanding of genre and text structure; to help them acquire and use new vocabulary and express understandings through conversation and writing; and to build a vital literary community centered around books and ideas.

Invite further academic investigation through collaborative unit projects, as described on pages 86–105 of this guide.

Pacing

The pacing for *Comprehension Clubs* is flexible and can accommodate different classroom needs, but each unit will typically last 2–3 weeks. See the Planning and Pacing Chart in this guide.

The Teaching Cards at a Glance

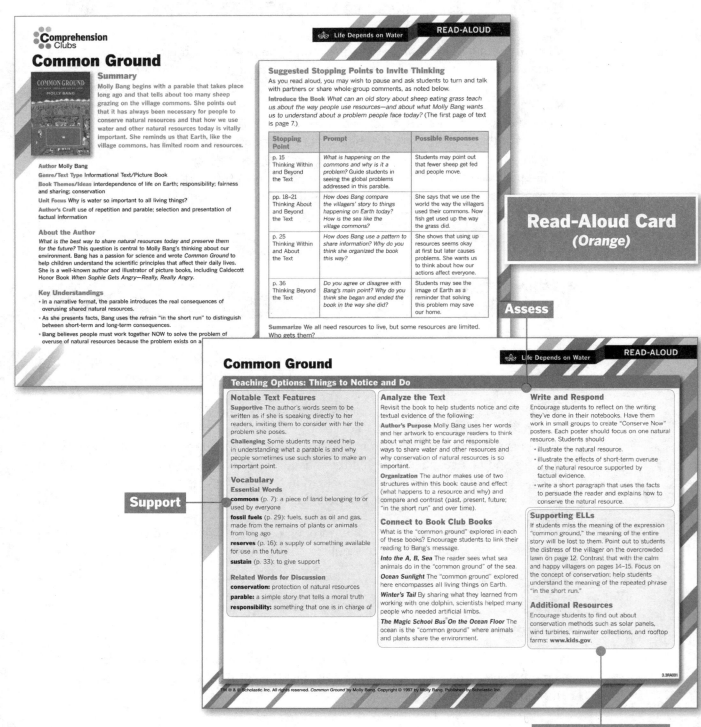

Common Ground

Read-Aloud Card (Orange)

Summary

Molly Bang begins with a parable that takes place long ago and that tells about too many sheep grazing on the village commons. She points out that it has always been necessary for people to conserve natural resources and that how we use water and other natural resources today is vitally important. She reminds us that Earth, like the village commons, has limited room and resources.

Author Molly Bang

Genre/Text Type Informational Text/Picture Book

Book Themes/Ideas interdependence of life on Earth; responsibility; fairness and sharing; conservation

Unit Focus Why is water so important to all living things?

Author's Craft use of repetition and parable; selection and presentation of factual information

About the Author

What is the best way to share natural resources today and preserve them for the future? This question is central to Molly Bang's thinking about our environment. Bang has a passion for science and wrote *Common Ground* to help children understand the scientific principles that affect their daily lives. She is a well-known author and illustrator of picture books, including Caldecott Honor Book *When Sophie Gets Angry—Really, Really Angry*.

Key Understandings

- In a narrative format, the parable introduces the real consequences of overusing shared natural resources.
- As she presents facts, Bang uses the refrain "in the short run" to distinguish between short-term and long-term consequences.
- Bang believes people must work together NOW to solve the problem of overuse of natural resources because the problem exists on a ...

Suggested Stopping Points to Invite Thinking

As you read aloud, you may wish to pause and ask students to turn and talk with partners or share whole-group comments, as noted below.

Introduce the Book *What can an old story about sheep eating grass teach us about the way people use resources—and about what Molly Bang wants us to understand about a problem people face today?* (The first page of text is page 7.)

Stopping Point	Prompt	Possible Responses
p. 15 Thinking Within and Beyond the Text	*What is happening on the commons and why is it a problem?* Guide students in seeing the global problems addressed in this parable.	Students may point out that fewer sheep get fed and people move.
pp. 18–21 Thinking About and Beyond the Text	*How does Bang compare the villagers' story to things happening on Earth today? How is the sea like the village commons?*	She says that we use the world the way the villagers used their commons. Now fish get used up the way the grass did.
p. 25 Thinking Within and About the Text	*How does Bang use a pattern to share information? Why do you think she organized the book this way?*	She shows that using up resources seems okay at first but later causes problems. She wants us to think about how our actions affect everyone.
p. 36 Thinking Beyond the Text	*Do you agree or disagree with Bang's main point? Why do you think she began and ended the book in the way she did?*	Students may see the image of Earth as a reminder that solving this problem may save our home.

Summarize We all need resources to live, but some resources are limited. Who gets them?

Assess

Support

Common Ground

Life Depends on Water — READ-ALOUD

Teaching Options: Things to Notice and Do

Notable Text Features

Supportive The author's words seem to be written as if she is speaking directly to her readers, inviting them to consider with her the problem she poses.

Challenging Some students may need help in understanding what a parable is and why people sometimes use such stories to make an important point.

Vocabulary

Essential Words

commons (p. 7): a piece of land belonging to or used by everyone

fossil fuels (p. 29): fuels, such as oil and gas, made from the remains of plants or animals from long ago

reserves (p. 16): a supply of something available for use in the future

sustain (p. 33): to give support

Related Words for Discussion

conservation: protection of natural resources

parable: a simple story that tells a moral truth

responsibility: something that one is in charge of

Analyze the Text

Revisit the book to help students notice and cite textual evidence of the following:

Author's Purpose Molly Bang uses her words and her artwork to encourage readers to think about what might be fair and responsible ways to share water and other resources and why conservation of natural resources is so important.

Organization The author makes use of two structures within this book: cause and effect (what happens to a resource and why) and compare and contrast (past, present, future; "in the short run" and over time).

Connect to Book Club Books

What is the "common ground" explored in each of these books? Encourage students to link their reading to Bang's message.

Into the A, B, Sea The reader sees what sea animals do in the "common ground" of the sea.

Ocean Sunlight The "common ground" explored here encompasses all living things on Earth.

Winter's Tail By sharing what they learned from working with one dolphin, scientists helped many people who needed artificial limbs.

The Magic School Bus On the Ocean Floor The ocean is the "common ground" where animals and plants share the environment.

Write and Respond

Encourage students to reflect on the writing they've done in their notebooks. Have them work in small groups to create "Conserve Now" posters. Each poster should focus on one natural resource. Students should

- illustrate the natural resource.
- illustrate the effects of short-term overuse of the natural resource supported by factual evidence.
- write a short paragraph that uses the facts to persuade the reader and explains how to conserve the natural resource.

Supporting ELLs

If students miss the meaning of the expression "common ground," the meaning of the entire story will be lost to them. Point out to students the distress of the villager on the overcrowded lawn on page 12. Contrast that with the calm and happy villagers on pages 14–15. Focus on the concept of conservation; help students understand the meaning of the repeated phrase "in the short run."

Additional Resources

Encourage students to find out about conservation methods such as solar panels, wind turbines, rainwater collections, and rooftop farms: www.kids.gov.

3.3RA001

Scaffold and Extend

Each teaching card for both the Interactive Read-Aloud and the Student Book Club titles provides teachers with options for supporting students' reading and comprehension, assessing students' understanding, and scaffolding and extending the lesson.

Comprehension Clubs
Winter's Tail

WINTER'S TAIL
How One Little Dolphin Learned to Swim Again

JULIANA HATKOFF, ISABELLA HATKOFF, CRAIG HATKOFF
SCHOLASTIC

Summary

This true story opens the door for a multifaceted discussion of what the story of the main character (Winter) has to teach us all about resilience. It offers opportunities to further discuss unit ideas, including the impact people have on the sea, on sea creatures, and on the interdependence of all life on Earth.

Authors Juliana Hatkoff, Isabella Hatkoff, and Craig Hatkoff

Genre/Text Type Informational Text/Photo Essay

Book Themes/Ideas interdependence of life on Earth; responsibility; resilience; overcoming obstacles; helping others

Unit Focus Why is water so important to all living things?

Author's Craft reporting style; factual evidence and photographs that give the sense of an eyewitness account

About the Authors

Craig Hatkoff and his young daughters Juliana and Isabella share in their introductory letter that they specialize in photo essays about animals that triumph over adversity. When a young fisherman rescues a dolphin caught in the ropes of a crab trap, the Hatkoffs knew that they had to tell the tale of how the dolphin was saved and learned to swim with a prosthesis after the loss of her tail.

Key Understandings

- The authors researched and interviewed people who had firsthand experience with Winter; her rescuer, her trainers, and the person who built her new tail. They even spent a day swimming with Winter.
- The authors had a compelling reason to write this book—to inspire people with disabilities by explaining how "Winter's uplifting spirit and her resilience helped her adjust and make the most of every situation." (p. 20)

Read • Cite Textual Evidence • Discuss

Set Expectations/Use Reader's Notebooks Tell students to notice and cite textual evidence of authenticity and how it contributes to the story structure as well as the theme of resilience, the authors' purpose for telling the story. (Story text starts on page 5.)

Remind students, as they read, to write in their notebooks what they want to talk about with their group, including any questions they have.

Textual Evidence of	Possible Citation: Analysis & Support	Page
Authors' purpose/Theme	*We dedicate this book to the millions of children around the world who struggle with disabilities of all kinds . . . .*	Copyright page
	. . . it was good that Winter was struggling—it showed she still had the heart and energy to try to protect herself.	p. 10
	Winter helps others understand what it means to have a disability and how people can adapt to almost any circumstance.	p. 18 caption
Story structure/Authenticity	The authors tell sequential events and demonstrate the passage of time at the aquarium: *On Winter's second day . . .; By the time Winter was about five months old . . .; When Winter was about a year old . . . .*	pp. 13, 14, 18
	Text and photos document how volunteers saved Winter's life and present information about her prosthetic tail.	pp. 10–11, 20–21

Reflect on Reading Have students make sure their questions have been addressed and then write in their notebooks the most important thing they learned from the discussion.

Book Club Card
(Blue)

Assess

Winter's Tail

Teaching Options: Things to Notice and Do

Notable Text Features

Supportive Engaging photographs and captions support the text and create a feeling of compassion within the reader.

Challenging Use sensitivity when explaining that a disability need not prevent people from meeting challenges—just as Winter's disability did not stop her from meeting hers.

Vocabulary
Essential Words

blowhole (p. 6): a dolphin's nostrils, located at the top of its head

buoy (p. 5): a floating object anchored to the bottom of a sea or lake

peduncle (p. 18): lower part of a dolphin's back to which its tail is attached

prosthesis (p. 19): a device used to replace a missing body part

Related Words for Discussion

adapt: to adjust to change

challenge: a difficult situation

inspiration: a person or thing that motivates one to try something new or do better

resilience: the ability to deal with difficult situations

Support

Developing Comprehension

Thinking Within the Text
Point out the importance of patience. Say: *Let's discuss sections in the book that show how Winter's patience and the volunteers' patience allow Winter to overcome her difficulties and thrive in her new home.*

Thinking Beyond the Text
Discuss how Winter became entangled in the crab trap. Ask: *Why is it important for humans to keep in mind all the life in the sea when they use equipment to catch fish and other seafood?*

Thinking About the Text
Remind students that *Winter's Tail* is a true story that the authors wrote by describing sequential events. Ask students what they think made the story so compelling—almost as if it were a fictional story.

Connect to Read-Aloud Books

Dolphins in the Sand Both the Hatkoffs and Arnosky include story details to help readers sympathize with dolphins in danger. Which kind of storytelling is more effective? Why?

Manfish Although Winter is not a person, in some ways the Hatkoffs tell Winter's story using

Common Ground How does Winter's getting caught in a crab trap support Molly Bang's message? What else about Winter's story supports Bang's ideas?

Life in a Coral Reef Like the Hatkoffs, Wendy Pfeffer includes an afterword in her book. How is an afterword helpful in an informational book?

Water Hole Waiting Recall how Jane and Christopher Kurtz show the passing of time in *Water Hole Waiting.* How does their technique compare with how the Hatkoffs show the passing of time in *Winter's Tail*?

Supporting All Learners

ELLs Help students link details shown in the photos with descriptions in the text.

Struggling Readers Listening to the audiobook will help students access more complex text and help them participate in book discussions. Listening to the narration will also help promote fluency.

Additional Resources

Share the book's afterword and website with students to continue exploring the subject of dolphins: **www.winterstail.com**.

For ideas about classroom management and helping students independently manage their book clubs, see page 76 of the guide.

Scaffold and Extend

3.3BC002

They also provide you with enough information to know what the Key Understandings are for each title, conduct an effective interactive read-aloud session, and actively support students when they might not be working effectively or need additional support and prompts to spark conversation.

Deepening Comprehension With the Interactive Read-Aloud

Research shows that reading aloud to children is one of the best ways to spend your instructional time with them. But reading aloud *plus* talking with children about the book you are reading is even better. Indeed, the research is indisputable. The most effective read-alouds are those in which children are not just sitting passively, listening, but are actively participating, absorbing the story, turning it over in their minds, asking questions, analyzing the text from multiple angles, and in all ways demonstrating their engagement. Known as *dialogic* or *interactive*, these read-alouds result in student gains in vocabulary (Hargrave & Sénéchal, 2000), comprehension strategies, and story schema (Van den Broek, 1997), and concept development (Wasik et al., 2001).

However, simply inviting students to talk during interactive read-alouds does not provide the needed learning boost. It's the *textual analysis*—deep, intentional conversation about the text—that makes the difference. You can lead your students into this sort of analytical thinking by modeling what it looks like and sounds like, by offering thoughtful comments, and by asking thought-provoking questions (Dickinson & Smith, 1994; Fountas & Pinnell, 2006, 2012; Harwayne, 2008; Serravallo, 2012). You can also model for them how to identify and cite textual evidence.

As the name suggests, the read-aloud is truly *interactive* (Fountas & Pinnell, 2006). As you read aloud to your students, invite them to participate, make comments, extend the ideas of their peers, evaluate the author's point of view, and ask and respond to questions. In ways that are akin to those of an orchestra conductor, help manage the conversation. This may include asking your students to turn and talk with a neighbor about their thinking, offering students opportunities to participate with safe, scaffolded support, such as the prompts suggested on the teaching cards, or simply modeling the internal questioning process of a good reader. Students quickly learn how to comment, critique, and claim their own thoughts beyond the usual "I liked it" or "I didn't like it."

During an interactive read-aloud, students learn to:

- focus on a text.

- use suitable language when talking about a text.

- listen actively and respect the ideas of others.

- build on the comments of others.

- back up their opinions with evidence from a text.

Preparing for the Read-Aloud

Your read-aloud sessions will be most successful if you establish a predictable structure that your students come to anticipate. The structure also makes clear that students are to assume an active role. To that end, make sure that every student can hear the text you are reading aloud and can see any illustrations.

In order to ensure that you get the most out of your read-aloud, spend time preparing, before you even start reading. Keep in mind these steps to guarantee your success—and the success of your students.

- Be sure to preview the book and the teaching card before you read the book aloud.

- Consider the book's content and the scaffolds you may need to provide for students' language and conceptual development.

- Slip in a few sticky notes to identify your stopping points—where you will pause to think aloud, guide a turn-and-talk, or ask questions about the text.

- Have in mind the instructional points you want to make as well as the deeply thoughtful moments you want to create.

Read-Aloud Cards for In-Depth Teaching

When using the Interactive Read-Aloud Teaching Card, take note of the following features.

Before the Interactive Read-Aloud

(1) Book Summary This information has been provided as a resource so that you have an understanding of the book itself and why it was chosen for inclusion in the text set. It is not intended to be read aloud or shared with students.

(2) Author

(3) Genre/Text Type Remember, form and format follow function. Helping students understand the characteristics of the genre and text type is important to overall comprehension.

Comprehension Clubs

🌿 Life Depends on Water | **READ-ALOUD**

Common Ground

(1) Summary
Molly Bang begins with a parable that takes place long ago and that tells about too many sheep grazing on the village commons. She points out that it has always been necessary for people to conserve natural resources and that how we use water and other natural resources today is vitally important. She reminds us that Earth, like the village commons, has limited room and resources.

(2) Author Molly Bang
Genre/Text Type Informational Text/Picture Book **(3)**
(4) Book Themes/Ideas interdependence of life on Earth; responsibility; fairness and sharing; conservation
Unit Focus Why is water so important to all living things? **(5)**
(6) Author's Craft use of repetition and parable; selection and presentation of factual information

(7) About the Author
What is the best way to share natural resources today and preserve them for the future? This question is central to Molly Bang's thinking about our environment. Bang has a passion for science and wrote *Common Ground* to help children understand the scientific principles that affect their daily lives. She is a well-known author and illustrator of picture books, including Caldecott Honor Book *When Sophie Gets Angry—Really, Really Angry.*

(8) Key Understandings
• In a narrative format, the parable introduces the real consequences of overusing shared natural resources.
• As she presents facts, Bang uses the refrain "in the short run" to distinguish between short-term and long-term consequences.
• Bang believes people must work together NOW to solve the problem of overuse of natural resources because the problem exists on a global scale.

(9) Suggested Stopping Points to Invite Thinking
As you read aloud, you may wish to pause and ask students to turn and talk with partners or share whole-group comments, as noted below.

(10) Introduce the Book *What can an old story about sheep eating grass teach us about the way people use resources—and about what Molly Bang wants us to understand about a problem people face today?* (The first page of text is page 7.)

(11)

Stopping Point	Prompt	Possible Responses
p. 15 Thinking Within and Beyond the Text	*What is happening on the commons and why is it a problem?* Guide students in seeing the global problems addressed in this parable.	Students may point out that fewer sheep get fed and people move.
pp. 18–21 Thinking About and Beyond the Text	*How does Bang compare the villagers' story to things happening on Earth today? How is the sea like the village commons?*	She says that we use the world the way the villagers used their commons. Now fish get used up the way the grass did.
p. 25 Thinking Within and About the Text	*How does Bang use a pattern to share information? Why do you think she organized the book this way?*	She shows that using up resources seems okay at first but later causes problems. She wants us to think about how our actions affect everyone.
p. 36 Thinking Beyond the Text	*Do you agree or disagree with Bang's main point? Why do you think she began and ended the book in the way she did?*	Students may see the image of Earth as a reminder that solving this problem may save our home.

(12) Summarize We all need resources to live, but some resources are limited. Who gets them?

SCHOLASTIC

4 **Book Themes/Ideas** These tie directly to the Unit Focus, to the Key Understandings and expected learning outcomes of the particular title, and to additional titles in the unit.

5 **Unit Focus** This focus was first highlighted on the unit folder and should remain foremost in your thinking as you read aloud.

6 **Author's Craft** In alignment with effective practices around mentor texts, *Comprehension Clubs* strives to point out to learners the craft behind the presentation of information.

Common Ground

🌿 Life Depends on Water   **READ-ALOUD**

Teaching Options: Things to Notice and Do

13 **Notable Text Features**

Supportive The author's words seem to be written as if she is speaking directly to her readers, inviting them to consider with her the problem she poses.

Challenging Some students may need help in understanding what a parable is and why people sometimes use such stories to make an important point.

14 **Vocabulary**

Essential Words

commons (p. 7): a piece of land belonging to or used by everyone

fossil fuels (p. 29): fuels, such as oil and gas, made from the remains of plants or animals from long ago

reserves (p. 16): a supply of something available for use in the future

sustain (p. 33): to give support

Related Words for Discussion

conservation: protection of natural resources

parable: a simple story that tells a moral truth

responsibility: something that one is in charge of

15 **Analyze the Text**

Revisit the book to help students notice and cite textual evidence of the following:

Author's Purpose Molly Bang uses her words and her artwork to encourage readers to think about what might be fair and responsible ways to share water and other resources and why conservation of natural resources is so important.

Organization The author makes use of two structures within this book: cause and effect (what happens to a resource and why) and compare and contrast (past, present, future; "in the short run" and over time).

16 **Connect to Book Club Books**

What is the "common ground" explored in each of these books? Encourage students to link their reading to Bang's message.

Into the A, B, Sea The reader sees what sea animals do in the "common ground" of the sea.

Ocean Sunlight The "common ground" explored here encompasses all living things on Earth.

Winter's Tail By sharing what they learned from working with one dolphin, scientists helped many people who needed artificial limbs.

The Magic School Bus® On the Ocean Floor The ocean is the "common ground" where animals and plants share the environment.

17 **Write and Respond**

Encourage students to reflect on the writing they've done in their notebooks. Have them work in small groups to create "Conserve Now" posters. Each poster should focus on one natural resource. Students should

• illustrate the natural resource.

• illustrate the effects of short-term overuse of the natural resource supported by factual evidence.

• write a short paragraph that uses the facts to persuade the reader and explains how to conserve the natural resource.

18 **Supporting ELLs**

If students miss the meaning of the expression "common ground," the meaning of the entire story will be lost to them. Point out to students the distress of the villager on the overcrowded lawn on page 12. Contrast that with the calm and happy villagers on pages 14–15. Focus on the concept of conservation; help students understand the meaning of the repeated phrase "in the short run."

19 **Additional Resources**

Encourage students to find out about conservation methods such as solar panels, wind turbines, rainwater collections, and rooftop farms: **www.kids.gov**.

3.3RA001

7 **About the Author** Providing students with information about the author, where appropriate, can deepen understanding and enliven conversation.

8 **Key Understandings** These reveal the heart of the instruction for every title and tie directly to information on the rest of the card, including stopping points for discussion as well as a deep analysis of author's craft.

9 **Suggested Stopping Points to Invite Thinking** These stopping points reinforce the Key Understandings and can be important moments for you to model citing textual evidence to support thinking within, about, and beyond the text.

10 **Introduce the Book** Provide students with a very brief introduction to the story and set a purpose for reading without giving away any of the deep thinking and analysis students are about to undertake as interactive listeners.

During the Read-Aloud: Reading the Text and Using the Shared Talk Routine

When a read-aloud is done well, it is a performance. In our view, reading aloud is an art akin to storytelling; the telling is as crucial to the listeners as is the tale itself. When reading aloud, your voice reflects and supports the meaning of the story.

11 **Use the Stopping Points and Prompts** Briefly comment, ask a question, or invite your students to share their thinking. Monitor comprehension, noting possible responses. Continue reading to the end of the book.

- Think about the book together, citing textual evidence to back up each observation and opinion. Your students may want to turn and talk with partners or share whole-group comments.

- Connect the book to other read-alouds or book club titles you've read and enjoyed together; note similarities and differences as well as recurring themes, big ideas, genres, text features, language and literary features, and vocabulary reflected across the text set.

Routines to Encourage Peer Talk

In shared text talk everyone is an equal partner in the meaning-making process. No one controls the conversation (although you facilitate, especially as your students are learning how to explore text analysis through an interactive read-aloud). What this means is that each member of the club must listen intently to what is being said, wait for an opening in the conversation, and slip in with his or her response. Help your students learn to use active listening and natural turn-taking.

You may feel uncomfortable allowing students to speak without first raising their hands. But try, over time, to help your students develop real conversational turn-taking, so you don't need a "traffic monitor" to signal who can speak and who must wait. To help your students succeed, spend time introducing each talk routine that encourages peer-to-peer talk.

We suggest three configurations:

Pair Talk One of the most effective ways to spark conversation and thinking is the instructional strategy, *turn and talk*. Try these guidelines:

- Students have an identified partner. At the signal "turn and talk" or "turn and talk about ____," they turn to each other (when seated on the floor or in chairs) and have time for one or two quick interchanges about the issue at hand. (If you have an uneven number of students, you can partner with a student.)

- Partners talk and then turn to another pair and quickly share a summary of what they have been saying.

Your students will easily learn the turn and talk routine with a quick share; both partners share their thoughts and always listen to each other thoughtfully and politely. After your demonstration with a partner, turn to your students and ask:

- Did you express your own ideas?
- Did you share quickly?
- Did you listen carefully to each other?

Threesome Talk After watching you demonstrate text talk with two partners, students try it themselves in a preassigned group of three. The routine is similar to pair talk, but students must be even more efficient and pace their talk so that all three can share.

Circle Talk in Two Pairs Again, demonstrate this configuration yourself before guiding your students to try it on their own. Have two partners turn to each other and talk about the text. Once your students are comfortable with this arrangement, they will be ready for the small group conversation of the book club.

After Sharing the Read-Aloud

12 **Summarize** Once you've completed the read-aloud, invite students to share their thinking. Share yours as well, but be careful not to dominate the conversation and overwhelm your students. The goal is to inspire them to talk—to engage in academic conversation about the book and topics. Acquiring the language of books and the language to talk about books is a cumulative process that builds over time, across books and discussions.

Support Student Learning

13 **Notable Text Features** It is important for you, as the teacher, to understand the supportive and challenging features of the text. Depending on the difficulties of a given text and your knowledge of your students' abilities, you may need to reread specific passages or point out additional items to either ensure or to deepen students' understanding.

14 **Vocabulary** We have distinguished between Tier 2 and Tier 3 words students will encounter during the read-aloud (Essential Words) from those that may not be in the book itself, but when understood, will enhance conversation and understanding (Related Words for Discussion). When meanings of words can be discovered through context, you can model and reinforce how to learn vocabulary from context clues. Where that isn't possible, you can define the words aloud for students, in student-friendly language. Definitions are provided here for your convenience.

Assess Understanding

(15) Analyze the Text and Cite Textual Evidence Help students discuss short, highlighted portions of the text in depth with their classmates. Help them feel confident in the skills they are building in extending their knowledge of textual analysis. Because students will not have the text in front of them for the read-alouds, it is important to read the relevant passages aloud again.

(16) Connect to Book Club Books Depending on where you are in your read-aloud and student book club cycle, you may need to modify the language provided here. But it is important to model comparing and contrasting topics, ideas, treatments, themes, genres, text features, language, literary features, and vocabulary across multiple texts.

(17) Write and Respond Encouraging students to write about text provides them with the opportunity to absorb content more deeply. It also provides you with an opportunity to evaluate their comprehension and their grasp of the key ideas and understandings—both of a given title and across the theme units.

Scaffold and Extend

(18) Supporting ELLs It is important to scaffold English Language Learners through the read-aloud process to ensure they are part of the growing learning community. Specific strategies are provided.

(19) Additional Resources These resources provide additional research opportunities and offer a relevant technology connection to each read-aloud title.

Supporting All Learning With Facilitated Student Book Clubs

Learning is often most effective as a facilitated activity. Within the safety and security of a book club we learn easily and joyfully. It's helpful to think of the book club discussion as a literature "investigation" in which participants, with guidance from the teacher, "try out tentative ideas, search for information to confirm or refute their thinking, and build on one another's ideas." Within their book clubs, students feel safe to take the risks that are necessary for learning and—thanks to the interactive read-aloud— they are thoroughly versed in effective "text talk" (Fountas & Pinnell, 2006).

In book clubs, students learn to control their own thinking, reading, writing, and talking with instructional guidance from you and with the collaborative meaning-making support of their peers. They learn to share their deep thinking about the book: thinking within, beyond, and about a text. And this text talk, coupled with the use of their readers' notebooks, bolsters their development as proficient readers. And remember: since the clubs are scaffolded with talk and a predictable structure and routines, students who are learning English or struggle with reading are able to listen in and participate. Additionally, the streaming audio for each student book club title adds indispensable support. (See page 144 for instructions on how to access *Comprehension Clubs* streaming audiobooks.)

As students and teachers come together in collaborative, heterogeneously grouped book clubs to discuss and engage with the books on multiple levels, everyone is given equal access to grade-level text, ideas, vocabulary, and language. Through reflective, academic conversation about books, teachers and students create the vibrant, literate classroom community that best supports high-level, quality comprehension. The collaborative, interactive nature of the student book club enables *all* students—including English Language Learners and struggling readers—to find the support they need to fully engage with the books. Each club member gains access to more expansive, deeper comprehension as he or she participates in an intricate network of meaning-construction through shared talk about each of the books in a unit.

Advantages of Using Book Clubs

Day et al. (2002) identify five primary benefits of student book clubs. Clubs accomplish the following:

- **Help teach—not merely check—comprehension.** Listening in on book clubs helps teachers pinpoint students' needs and deliver the precise instruction they need to move forward in their development as proficient readers.

- **Enable teachers to teach multiple facets of comprehension.** Book clubs help students move beyond superficial facts about a book. The analytical talk that book clubs make possible fosters deep, multifaceted comprehension.

- **Encourage students to learn from one another.** The rich, analytical talk of book clubs supports all members, including ELLs and those who find reading a challenge.

- **Motivate students naturally.** Book clubs give all students an opportunity to share their thoughts, questions, and theories, and, in the process, students are ultimately led to think much more deeply about a book than they could have accomplished on their own.

- **Promote discussion more effectively than whole-group structures allow.**

Preparing for Effective Student Book Club Sessions

Timing is everything when it comes to running effective student book clubs. In our estimation, each *Comprehension Clubs* unit should take approximately 2–4 weeks to complete. Ideally, you will read aloud on each of five consecutive days, but Day 2 of the first week should be set aside for a brief booktalk about each of the student book club selections.

To conduct an effective booktalk, hold the book up so your students can see the cover, and then give a very brief synopsis of the book. Without giving away too many details, explain why you think it's a worthwhile read. Once you have introduced the four book club titles, depending on the size of your class, invite your students to choose the book they most want to read.

Ask students to vote for their first, second, and third book choices on a slip of paper that you collect. Later, you can find a quiet moment to quickly sort your students into their clubs based on their written choices. If a student fails to get her first book choice, reassure her that she'll get another chance to read the book when groups form again. You'll want to make sure the groups feature students who work well together, reflect a diversity of opinion, and provide a balance of proficient readers with those who may need more support.

With the booktalks out of the way, students can read and prepare for their book club discussions over the next week.

A circle of chairs or chairs grouped around a table works best for student book club meetings. Use the corners of your classroom to create semiprivate meeting spaces for book club meetings and keep the talk volume low so as not to bother other readers. Remember that your students need to prepare for the book clubs by reading on their own or with a partner, so you'll want to create structures and provide resources that support independent reading, too. For example, include containers to hold students' book club books and readers' notebooks, and a listening center for students who choose to listen to the streaming audiobooks. (See page 144 for the instructions on how to access *Comprehension Clubs* streaming audiobooks.)

Groups and Guidelines

There are multiple ways to organize book club meetings. Initially, meetings may last only 15 minutes for younger children, whereas older students may meet for about 25 to 30 minutes. You can extend these times as your students become more adept at discussion. Either way, you will play a critical role in the clubs and should facilitate discussions until students develop a measure of independence (Fountas & Pinnell, 2006).

Each club tends to follow the same structure:

1. **Students Prepare** Students will read the book in class and at home keeping in mind the upcoming discussion. What will they want to share with their peers? What questions do they have? Remind your students to use their readers' notebooks as tools (see pages 40–43 for more information). During each independent reading session, they can make notes and identify page numbers. By the time they finish their book they will have notes to use to guide their discussion. Alternatively, they can place a few sticky notes at places they want to talk about.

   You may have students negotiate with you and with each other a date by which they will have read their book, or you may also simply assign a date. Either way, the understanding is that by this date, they will be fully prepared to discuss the book in their book club meeting. They may have placed stick-on notes in places they want to talk about or may have taken notes or written down a few questions. They are ready to launch into an engaging discussion about the text. Students quickly learn that it is their responsibility to bring their own thinking to the group. When they don't prepare, they don't have anything to bring to the group.

2. **Students Discuss** Students meet to discuss their book or books for a designated time, typically 15–30 minutes, depending on their age and experience. At first, they may run out of things to say; that's where you come in, prompting and demonstrating how to analyze and respond to a book. After participating in multiple groups, students will look forward to their meetings and arrive bursting at the seams, eager to share, question, analyze, and discuss.

3. **Students Summarize and Evaluate** Encourage student evaluation at the end of each group meeting: What went well? Did everyone share their thinking? What didn't go as well, and why? What can be done next time to improve the group dynamics? Students will evaluate both the group and their individual performance within it.

The Teacher's Role

Your role in a facilitated book club is key. You demonstrate the stance and language of literary analysis. What does it look like and sound like to engage in an analytical discussion about a book, whether literary or informational? What language do you use? How do you draw on evidence from the book to support your position? Students will learn as you prompt and model—not only in their book clubs, but throughout the day. You can also create a rich, analytical classroom culture during the interactive read-aloud as well as in your small-group instruction.

Demonstrate the components of literary analysis: plot, characters, setting, theme, style and language, mood, point of view, illustrations, and symbols, as well as the features of informational text such as organization, style, tone, illustrations/graphics, accuracy, and mood. What do you notice about the language the author uses, the perspectives he or she assumes? Prompt, model, and continually monitor the discussion. What do your students understand? Where do they need more support?

You will need to be closely involved with your student book clubs in order to set routines; select books; assign groups; and monitor, guide, and assess the discussions. Once a book club is established and is enjoying a second or third discussion, you may step away to listen in on another group or help a small group of students with a theme project. But, in general, the clubs work best when you are present. After all, book clubs represent key instructional time. You won't want to miss out on the many instructional and assessment opportunities every book club meeting makes possible.

Designate where and when the clubs will meet. Encourage members to come prepared by having read the selected book, spent some time thinking about it, and decided on information and ideas to share. Have students, in class, sit in a circle on the floor, in chairs, or around a table, so they can see one another. You may want to post a list of text elements for fiction and informational text for the group to refer to as they discuss the book. Book club meetings will normally last about 15 minutes for younger students and up to 30 minutes for older, more experienced students.

More specifically, you can participate by helping groups get their discussions started, move beyond a sticking point, or continue when students think they have run out of things to say. Note how group members work with each other, and be sure they back up their opinions with evidence from the text. Encourage students to ask questions, especially when they don't understand something. As students become more experienced in discussing books, you can move gradually into the role of observer, taking notes and collecting assessment data.

Your observations are also an important part of informal assessment. As you observe book discussions, pay attention to both process and content. Some groups may be proficient at the process of talking about a book but not about the vital content, so they end up saying little about the deeper meaning of a book. Students need to explore the meaning of a text, analyze how the text was crafted, and express their thinking about its meaning. Other groups may have many ideas to share, but they don't know how to organize their meeting. You may need to spend some time with these groups to remind them how to structure a discussion, let everyone have a turn, listen when others are speaking, and participate in the discussion building on each other's comments.

Note, too, whether students arrived to the group fully prepared, having read the book. Notice the depth of students' thinking. Observe: Are students able to build on peers' meanings? Do they identify literary elements? Text features?

Pay particular attention to students' ability to cite textual evidence. Were their conversations grounded in the text? Were they able to skillfully and efficiently find passages and quotes from the book to back up their thinking? How adept were they at building on the meaning their peers shared? Were they good listeners who used the ideas of others to extend their own thinking and understanding? Could they compare critical thinking appropriately across texts?

You will find several reproducible forms to help you document your observations in the assessment section of this guide (see pages 130–143).

Book Club Cards for In-Depth Teaching

When using the Book Club Teaching Card, take note of the following features.

Encourage Student Preparation and Discussion

(1) Summary This information has been provided to you as a resource so you have an understanding of the book itself and why it was chosen for inclusion in the text set. It isn't intended to be read aloud, nor shared with students, though it may help structure your introductory booktalk for each book club title.

(2) Author

(3) Genre/Text Type Remember, form and format follow function. It is particularly important for students to start to understand key genre features as they prepare to read independently.

 **Comprehension Clubs**

🍃 Life Depends on Water   **BOOK CLUB**

Winter's Tail

(1) Summary

This true story opens the door for a multifaceted discussion of what the story of the main character (Winter) has to teach us all about resilience. It offers opportunities to further discuss unit ideas, including the impact people have on the sea, on sea creatures, and on the interdependence of all life on Earth.

(2) Authors Juliana Hatkoff, Isabella Hatkoff, and Craig Hatkoff

Genre/Text Type Informational Text/Photo Essay **(3)**

(4) Book Themes/Ideas interdependence of life on Earth; responsibility; resilience; overcoming obstacles; helping others

Unit Focus Why is water so important to all living things? **(5)**

(6) Author's Craft reporting style; factual evidence and photographs that give the sense of an eyewitness account

(7) About the Authors

Craig Hatkoff and his young daughters Juliana and Isabella share in their introductory letter that they specialize in photo essays about animals that triumph over adversity. When a young fisherman rescues a dolphin caught in the ropes of a crab trap, the Hatkoffs knew that they had to tell the tale of how the dolphin was saved and learned to swim with a prosthesis after the loss of her tail.

(8) Key Understandings

• The authors researched and interviewed people who had firsthand experience with Winter; her rescuer, her trainers, and the person who built her new tail. They even spent a day swimming with Winter.

• The authors had a compelling reason to write this book—to inspire people with disabilities by explaining how "Winter's uplifting spirit and her resilience helped her adjust and make the most of every situation." (p. 29)

(9) Read • Cite Textual Evidence • Discuss

(10) Set Expectations/Use Reader's Notebooks Tell students to notice and cite textual evidence of authenticity and how it contributes to the story structure as well as the theme of resilience, the authors' purpose for telling the story. (Story text starts on page 5.)

Remind students, as they read, to write in their notebooks what they want to talk about with their group, including any questions they have.

Textual Evidence of	Possible Citation: Analysis & Support	Page
Authors' purpose/Theme	*We dedicate this book to the millions of children around the world who struggle with disabilities of all kinds . . . .*	Copyright page
	. . . it was good that Winter was struggling—it showed she still had the heart and energy to try to protect herself.	p. 10
	Winter helps others understand what it means to have a disability and how people can adapt to almost any circumstance.	p. 18 caption
Story structure/ Authenticity	The authors tell sequential events and demonstrate the passage of time at the aquarium: *On Winter's second day . . .; By the time Winter was about five months old . . .; When Winter was about a year old . . . .*	pp. 13, 14, 18
	Text and photos document how volunteers saved Winter's life and present information about her prosthetic tail.	pp. 10–11, 20–21

Reflect on Reading Have students make sure their questions have been addressed and then write in their notebooks the most important thing they learned from the discussion.

■ SCHOLASTIC

4 **Book Themes/Ideas** These tie directly to the Unit Focus, to the Key Understandings and expected learning outcomes of this particular title, and to additional titles in the unit.

5 **Unit Focus** This focus was first highlighted on the unit folder and should remain foremost in your thinking as you facilitate student book club discussions.

6 **Author's Craft** In alignment with effective practices around mentor texts, *Comprehension Clubs* strives to point out to learners the craft behind the presentation of information.

Winter's Tail

🌱 Life Depends on Water   **BOOK CLUB**

Teaching Options: Things to Notice and Do

11 **Notable Text Features**

Supportive Engaging photographs and captions support the text and create a feeling of compassion within the reader.

Challenging Use sensitivity when explaining that a disability need not prevent people from meeting challenges—just as Winter's disability did not stop her from meeting hers.

12 **Vocabulary**

Essential Words

blowhole (p. 6): a dolphin's nostrils, located at the top of its head

buoy (p. 5): a floating object anchored to the bottom of a sea or lake

peduncle (p. 18): lower part of a dolphin's back to which its tail is attached

prosthesis (p. 19): a device used to replace a missing body part

Related Words for Discussion

adapt: to adjust to change

challenge: a difficult situation

inspiration: a person or thing that motivates one to try something new or do better

resilience: the ability to deal with difficult situations

13 **Developing Comprehension**

14 **Thinking Within the Text**

Point out the importance of patience. Say: *Let's discuss sections in the book that show how Winter's patience and the volunteers' patience allow Winter to overcome her difficulties and thrive in her new home.*

15 **Thinking Beyond the Text**

Discuss how Winter became entangled in the crab trap. Ask: *Why is it important for humans to keep in mind all the life in the sea when they use equipment to catch fish and other seafood?*

16 **Thinking About the Text**

Remind students that *Winter's Tail* is a true story that the authors wrote by describing sequential events. Ask students what they think made the story so compelling—almost as if it were a fictional story.

17 **Connect to Read-Aloud Books**

Dolphins in the Sand Both the Hatkoffs and Arnosky include story details to help readers sympathize with dolphins in danger. Which kind of storytelling is more effective? Why?

Manfish Although Winter is not a person, in some ways the Hatkoffs tell Winter's story using techniques similar to ones used in a biography. Describe the similarities.

Common Ground How does Winter's getting caught in a crab trap support Molly Bang's message? What else about Winter's story supports Bang's ideas?

Life in a Coral Reef Like the Hatkoffs, Wendy Pfeffer includes an afterword in her book. How is an afterword helpful in an informational book?

Water Hole Waiting Recall how Jane and Christopher Kurtz show the passing of time in *Water Hole Waiting*. How does their technique compare with how the Hatkoffs show the passing of time in *Winter's Tail*?

18 **Supporting All Learners**

ELLs Help students link details shown in the photos with descriptions in the text.

Struggling Readers Listening to the audiobook will help students access more complex text and help them participate in book discussions. Listening to the narration will also help promote fluency.

19 **Additional Resources**

Share the book's afterword and website with students to continue exploring the subject of dolphins: **www.winterstail.com**.

For ideas about classroom management and helping students independently manage their book clubs, see page 76 of the guide.

3.3BC002

Using a Reader's Notebook

Informal This is writing students do to capture and guide their own thinking. Katherine Schlick Noe (Schlick Noe & Johnson, 1999) calls it "thinking aloud on paper." Quick notes, lists, sketches, predictions, confirmations, questions, favorite language, diagrams, and the like help capture and shape students' evolving thinking about a book or jog their memories for upcoming book discussions.

Formal Writing that is more formal can serve as an assessment tool demonstrating what students have learned or thought as they read (Serravallo, 2012). This is writing that is meant to be shared in a more public and polished way—for example, detailed book notes and quotes that lead to a book review in a class newspaper, or a list of essential questions and the answers obtained through a collaborative inquiry project. Other more formal writing projects might include author or illustrator studies, literary essays, genre studies, biographical sketches, and news articles.

7 **About the Author** Providing students with information about the author, where appropriate, can deepen understanding and enliven conversation.

8 **Key Understandings** These reveal the heart of the instruction for every title and tie directly to information on the rest of the card, including suggested points of evaluation and textual analysis and citation as well as a deep analysis of author's craft.

9 **Read • Cite Textual Evidence • Discuss** These suggestions for where to draw readers' attention, how to cite textual evidence, and what to write about in their readers' notebooks as they prepare for their book club sessions help ensure that deep comprehension of the Key Understandings is achieved.

10 **Set Expectations/Use Readers' Notebooks** During facilitated book clubs, writing in a reader's notebook serves two broad purposes: one informal and personal; the other, more formal and public.

Support Student Learning

11 **Notable Text Features** It is important for you, as the teacher, to understand the supportive and challenging features of the text. Depending on the difficulties of a given text and your knowledge of your students' abilities, you may need to query students' understanding of difficult passages as they meet in their student book clubs. Challenge students to work together to unpack meaning from the text.

12 **Vocabulary** When meanings of words can be discovered through context, you can model and reinforce how to learn vocabulary from contextual clues. Where that isn't possible, you can define the words aloud for students, in student-friendly language. Help students to note new vocabulary they encounter as they read. Encourage them to guess the meaning from context clues and write their guesses in their notebooks to discuss and share with others.

Offer Tools for Oral or Written Response

Here are some prompts designed to support discussion and writing in a reader's notebook. (See also Fountas & Pinnell's Prompting Guides, 2012.)

- To lead students to revisit the text, provide open-ended questions and prompts, such as:
  - ❏ What are one or two of the most important ideas about this story?
  - ❏ What struck you as the most intriguing part of the story?
  - ❏ What surprised you? Why?
  - ❏ Given the title, what did you think the book might be about? Were your expectations confirmed? Why or why not?
  - ❏ Why do you think the author might have written the book?
  - ❏ If you could interview the author, what might you ask?
  - ❏ Would you read another book by this author? Why or why not?
  - ❏ Which character did you like best? Least? Why?

- Ask questions about genre:
  - ❏ Why might the author have chosen this particular genre?
  - ❏ What elements that are unique to this genre did you notice?
  - ❏ Do you have a favorite genre and, if so, what do you enjoy about it?
  - ❏ If you were going to write a piece to share, what genre would you choose? Why?

Assess Understanding

13 **Developing Comprehension: Thinking Within, Beyond, and
About the Text** Readers access a wide range of information
that is both visible and invisible. Visible information
includes the words and art on the page. As they read,
readers recognize letters, words, punctuation, format, and
text structures.

As we note in *Genre Study: Teaching With Fiction and
Nonfiction Books* (2012), readers employ systems of
strategic actions that sustain reading across a text. Each
system is a large and complex body of understandings and
actions; all are taking place simultaneously in the brain as
we look at print and pictures. We divide these systems into
three broad categories of thinking in which readers process
twelve "systems of strategic actions" as described in the
sidebars on this page and the next.

14 **Thinking Within the Text** includes the strategic actions
readers use to process the text and gain a satisfactory
literal meaning of the text. Text matters, and readers
need to understand what happened in a fictional story
or account for the facts in an informational text. It's
from this base that readers are able to extend and refine
their understanding.

15 **Thinking Beyond the Text** showcases what the reader
knows—prior knowledge in the reader's head—together
with what is cued by the text. Proficient readers
continuously draw from their own knowledge of the
world to make predictions about the text that's unfolding
before them, infer implied understandings, absorb
new understandings, and connect to their own known
experiences culled from the wider world or the pages of
other texts.

(16) **Thinking About the Text** invites analysis of the text itself: how is it structured and framed? If it's a fictional piece, what literary elements does it feature? If it's an informational text, what components does it showcase? This is an opportunity for readers to critique the author's craft and consider what's effective and what's not.

(17) **Connect to Read-Aloud Books** Depending on where you are in your Read-Aloud and Book Club cycle, you may need to modify the language provided here. But it is important to model comparing and contrasting topics, ideas, treatments, themes, genres, text features, language and literary features, and vocabulary across multiple texts.

Scaffold and Extend

(18) **Supporting All Learners** It is important to scaffold English Language Learners through the book club process to ensure they are part of the growing learning community. Specific strategies are provided. Struggling readers may benefit from using streaming audio which may be accessed at *http://www.comprehensionclubs.scholastic.com*. Type in the user ID "hear" and the password "books" to access audios.

(19) **Additional Resources** These resources provide additional research opportunities and offer a relevant technology connection to each Read-Aloud title.

---

(15) **Strategic Actions: Thinking Beyond the Text**

Predicting Considering what is already known about the text to predict what might happen next—and then, in the midst of continuous reading, either confirming or discarding based on what unfolds in the text

Making Connections Connecting their reading to their own personal experiences, to other texts they've read, as well as to their understandings about the world beyond

Inferring Developing understandings that are not directly stated in the text but are implied by the author

Synthesizing Drawing together information and understandings from the text with the reader's own understandings and perceptions to create a deeper, multifaceted understanding

(From Fountas & Pinnell, *Teaching for Comprehending and Fluency*, 2006.)

---

(16) **Strategic Actions: Thinking About the Text**

Analyzing Noting how the text is constructed; identifying characteristics of the genre; observing how the author uses language and literary devices or, for informational texts, provides information such as comparing and contrasting and cause and effect

Critiquing Using their own knowledge to think critically about ideas and evaluate the quality and authenticity of the text— beyond simple likes and dislikes. In this way, readers come to understand how texts work, how different genres are structured, and what good-quality writing looks and sounds like.

(From Fountas & Pinnell, *Teaching for Comprehending and Fluency*, 2006.)

Using a Reader's Notebook

What seems to distinguish students who succeed as readers from those who don't is the ability to engage independently in a close analysis of demanding text (ACT, 2006)—and there may be no better way to accomplish that goal than through writing. Writing has a strong and consistently positive impact on reading comprehension. "Transforming a mental summary of text into writing requires additional thought about the essence of the material, and the permanence of writing creates an external record of this synopsis that can be readily critiqued" (Graham & Hebert, 2010).

Writing about text provides students with a way into the text that enables them to crack it open and construct meaning and knowledge in ways that are more effective and precise than would be possible if they were only reading and rereading or reading and discussing the text. The benefits of writing about text are both abundant and profound—and mirror the thinking we want our students to do when they are reading:

- Engage in deep thinking about ideas
- Draw on their own knowledge and experience
- Consolidate and review information
- Reformulate thinking
- Organize and integrate ideas
- Be explicit about text evidence
- Be reflective
- Note personal involvement
- Capture reading experience in their own words

(Fountas & Pinnell, 2012)

Inviting students to write about a text enhances reading comprehension because it affords greater opportunities to think about ideas in a text, requires them to organize and integrate those ideas into a coherent whole, fosters explicitness, facilitates reflection, encourages personal involvement with texts, and involves students transforming ideas into their own words. In short, writing about a text enhances comprehension because it provides students with a tool for visibly and permanently recording, connecting, analyzing, personalizing, and manipulating key ideas in text (Fountas & Pinnell, 2006; Graham & Perin, 2007).

The ways in which your students use their readers' notebooks will depend, of course, on their grade level. But, in general, the reader's notebook serves as a lifeline to books and the conversations about books that you and your students enjoy through interactive read-alouds and book clubs. Through their writing, your students develop an intellectual and emotional bond with each book they read. The notebook also helps students organize their thinking and become more analytical as they revisit their thinking and extend and refine their original ideas. Writing captures their thinking and makes it concrete so they can return to it and revise it with new insights and questions.

Here are some ways in which your students might use their readers' notebooks to support book club discussions:

Book Clubs In the fast-paced conversation of a book club, your students will find the notebooks helpful as a record of thinking and growth.

- **New Ideas** Students can use their readers' notebooks to remember some of their fellow club members' most interesting ideas about the book under discussion. Their notes also work to hold their places and jog their memories— so when it's their turn to talk, they can recall precisely what they wanted to share.

- **Personal Record of Growth** Your students can make notes before or after the discussion and will enjoy keeping track of the range of ideas and topics they covered in their book clubs; over time, they can see how their thinking has deepened and their engagement with books become more analytical. The reader's notebook becomes a wonderful record of their personal relationship with books and their developing journey as proficient readers.

Organizing the Reader's Notebook

We have written extensively about creating readers' notebooks as vessels for students' thinking (2001, 2006, 2012). You can make notebooks with sections or involve your students in creating their own notebooks. We have suggested that the notebook have a clear structure with tabs or labeled sections that may include those listed below.

1 A Reading List

Students list the book, date, and genre when they start reading and the date when they finish.

2 Books to Read

Students keep a list of books they are interested in reading.

3 Reading Requirements

Students tally the books they read in each genre.

4 Reading Mini-Lessons

Students take notes from the mini-lessons to use as a reference. Alternatively, they can paste in a handout with the important points.

5 Writing About Reading

Students share their thinking about their reading by writing in a variety of formats such as dialogue, letters, two-column entries, or graphic organizers.

Measuring the Success of a Facilitated Book Club Session

In an ideal world, we hope that all members of the book club jump right into the discussion—which typically, depending on the age of your students, runs about 15 to 30 minutes—expressing their opinions, citing important textual details from the story, making connections to other books the group may have read. We hope that all students assume an analytical stance as they explore together the meaning of the text.

However, especially in the beginning, listen in and monitor the discussion, stepping in as needed to reorient the group or spark a new line of thinking. You are definitely not asking comprehension questions or dominating the conversation. Indeed, you're holding back, even keeping your eyes down (perhaps recording notes) so the club members will not try to catch your eye and engage you, but, instead, will look at and talk to each other.

Text talk in a book club is all about deeply satisfying peer-to-peer conversation with teacher guidance as needed to keep the discussion centered on text and analytical. Over time, as your students become more-skilled conversationalists, you'll notice exciting changes. We outline the developments you might observe:

- **Texts become more sophisticated and demanding, prompting richer discussion.**

- **Children develop as conversationalists who know how to probe the text and talk with one another about texts.**

- **Students become more adept at close reading, understanding how to return to the text for another read to make a particular point or check up on meaning.**

- **Children become more competent readers and their interests change, perhaps broadening as they take in more of the world through their wide reading and shared conversations.**

(Fountas & Pinnell, 2006)

Once the students wrap up their discussion, you might ask them to take a moment and, using their readers' notebooks for reference, evaluate how things went and consider what they might do differently next time. You may also want to evaluate individual students' preparation and comprehension, but it seems especially important that your students have a strong sense of what makes for an excellent discussion and what they might do differently to improve it next time they meet.

Book Club Resources

We include here two self-assessment forms, one for primary (p. 45) and one for intermediate grades (p. 46), that you and your students might find useful.

Additional student reproducible forms relevant to Facilitated Student Book Clubs can be found in the Assessment & Forms section that begins on page 130. These include Reading Log (p. 134), Close Reading & Text Evidence (p. 135), Quotations & Responses (p. 136), and Student Book Club Discussion Tracker (p. 137).

Name _____ **Date** _____

Book Title _____

Today in Book Club, I . . .

☐ Listened to others.

☐ Looked at the person who was speaking.

☐ Responded to many of the people who were speaking.

☐ Asked questions of other people who were speaking.

☐ Spoke loud enough for others to hear.

☐ Talked my fair share—not too much and not too little.

☐ Was polite to others.

☐ Tried to include others.

Additional Notes: _____

_____

_____

_____

Comprehension Clubs

Name _____ Date _____

Book Title_____

Thinking About Our Book Club Discussion

☐ We shared our thinking in clear, appropriately loud voices that everyone could hear.

☐ Everyone in the group had a turn.

☐ We listened to and looked at the person who was speaking.

☐ We stayed on the topic as long as someone wanted to speak.

☐ We used signals to get a turn and to change the topic.

☐ We were polite to each other.

☐ We asked each other questions when we didn't understand.

☐ We called each other by name.

☐ We had examples from the book to support our thinking.

Our goals for the next book club discussion are: _____

_____

_____

_____

Effective Text Talk

Thanks to the many deep conversations about books that your students have enjoyed during the interactive read-aloud, they know what effective text talk feels like and sounds like. They understand the turn-taking nature of the conversation and what it means to build on a peer's ideas and insights as you push forward as a group to make sense of the book under discussion.

This is how we characterize effective text talk:

- The club members have a shared, continually growing language they use to talk about text.

- The talk is anchored to the particular text being discussed.

- The talk centers on the text as well as the reader's personal response.

- Club members may connect the text to other texts they have read.

- One idea sparks another, so club members "piggyback" their comments.

- Club members listen actively and carefully to one another.

- Club members ask one another questions to clarify or extend the meaning they are sharing.

- The club maintains ownership of the conversation; the text is the focus.

- Club members stay on a topic long enough to gain depth and get several perspectives.

- The shared "club talk" often changes the thinking of individual members in some way.

- The conversation builds relationships and develops a sense of community among members.

- Club members care about what other members think.

- Members know how to disagree respectfully; constructive disagreement is valued rather than avoided.

- Club members can change opinions and understandings during the course of a discussion; book clubs promote fluid discussion and a flexible search for meaning.

(Fountas & Pinnell, 2006)

With every book club meeting, your students become more adept at holding deep conversations about books. It takes time and experience to learn how to analyze texts and share your analysis with others through rich, multifaceted text talk. As always, thinking within, beyond, and about the text serves as an invaluable framework to shape the talk.

The *Comprehension Clubs* Classroom

The Scholastic *Comprehension Clubs* program supports high-quality literacy learning by integrating interactive read-alouds and independent student book clubs in your classroom. Here's what a *Comprehension Clubs* classroom might look like.

Consider the rich and varied literacy experiences you want to orchestrate in your classroom:

- Whole-class activities, such as the Interactive Read-Aloud
- Small-group work such as Book Club discussions or unit projects
- Independent reading time

Students need different levels of support as they engage with a variety of texts and purposes for reading and writing. So, before the school year even begins, consider the activities you plan for your class and the physical layout of your room. The way in which you set up your classroom can facilitate the ways in which your students work and are assessed.

1. **Technology Center** Technology-led independent and small-group practice with streaming audiobooks

2. **Student Tables** Independent writing and follow-up practice

3. **Whole-Group Instruction** Whole-class instruction on Interactive Read-Alouds

4. **Classroom Library** Independent Book Club reading

5. **Book Club Discussion Group** Teacher/student-led small-group instruction and assessment

6. **Teacher Desk** Professional development

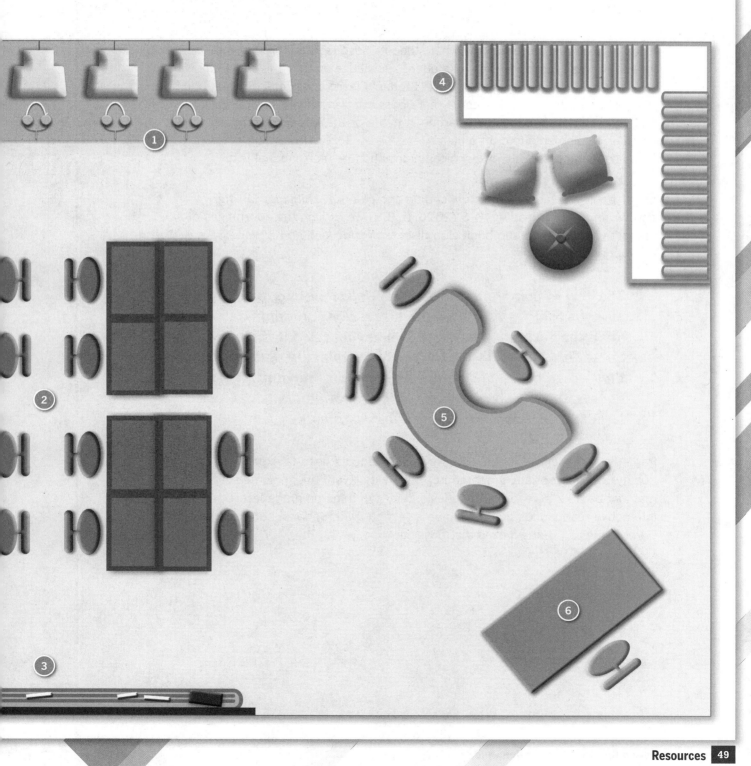

Book Selection

The interactive read-aloud is an ideal instructional context for studying topics, themes, genre, text types, text features, and literary elements. As you read aloud to your students, stop and address these aspects of text. Demonstrate close reading, finding and citing textual evidence, and engaging in the deep and thoughtful analysis of text.

Book club discussions reinforce what students have learned through the interactive read-aloud, deepening student knowledge as they think and talk with their peers. The learning is generative. Students learn a way of looking at and thinking about texts. They become more observant and analytical, noticing the text characteristics unique to a particular genre or the way in which authors use literary elements to craft a literary text or use text features and graphics to enhance the accessibility of technical information in informational text.

In our book *Teaching for Comprehending and Fluency: Thinking, Talking, and Writing About Reading, K–8* (2006, p. 218) we explain the advantages of interactive read-aloud and book club discussions focused on high-quality, age-appropriate books.

> **" *The text is complete, the writer's decisions are made, and all its attributes are there for discussion. Students can 'hold the text still,' examine it, and think about the writer's decisions. The texts they access, the thinking and talking they do, and the close analysis in which they engage develop a repertoire of possibilities that students can use to boost their reading and writing abilities.* "**

Regardless of their current reading level, all students need to experience high-quality, age-appropriate, grade-appropriate texts. Even though some students may not be able to read on grade level, they can think on grade level—and the interactive read-alouds and book club selections with optional audio support in *Comprehension Clubs* makes that possible.

Genre/Text Type:
Descriptions and Key Features

Comprehension Clubs provides a wide variety of genres and text types at every grade level, including many of those described below.

Fiction	
Realistic Fiction	Realistic fiction tells a story that could possibly happen to real people. The characters appear to have problems and goals that real people have, and attempt to solve these problems or reach goals with plausible actions. Readers often experience realistic fiction as truthful and can identify with and see themselves in the characters.
Key Features	• believable characters with human problems and desires • setting that reflects real places and time • character-driven events • reasonable outcomes that reflect real life • humor may be an element
Mystery	A mystery is a special type of fiction that centers on a problem that needs to be solved. The problem can be missing or stolen objects, puzzles, criminals to be identified and caught, or strange behavior that needs to be explained. Suspense and sometimes danger and fear play an important part in the action.
Key Features	• characters involved in solving a problem such as a puzzle or crime • setting that may be mysterious or ordinary • plot that carries the story as characters follow clues to solve the mystery • suspenseful mood • forms such as detective stories, strange adventures, and tales of espionage and crime
Historical Fiction	Realistic fiction that takes place in the past is considered historical fiction. The story combines imagination and fact with characters as part of a fictional plot placed in a real historical setting. The setting is often integral to the plot as it affects how characters live and act as well as the events they are a part of.
Key Features	• believable characters • setting that reflects a historical time and place • details of how people live and work that fit the time and place • real historical people who appear as characters; dialogue and actions fictional unless historically documented
Fantasy	Fantasy includes stories that are not possible in real life. Characters or settings may be imaginary, or the events and characters' actions or abilities are not realistic. Once readers willingly accept the fantasy, the characters may be plausible with realistic problems, and the outcome may be reasonable.
Key Features	• characters that may be imaginary, have magical abilities, and/or include personified animals • settings that may be imaginary but seem real • simple plot that may involve a conflict between good and evil

Fiction	
Science Fiction	Science fiction is a type of fantasy that tells about events that have not happened yet or that could not happen in real life as it is known today. The imaginary elements are technology-driven instead of magical. The science established in a science fiction story may not be explained, but it must remain consistent to be believable.
Key Features	• stories that may take place in outer space, on other worlds, or in alternate dimensions • science and technology used to create a world or characters that are not possible in present life • setting that affects characters and their actions
Traditional Literature	Traditional literature encompasses stories that have been passed down orally through many generations. Different versions of the same tale often appear in many cultures. Readers expect recurring themes and structures, such as three wishes, journeys or quests, tricksters, or heroes who are often young.
Key Features	• Folktale An often humorous story that comes from a particular culture and is told orally until it is eventually recorded; includes stock characters that fill one function, simple conflicts and goals, fast action, repetitive events often in threes, and a definitive outcome • Fable A brief story, usually with animal characters, that reaches a moral or a lesson that can be stated or unstated • Fairy Tale A short story with magical characters and events; characters are usually all good or all bad; repetition in characters and actions; often begins with "once upon a time" and ends with "and they lived happily ever after"; has a more elaborate structure than a folktale
Adventure	An adventure tells a story that involves characters in exciting, and often risky, situations. Characters may accomplish heroic feats.
Key Features	• setting that may be real or imaginary • plot that may involve danger • hero who is brave

Informational Text	
Informational Text	Informational text provides factual information. Content may be scientific or social, exploring the natural and physical world or people and places in the past or present. Informational text can be presented in a variety of formats including reference books, books on specific subjects or processes, magazines, CDs, or filmed documentaries.
Key Features	• information on a whole class of things, places, or people • text that describes and explains • text that compares and contrasts • technical vocabulary • headings and subheadings to divide text • information presented through graphics such as photographs, charts, diagrams, and maps as well as text

Informational Text

Biography/ Autobiography	A biography or autobiography is about a single historical or current person. It may cover the person's whole life or a significant period. An autobiography is written by the person who is the subject of the story. An autobiography may take the form of a memoir in which the person relates his or her experiences during a meaningful time. A biography is written by an author about a person who is the subject of the book.
Key Features	• covers one person's life or a significant period of that person's life • is usually written about an important person • may include photographs and illustrations • may include a table of contents, an index, and/or a bibliography • is based on research

Text Types

Picture Book	A picture book has illustrations that help tell the story or photos to convey information.
Key Features	• pictures that show characters, setting, and plot in fictional text • photographs and graphics that help add content to informational text
Play	A play is a story that is intended to be performed. Plays are character-driven, as they are told through what the characters say and do.
Key Features	• dialogue form, with character names identifying the speaker • character actions and expressions briefly indicated, often parenthetically • one or more acts, with a clearly identified setting • list of characters and their characteristics such as name, age, and identity or profession
Chapter Book/ Novel	A chapter book is a work of fiction that contains all story elements, including characters, setting, plot, and theme. A novel is a longer work. Because of its longer length, a novel can more fully develop characters over time and place. The length of a novel requires readers to develop reading stamina and the ability to follow plots and characters over an extended period of time and several reading sessions.
Key Features	• story usually divided into chapters • several major and minor characters that may be fully developed • story background included in the beginning or as the story unfolds • plot that may include many events as the action rises and falls • several subplots • events and resolution that follow the climax or turning point
Graphic Novel	Graphic novels are similar to comic books, but they tell a more complete story with a beginning, middle, and end. A graphic novel often resembles a novel in length and narrative. The term *graphic* refers to the pictorial nature of the novel.
Key Features	• story told through pictures • dialogue included in speech balloons • narrative within story frames or at the top of a page • characters developed through dialogue and illustration
Short Stories	A short story is a short work of fiction that includes the story elements of characters, setting, plot, and theme.
Key Features	• usually part of a collection • of any fictional genre

Writing About Reading

Using *Comprehension Clubs* in your classroom means your students will be thinking and talking about texts in productive and meaningful ways. The teaching cards offer prompts and suggestions to encourage students to share their thinking through both talking and writing. Writing is an essential part of each unit of study because understanding text begins with thinking, talking, and representing ideas. Students' writing makes their comprehension visible (Fountas & Pinnell, 2006, p. 438):

" *When young children are asked to write (and draw) in response to their reading from the beginning, they will be able to use this tool in response to reading and to expand their own thinking about texts.* **"**

The Writing-Reading Connection

As Graham & Perrin (2007) and others have noted, the empirical evidence is clear: writing about a text provides students with a way into the text that enables them to construct meaning and build knowledge in ways that are more effective and precise than would be the case if they were only reading and rereading the text or reading it and discussing it. As students expand their thinking, they not only deepen their understanding—they also become better writers. The kind of writing students do in *Comprehension Clubs* is based on the close analysis of text and therefore will serve them well when they take high-stakes tests that demand that they demonstrate in writing their comprehension of texts.

Assessing Writing

The writing prompts on the *Comprehension Clubs* teaching cards are designed to help students show their thinking within, beyond, and about the text. To help students grasp what is being asked of them, we suggest you do some shared writing or interactive writing so that you can model how to respond to texts through writing, including how to revise and add to a text in order to better represent ideas.

The grade-by-grade examples on the following pages illustrate a few of the writing prompts found at each grade and the kinds of strategic actions that may be assessed when you review students' writing. Keep in mind that additional opportunities for writing are found in the Unit Projects section of this guide.

Examples of *Comprehension Clubs* Writing

Kindergarten

Overview In kindergarten, the kinds of writing tasks that children are asked to produce emphasize drawing and telling. "Telling" can mean that children dictate their responses for you to write down. However, some children will be eager to write on their own using invented spelling.

Support Children will also enjoy and greatly benefit from responding as a group to writing prompts. They may then be able to participate in more-challenging writing, with you modeling and leading shared writing sessions. In shared writing, a group of children work together to compose, on chart paper or on a whiteboard, a text that children can then illustrate. You may wish to make these sessions more interactive by inviting individual children to come up and add a letter, word, or picture to the text you and the group are creating.

Examples From the Teaching Cards

WRITING ABOUT READ-ALOUDS	BOOK CLUB WRITING
from Telling Tales: *Chicken Little*	**from Telling Tales: *Let's Play in the Forest***
Write and Respond Have children draw another animal that Chicken Little might have met along the way. Then have them write in large letters a sound word that shows what sound might have been made when Chicken Little and the new animal collided.	**Set Expectations/Use Readers' Notebooks** Help children notice and think about the pattern used in the story and what the author does at the end to surprise them. *How does the writer tell the story in an interesting way?* (Story Structure) *What happens in the story that you did not expect to happen?* (Plot) Ask children to draw and tell about their favorite picture from the story.
Behaviors to Notice and Support	**Behaviors to Notice and Support**
• **Thinking Beyond the Text** to compose innovations on *Chicken Little* • **Thinking About the Text** to borrow the style or expressions the writer used to show what happened each time Chicken Little bumped into another animal	• **Thinking Within the Text** to notice and use information about events and characters • **Thinking Beyond the Text** to express opinions about the story • **Thinking About the Text** to recognize the pattern in the text structure
from Trees & Other Plants: *Up, Down, and Around*	**from Trees & Other Plants: *Wonderful Worms***
Write and Respond Encourage children to create charts that show which vegetables grow up, which grow down, and which grow around. Give children paper folded in thirds. Children should write "Up," "Down," and "Around" at the top of the three columns on their papers. Then, have children draw pictures of the appropriate vegetables under each word and write or dictate a sentence that tells what they learned about growing fruits and vegetables.	**Set Expectations/Use Readers' Notebooks** Help children notice and think about who is telling the story and how the narrator provides information about worms. *Who is telling us about worms in this book?* (Perspective) *How would you describe how worms look? What words could you use to describe them?* (Descriptive Language/Sensory Details) Ask children to draw and tell about how earthworms move.
Behaviors to Notice and Support	**Behaviors to Notice and Support**
• **Thinking Within the Text** to compose and combine lists into a chart and tell important information from their reading and to write and draw about interesting facts	• **Thinking Within the Text** to notice and use words to describe worms and tell how they move as well as to notice who is telling the story • **Thinking About the Text** to notice who is telling the story

Grade 1

Overview In Grade 1, the kinds of writing tasks children are asked to produce move beyond telling to encompass more writing. However, drawing continues to be an important part of the way in which children communicate their ideas. Much of the writing that children produce may be labels for diagrams they create, captions for pictures, lists, or simple summaries. Invented spellings are often still used, but many first graders' writing demonstrates an emerging ability to spell words correctly and use punctuation.

Support Children continue to enjoy and greatly benefit from responding to writing prompts as a group, and therefore may participate in more-challenging writing, with you modeling and leading shared writing sessions. In shared writing, a group works together to compose a text, on chart paper or on a whiteboard, that children can then illustrate. You may wish to make these sessions more interactive by inviting individual children to add a word, phrase, or picture to the text you are creating together. To express ideas, use complete sentences whenever possible.

Examples From the Teaching Cards

WRITING ABOUT READ-ALOUDS	BOOK CLUB WRITING

from It Happened to Me: *The Ugly Vegetables*

Write and Respond Discuss with children the steps that the mother and daughter followed to begin their garden. Then ask children to draw four pictures to show the first four things the girl and her mother did in their garden (dig, plant seeds, water, and write labels). Have children write a sentence to describe each picture.

Behaviors to Notice and Support

- **Thinking Within the Text** to use the text as a resource for words and ideas and to write sentences that summarize important details from the story
- **Thinking About the Text** to notice and apply organization of events and to use drawings to represent a sequence of events

from It Happened to Me: *Knuffle Bunny*

Set Expectations/Use Readers' Notebooks Help children notice and think about how the author shows Trixie's problem and how the artwork gives additional details and makes the story funny. *When Trixie tries to tell her father what is wrong, why does she get so upset? How does the author/illustrator show this?* (Developing Conflict) *What is the turning point in the story? How does the author/illustrator let you know?* (Illustrations: Humor/Story Details) Ask children to write about Knuffle Bunny's experiences.

Behaviors to Notice and Support

- **Thinking Within the Text** to represent characters and a sequence of events through drawing and writing
- **Thinking Beyond the Text** to infer how Trixie feels
- **Thinking About the Text** to notice how the book is organized and identify the turning point or shift in the story

from Animal Stories: *Julius, the Baby of the World*

Write and Respond Ask children to extend the story by drawing and writing a scene that might take place after Lilly changes her mind and decides she likes Julius. Children should draw Lilly playing with Julius and write sentences that explain what Lilly and Julius are doing.

Behaviors to Notice and Support

- **Thinking Within the Text** to represent story characters through drawing and writing
- **Thinking Beyond the Text** to reflect what the character is really like and produce innovations on the text
- **Thinking About the Text** to borrow the style or some language from author Kevin Henkes

from Animal Stories: *Bear Wants More*

Set Expectations/Use Readers' Notebooks Help children to notice and think about the repeated pattern used in this fantasy and how pictures help readers understand the ways in which the animals act like people when they help Bear solve his problems. *Every time you read the words, "But the bear wants more," something happens to let the bear eat more food. What happens?* (Language) *After Bear's friends help him find more food to eat, what else do they help him with?* (Plot) Ask children to write about one of the characters that help Bear find food.

Behaviors to Notice and Support

- **Thinking Within the Text** to represent a character through writing and summarize details from the story
- **Thinking About the Text** to notice the pattern in the plot and interesting language from the story

Overview In Grade 2, children are taking on more independent writing and producing longer written responses. Children's writing also shows increasing mastery of proper spelling and writing conventions. Children are also expanding their repertoire of writing forms. They are more readily able to represent in their own writing the elements of a genre they have read, as well as mimic a favorite author's style and use of language.

Support Children still enjoy and greatly benefit from responding to writing prompts as a group, and therefore may be able to participate in more-challenging writing, with you modeling and leading shared writing sessions. In shared writing, a group works together to compose a text, on chart paper or on a whiteboard, that children can then illustrate. You may wish to make these sessions more interactive by inviting individual children to add a word or sentence to the text you are creating. Children may also benefit from working in pairs or small groups without your guidance for some of their writing activities.

Examples From the Teaching Cards

WRITING ABOUT READ-ALOUDS	BOOK CLUB WRITING

from It Happened in School: *Crazy Hair Day*

Write and Respond Saltzberg ends *Crazy Hair Day* by showing how the class solves Stanley's embarrassing problem. Ask children to think about what the class must have been doing while Stanley was hiding in the bathroom. Then have partners write a short conversation that takes place between members of the class and the teacher, Mr. Winger. Students should begin with Larry's "progress report" on Stanley when he returns from the bathroom the first time. They also should use a separate line for each speaker.

Behaviors to Notice and Support

- **Thinking Within the Text** to represent story characters and how they solved problems
- **Thinking Beyond the Text** to produce an innovation on the text and infer and describe characters' motivations and feelings
- **Thinking About the Text** to create dialogue that has some of the characteristics of conversations from the book

from It Happened in School: *Make Way for Dyamonde Daniel*

Set Expectations/Use Readers' Notebooks Ask children to notice and think about how Nikki Grimes conveys Dyamonde Daniel's character and how she uses different locations to frame Dyamonde's relationship with Free. Ask children to write about how knowing Free changes Dyamonde. Remind them to think about what they will want to talk about with their group when they write.

Behaviors to Notice and Support

- **Thinking Within the Text** to represent important information about the characters and setting and to note significant events within the book
- **Thinking Beyond the Text** to describe Dyamonde's feelings and motivations and express opinions about her and her friendship with Free
- **Thinking About the Text** to notice how the author has organized the story and uses interesting language to describe her characters

from Wishes & Promises: *Mouse & Lion*

Write and Respond Have children write a brief summary that tells about King Lion's experience with the brave and loyal Mouse and includes the lesson King Lion learns at the end of the story. Ask children to include in their summary the most important things that happened in the story and tell what lesson King Lion learned about the small creatures in his environment.

Behaviors to Notice and Support

- **Thinking Within the Text** to create a summary that reflects important information
- **Thinking Beyond the Text** to express a new understanding gained from the story
- **Thinking About the Text** to show awareness of cause and effect

from Wishes & Promises: *The Magic Fish*

Set Expectations/Use Readers' Notebooks Ask children to notice and think about how the author uses repetition of events to move the story along and dialogue to tell about the characters in this well-known tale. Ask children to complete a story map of events. Remind them to think about what they will want to talk about with their group.

Behaviors to Notice & Support

- **Thinking Within the Text** to report information from the text
- **Thinking Beyond the Text** to use story dialogue to infer the characters' feelings and motivations
- **Thinking About the Text** to explain the pattern of events in the story and produce a story map that represents the progression of events in this tale

Grade 3

Overview In Grade 3, students are becoming able to write more-detailed responses and to delve more deeply into different forms and genres of writing. They continue to do some drawing but are now likely to record more of their thoughts in writing. They are becoming more skilled at listing, summarizing, writing informational texts, and explaining their own ideas. As their vocabulary grows, some students are willing to take risks and incorporate more precise terms in their own writing. They continue to make progress with conventions and spelling, but may need to be reminded to take the risk of using the best words they can think of—even if students are uncertain about spelling.

Support When you lead shared writing sessions, students are likely to be eager to contribute their ideas, but sharing more ideas also means that students may need more help organizing their thoughts. Consider modeling how to use graphic organizers such as word webs, T-charts, and the charts on pages 135–136 of this guide as resources for different forms of writing. Model revising for different purposes so that students can see the difference between informal writing, used to record and refine their own thinking, and more-formal writing that will be published in some form. Students will take on doing more independent writing but will also benefit from working with a partner some of the time.

Examples From the Teaching Cards

WRITING ABOUT READ-ALOUDS	BOOK CLUB WRITING
from Life Depends on Water: *Manfish*	**from Life Depends on Water: *Ocean Sunlight***
Write and Respond Have students write a letter to Jacques Cousteau, thanking him for the information and ideas he shared with the world. Students should base their letter on information from the book and tell which of his achievements they think is most significant and why.	**Set Expectations/Use Readers' Notebooks** Tell students to notice and cite textual evidence of Bang and Chisholm's use of scientific facts combined with poetic language (personification) to relate information. Remind students, as they read, to write in their notebooks what they want to talk about with their group, including any questions they may have.
Behaviors to Notice and Support	**Behaviors to Notice and Support**
• **Thinking Within the Text** to include important details from this biography • **Thinking Beyond the Text** to provide evidence from the text and from personal experience to support statements students write • **Thinking About the Text** to express opinions about the text and back them up with specific reasons	• **Thinking Within the Text** to note important scientific information as well as details that illustrate the use of personification • **Thinking Beyond the Text** to reflect awareness of the author's craft and underlying message • **Thinking About the Text** to analyze the author's craft and how they have organized the book
from Mystery: *What Really Happened to Humpty?*	**from Mystery: *The Talking T-Rex***
Write and Respond Discuss with students the clues that helped Detective Joe Dumpty solve the mystery of what made Humpty fall. Then have students write another possible solution to the mystery. Students should use clues from the story to explain their solutions and incorporate other details from the story into their explanation, such as the setting and the use of modern technology. They may also draw an illustration if they wish.	**Set Expectations/Use Readers' Notebooks** Tell students to notice and cite textual evidence of suspense, important details that serve as clues, and dialogue that reveals characters' thoughts and feelings. Remind students, as they read, to write in their notebooks what they want to talk about with their group, including any questions they have.
Behaviors to Notice and Support	**Behaviors to Notice and Support**
• **Thinking Within the Text** to revisit the text for relevant details and use significant and appropriate events from the story • **Thinking Beyond the Text** to include evidence from the book to support thinking about the new solution • **Thinking About the Text** to show awareness of cause and effect and problem/solution in a mystery story	• **Thinking Within the Text** to represent important details that serve as clues and to reflect both prior knowledge and textual evidence in their writing • **Thinking Beyond the Text** to infer the characters' thoughts, feelings, and motivations • **Thinking About the Text** to describe how the author builds suspense

Grade 4

Overview In Grade 4, students are becoming more aware of the way in which authors use word choice, organization, and other techniques to accomplish their purpose. They may enjoy working with a partner on some writing assignments but over the year, their stamina increases and they produce more thoughtful writing on their own—including creative innovations on texts they have read.

Support Shared writing in which you model and have students contribute to graphic organizers—word webs, T-charts, and others—will help students see how to use these tools to record and expand thinking, as well as help them plan for specific writing projects. Use the graphic organizers on pages 135–136 of this guide as resources for different forms of writing. Also, model, as you work together on different forms of writing, how refining word choice to create richer descriptions and organization helps writers get their messages across. Working with groups or partners may also help students grow as writers.

Examples From the Teaching Cards

WRITING ABOUT READ-ALOUDS	BOOK CLUB WRITING

from Taking Responsibility: *Wangari's Tree of Peace*

Write and Respond Have students write a summary of the book. Students should describe the land of Kenya and Wangari's life before she left to study in America, describe Kenya after Wangari returned, and explain what Wangari did about the problem she found—and what happened as a result of her actions.

Behaviors to Notice and Support

- **Thinking Within the Text** to include accurate and significant details about Wangari's life
- **Thinking Beyond the Text** to infer Wangari's feelings and motivations
- **Thinking About the Text** to notice and write about Jeanette Winter's underlying message

from Taking Responsibility: *Dexter the Tough*

Set Expectations/Use Readers' Notebooks Tell students to notice and cite textual evidence of the main character's growing self-awareness as he deals with his inner conflicts. Have students cite examples of narration and of Dexter's voice. Remind students, as they read, to write in their notebooks what they want to talk about with their group, including any questions they have.

Behaviors to Notice and Support

- **Thinking Within the Text** to notice and comment on details and vocabulary that reveal Dexter's character and tell about his relationship with Robin and with his teacher
- **Thinking Beyond the Text** to infer Dexter's emotions and express changes in understanding as the book develops
- **Thinking About the Text** to analyze how the author intentionally uses dialogue and narration to reveal Dexter's growing self-awareness

from The Artist's Eye: *An Eye for Color*

Write and Respond Gather the materials needed for one or more of the activities on page 38 and have students follow the directions. Then have students write about the outcome. Remind students to explain what they did and what they observed, tell what they did or did not like about the outcome, and connect their observations to what they learned about Josef Albers's work.

Behaviors to Notice and Support

- **Thinking Within the Text** to access information from both print and graphics
- **Thinking Beyond the Text** to show connections between Albers's ideas about colors and students' own observations
- **Thinking About the Text** to describe how illustrations contributed to students' understanding of Albers's work and show awareness of the role of cause and effect in perception of images as the colors change

from The Artist's Eye: *Frida Kahlo*

Set Expectations/Use Readers' Notebooks Tell students to notice and cite textual evidence of how the time and place in which Kahlo lived and the events in her life influenced and shaped her art. Remind students, as they read, to write in their notebooks what they want to talk about with their group, including any questions they have.

Behaviors to Notice and Support

- **Thinking Within the Text** to access information from both print and graphics about Kahlo, the setting, and her art
- **Thinking Beyond the Text** to relate ideas about Kahlo's art to her personal experiences
- **Thinking About the Text** to use genre (biography) to interpret the text and to comment on the writer's use of artwork, photos, and cartoons to support and extend the text

Grade 5

Overview Grade 5 students are becoming more adept at producing complex responses, moving toward essays, speeches, and other works to present a well-reasoned argument. As they begin to understand the complexities and conflicts presented in the texts they read, students will gravitate toward specific vocabulary and greater precision in their word choices. They will construct complex sentences and paragraphs to express increasingly sophisticated opinions and ideas.

Support As you offer help to students with their writing, you can model using graphic organizers (see pp. 135–136 of this guide) as a preliminary step to students' formulations of ideas and responses. Point out that, when responding to longer readings, it is often helpful to focus on a specific section of the book to exemplify an overarching idea. Remind students also that, although they may be writing an essay or fact-based piece, the language they use can still be vivid and evocative. As a group, write a detailed description that conveys a strong mental picture, and then another description that is general and/or uses less vivid vocabulary. Invite students to compare the two and discuss their relative effectiveness.

Examples From the Teaching Cards

WRITING ABOUT READ-ALOUDS	BOOK CLUB WRITING

from Better Together: *The Yellow Star*

Write and Respond Have students recall that the Nazis wanted all the Jews to wear yellow stars and that the king came up with a solution to this problem. Have students briefly summarize the king's solution and challenge them to use examples from the book to compare and contrast what the Nazis wanted the star to symbolize with what the star came to symbolize for the Danes.

Behaviors to Notice and Support

- **Thinking Within the Text** to remember significant details from the Danes' actions and use these details to analyze and understand the story
- **Thinking Beyond the Text** to make connections between historical and cultural awareness of the Nazi occupation of Denmark and the story told in the text
- **Thinking About the Text** to comment on how the author revealed the underlying message of Denmark's act of resistance to the Nazis

from Better Together: *The Tiger Rising*

Set Expectations/Use Readers' Notebooks Tell students to notice and cite textual evidence of the symbols and metaphors the author uses throughout the story, what they stand for, and the language the author uses to describe characters. Remind students, as they read, to write in their notebooks what they want to talk about with their group, including any questions they have.

Behaviors to Notice and Support

- **Thinking Within the Text** to notice and comment on the language used to describe Rob's grief and his emergence from it
- **Thinking Beyond the Text** to infer the meanings of the symbols and metaphors the author used to communicate Rob's evolution over the course of the story
- **Thinking About the Text** to comment on Kate DiCamillo's use of language to create subtle shades of meaning and mood

from Watch Out!: *The Odious Ogre*

Write and Respond Have students write a newspaper-style article describing the girl's defeat of the Ogre. The article should begin with a catchy headline and lead sentence, describe the Ogre's terrifying qualities, summarize ways in which the girl tried to be friendly to the Ogre, and include made-up quotes from the girl that show what she thought about the Ogre.

Behaviors to Notice and Support

- **Thinking Within the Text** to provide details that are important to understanding the relationships among the girl, the Ogre, the girl's viewpoint, and the events that lead to the Ogre's defeat
- **Thinking Beyond the Text** to infer the girl's feelings and motivations and give text evidence to back up students' claims
- **Thinking About the Text** to show awareness of the author's language and imagery as a basis for creating students' own news article about the girl's defeat of the Ogre

from Watch Out!: *Skeleton Man*

Set Expectations/Use Readers' Notebooks Tell students to notice and cite textual evidence of first-person point of view, the building of suspense, and references to Native-American heritage. Remind students, as they read, to write in their notebooks what they want to talk about with their group, including any questions they have.

Behaviors to Notice and Support

- **Thinking Within the Text** to represent ways in which this text's use of Native-American cultural details and Molly as narrator help contribute to the sense of suspense
- **Thinking Beyond the Text** to make connections between Native-American culture and the characters and events in the story
- **Thinking About the Text** to recognize the narrative voice of Molly and discuss how experiencing the story from her viewpoint affects the reader's perception of characters and events

Comprehension Clubs and the Struggling Reader

As many as one in three American children finds learning to read challenging (Adams, 1994). This makes our goal—to help all readers achieve grade-level independent reading—all the more urgent and essential. Typically, the children who get off to a poor start in reading rarely succeed in catching up. On this point, the research is both extensive and unequivocal (Neuman & Dickinson, 2001; Snow, Burns, & Griffin, 1998). As Juel first noted in 1988, a child who struggles to read in the first grade is 88 percent more likely to struggle in the fourth grade as well. Clearly, the early prevention of reading difficulties is critical (Clay, 1991; Pinnell & Fountas, 2009) and, to that end, we need always to keep in mind those students in our classrooms who find reading challenging.

Text Support: High Quality, Spiraling Complexity, Print, and Audio

Hargis (2006) discovered that the typical fourth-grade classroom reflects a reading range that spans second grade to ninth. Clearly, teachers and students need access to a wide range of text—unleveled for independent reading and leveled for guided reading. As Richard Allington reminds us, "Good readers read with accuracy almost all the time." If we want our kids to sprint ahead—to become reading champions on their way to college and beyond—they must read with 98 percent accuracy or higher. Not only do our kids miss out on accelerated reading when their accuracy rate slips to 90 percent or below, but also, even more alarmingly, they fail to make any reading progress at all (Allington, 2012). Our students grow as readers when they read books they can understand; it's just that simple—and that critical. We can't take chances with our students' reading lives.

Fortunately, the support we offer our students through *Comprehension Clubs* is exactly what all students need: text, talk, and teaching. These are the essential literacy experiences that all children need on their way to becoming proficient readers.

Because the texts within it are thematically related, *Comprehension Clubs* works especially well for students who find reading challenging. Students benefit immeasurably from reading across a set of books that are conceptually related; text sets automatically create a network of shared meaning that serves as a safety net for those students most in need. They more easily learn the big ideas and shared vocabulary related to a specific unit of study, and that, in turn, enables them to more easily read and write about the topic of study.

Plus, the books form a spiral of increasing complexity—each subsequent text set across the year and across the grades becomes more challenging, requiring students to use their developing strategic reading actions. You can help your struggling readers by reading each book multiple times, pairing them with a more capable partner, and inviting students to listen to the audiobooks. And also, surround each book with lively text talk and writing. What's more, at every opportunity, tuck in quick mini-lessons about word solving, comprehension strategies, writing to refine meaning, and the like, as your observations reveal the need.

Through the interactive read-alouds, book clubs, and coherent, thematically related, content-rich collection of books *Comprehension Clubs* provides, you're able to easily provide the essential literacy experiences—and the talk, texts, and teaching—your challenged readers need to achieve reading success. Let's explore each in turn.

Text

Text matters—hugely—and we have long showcased text as a critical component of the reading process. All texts share certain essential reading components. Readers must solve the words, recognize how the text is organized (the text structure), make sense of the sentences and paragraphs (language structure), and understand what they are reading. . . . To be a skillful comprehender, readers need exposure—with teaching—to a wide variety of texts. Learning to make adjustments to accommodate different kinds of texts requires this exposure (Pinnell & Fountas, 2009).

Talk

Students learn to talk by talking. Their talk represents their thinking. *Comprehension Clubs* multiplies the opportunities for students to learn from talking and benefit from the language and thinking of others.

Teaching

Your teaching involves the essential moves you make to expand students' thinking. When you demonstrate, prompt for, or reinforce thinking, students expand their ability to engage with text. Struggling readers benefit greatly from your skillful use of language to support their thinking.

Audiobooks

Struggling readers need help with fluency and comprehension as well as building their confidence to handle both. One of the most effective ways to help is to invite them to read along with audiobooks, such as the streaming audiobooks in *Comprehension Clubs*. In this way, students learn about fluency, expression, and reading at an appropriate rate. They also learn about the role of punctuation and the ways in which the various punctuation marks they encounter while reading affect their reading style and pace. Fluency and pace affect comprehension (Rasinski, 2010), so this creates a winning cycle of support for challenged readers. What's more, with the aid of the audiobook, students can read more challenging text than they could otherwise handle on their own—and then they are able to participate in the book clubs, which provide additional support.

Make sure that while they are listening to the streaming audio, every student has a copy of the book and follows along with the text if they are able. (See page 144 for instructions on how to access *Comprehension Clubs* streaming audiobooks.)

Educator Margo Dill (2010) points out that audiobooks help even the playing field for challenged readers:

> **"Using books on tape for struggling readers exposes them to literature above their reading levels. Struggling readers . . . are often reading different books than their classmates, and these books are not on grade level. Sometimes students reading below grade level want to read the same books as their classmates, but they are not able to. Books on tape can help students to feel self-confident and improve reading skills."**

Comprehension Clubs and Supporting All Learners (RTI)

With nearly one in three U.S. high school students failing to graduate with a diploma—approximately 1.2 million students drop out each year—no one disputes the fact that we're facing a devastating challenge. Among students of color, the problem is even more severe, with nearly 50 percent of African-American and Hispanic students not completing high school on time. And almost always, the dropouts are students who have struggled with reading, often from the beginning of their school careers, and consequently fall farther and farther behind in their course work (Hunter, 2012; Tatum, 2013; America's Promise Alliance, 2010).

Response to Intervention (RTI) originated in 2002 with the Individuals with Disabilities Education Act (IDEA). While its premise was simple, its results have been revolutionary: students who struggle with reading no longer face a battery of diagnostic tests administered by a school psychologist which, in years past, typically led to a special education placement. Now, thanks to the RTI breakthrough, classroom teachers use a series of systematic assessments to determine the strengths and weaknesses of their struggling readers. With that information in hand, they are able to create a thoughtful program of systematic, sensitive support for these students inside the comfort of their own classrooms and core reading programs. In other words, rather than referring struggling readers to the school psychologist and special education, a process which can take months, classroom teachers intervene with targeted small-group instruction, typically framed around three tiers that represent a "continuum of supports" (National Center on Response to Intervention, 2010, 4). The advantage of using RTI is that students who are at risk of having reading difficulties are identified early. Early identification can prevent some students from being placed in special education despite the fact that all they need is a short period of intense intervention. Further, student progress is carefully monitored.

Since its authorization, RTI is now being combined with social/emotional considerations for learners, in recognition of the reciprocal nature of academic performance and social/emotional response. Multitiered Systems of Support frameworks encourage districts to integrate RTI for academics and behavior. In practice this can and will look very different from school to school, as it is tailored to fit specific situations and students.

In the typical three-tier model, Tier 1 is intended to represent high-quality core classroom instruction for all children. *Comprehension Clubs*—ideally in tandem with guided reading or small-group instruction—provides the foundational support needed for Tier 1 intervention. Tier 2 gives more support to children who are not showing adequate progress. This is often accomplished through small-group or one-on-one instruction and more-frequent progress monitoring so that instruction can be tailored to each student's needs. Tier 3 instruction is typically an intensive, often one-on-one intervention conducted by a specialized teacher.

Tier 1

***Comprehension Clubs*—Ideal Core Support for RTI** Tier 1, or primary intervention, centers on core reading instruction—informed by the best available information on how to teach reading. To that end, *Comprehension Clubs*, ideally coupled with guided reading, provides a setting within which the explicit teaching of strategic processing behaviors—word solving, comprehending, and reading with fluency—is most effective. Indeed, CIERA (Center for the Improvement of Early Reading Achievement) investigated the practices of accomplished classroom teachers who were helping strugglers beat the odds and achieve. What they found is noteworthy: "Time spent in small-group instruction for reading distinguished the most effective schools from the other schools in the study" (Taylor et al., 2000). Tier 1 intervention is accomplished through the use of high-quality reading materials and carefully selected leveled texts that meet the needs of all students. *Comprehension Clubs* and guided reading instruction align perfectly with the goals and targeted support of Tier 1 intervention. You'll recognize the framework of *Comprehension Clubs* in this list of essential instructional moves for Tier 1:

- Introduce text to students, providing background information and pointing out elements such as structure, topics, vocabulary, plot, illustrations, and other graphics.

- Intervene as needed to demonstrate specific comprehension strategies as well as to prompt and reinforce students' thinking.

- Reinforce effective problem solving of words using the word's meaning, language, and print.

- Demonstrate, reinforce, or prompt using punctuation to aid meaning, reading with phrasing, pausing appropriately, stressing the correct words, or using expression.

- Guide a discussion—after students have read—that probes for deeper meaning and helps students extend their thinking.

- Link to writing as yet another way to extend thinking.

The majority of readers, both on-level and vulnerable, will thrive and succeed with Tier 1 intervention. Allington (2012) notes that informed, strategic, small-group reading instruction coupled with engaged text that students can read is the key to success for most struggling readers.

And the *Comprehension Clubs* emphasis on *text*, *talk*, and *teaching* provides just the right foundational support. Indeed, because the collection is thematically organized and backed up with books on tape, your students, even those for whom reading is a challenge, will find the support they need to access the content.

All students thrive in classrooms that are filled with books, classrooms in which the teacher celebrates books—creating colorful book displays and giving booktalks that promote favorite titles—and students are given some choice in what they read and time and support to read it (Pressley et al., 2006).

Tier 2

On the other hand, if students fail to respond successfully to Tier 1 intervention, the next step is to increase and intensify the intervention. Tier 2 work is characterized by small-group work that provides explicit, scaffolded, targeted intervention. During Tier 2 intervention, it is key to demonstrate, prompt for, and reinforce problem-solving strategies alongside daily core instruction. Again, guided reading (Fountas & Pinnell, 2006) provides an ideal instructional setting for this intensive teaching. Guided reading supports and encourages teachers to

- draw attention to the ways in which words work, for example, pointing out first letters, plurals, word endings, consonant clusters, vowel pairs, syllables, and the like.

- watch for opportunities to teach, prompt, and demonstrate how to take words apart, as well as opportunities to teach word-solving rapidly and efficiently.

- engage students to develop the automatic word recognition and comprehending strategies that enable fluent reading.

- demonstrate, prompt for, and reinforce all the strategies that accelerate proficient reading—comprehending, phonics, and fluency.

Tier 3

Occasionally, despite best efforts through your Tier 1 core reading instruction and the intensive intervention of Tier 2, a few at-risk strugglers may need even more extensive intervention. Within Tier 3, intense extensive guided reading support coupled with a wide range of texts students can read is still the best bet for moving kids into successful, proficient reading. Teachers may work one-on-one with students and engage the services of a literacy specialist or, as needed, may consider recommending at-risk students for special education testing and services.

RTI, coupled with *Comprehension Clubs* and guided reading, accomplishes two goals: It 1) develops a more valid way of identifying students who are struggling as readers; and 2) supports, through early intervention, students at risk of failure. At the same time, RTI elevates teachers' professional understanding of effective reading instruction and improves the overall approach to helping students who don't initially "get" reading. Ultimately, RTI moves us away from a model of failure to one of prevention.

Comprehension Clubs offers multiple opportunities to provide the extra support struggling readers need. You can tuck word-solving strategies into your interactive read-aloud and work closely with book clubs to scaffold challenged readers, leading them through the framework for developing comprehension: thinking within, beyond, and about the text. The reader's notebook, too, offers essential support especially for those children who find the written language they create through their own writing an easier entry point into literacy.

Comprehension Clubs and English Language Learners

The most obvious challenge for English Language Learners (ELLs) is the phonological system of our English language—the sounds and letters (in written language)—which may differ significantly from that of the student's primary language. Nonnative speakers may also find English-language vocabulary challenging—especially the Tier 2 academic words. Still, text, talk, and teaching—not isolated skill and drill separated from meaningful text—are exactly what our ELLs need.

Get to Know Your English Language Learners

It is always important to keep in mind the literacy foundation of each student in question. An English Language Learner designation applies to students "who vary by age, country of origin, mother tongue, socioeconomic status, degree of access and exposure to formal schooling, and so on. Variations among these factors influence the extent to which instruction practices can favorably impact learning to read in a second language" (Carlo, 2007). In other words, an ELL who arrives in your classroom without any formal schooling faces a different set of challenges than an ELL who is already a sophisticated reader and writer in his or her own language.

Clearly, your first order of business, then, is to get to know your English Language Learners; in order to effectively plan your instruction, you'll want to collect the following basic information:

- the student's name and age
- the student's first language and country of origin
- information about the student's prior educational experiences
- information the student would like to share about his or her social interactions with other children, and about the situations in which he or she learns best
- the student's place of birth

Questions such as these can also elicit vital and useful information from English Language Learners:

- When did the student arrive in the country?
- How long has the student been in school in this country and/or in his or her country of origin?
- Does anyone read to the student in his or her first language?
- Does the student have books in his or her first language?
- What general topics have been covered in the student's class so far?

(adapted from Bank Street College of Education: http://bankstreet.edu/literacy-guide/english-language-learners/strategies-working-english-language-learners/strategies-contact/)

Communication Strategies for Working With English Language Learners

With this information in hand, you'll know how best to implement *Comprehension Clubs* for your ELLs; as you draw them into the interactive read-alouds and book clubs, use these basic communication strategies to lend extra support:

- Simplify your language by using short, clear sentences when speaking to a student for whom English is a new language.

- Accompany your words with pictures, gestures, and movements that will help to convey meaning.

- Slow down when you speak with your student.

- Do not raise your volume when speaking. Loudness does not compensate for lack of understanding, and may be interpreted as anger toward the student.

- Accept a student's initial silence as a natural stage of development.

- Avoid correcting the student's errors when she or he attempts to speak English. Instead, model the correct form in your response.

- Allow plenty of time for the child to answer a question or wait a bit and then rephrase the question in simpler language. Remember, when answering a question, your student first must be sure to understand the English words you have used, then he or she must figure out a response to your question, and then she or he must remember the English way of saying that response. Keeping these steps in mind will help you to allow your student plenty of time for considering and responding to your questions.

(Bank Street College of Education, 2010)

Creating a Safe, Supportive Classroom Environment

Never lose sight of the emotional challenge of learning a new language; above all, English Language Learners need a safe, supportive environment in which to take the risks necessary in order to learn. To that end, also keep in mind these basic guidelines:

- Be mindful of the complexities of learning a new language and culture. There are many different circumstances that bring families to a new country: job transfer, planned migration, war, or refugee status.

- Be aware of your body language and tone of voice around your students. Children are extremely sensitive, and they feel acceptance or rejection from you long before you utter your first word.

- Be positive and encouraging when your students begin to experiment with new words; focus on the meaning of a student's effort to communicate rather than on the pronunciation, grammar, or correct choice of vocabulary.

- Your interest in the child's culture and language should be infused into each of your sessions. For example, ask your student to make connections between your activities and the student's prior activities.

(Bank Street College of Education, 2010)

With these guidelines in place, your English Language Learners will fully benefit from the text, talk, and teaching you introduce through *Comprehension Clubs*.

High-Quality, Content-Rich Text: The Best Support for English Language Learners

Books are powerful instructional tools for meeting the needs of a variety of students with diverse learning styles. The same language-rich environment—with lots of books and talk about books—that helps all children acquire literacy also helps English Language Learners add English to their home language. Therefore, you'll want to be sure that in your classroom reading and writing are easy to access and always appeal to all your students. To this end, there's nothing better than independent reading—scaffolded with engaging, content-rich text and lots of text talk. Through wide reading in English and immersion in meaningful conversation, ELLs learn vocabulary and grammar and improve their fluency, oral/aural language ability, and spelling and writing (Krashen, 2004).

In sum, ELLs need intensive and comprehensive oral English Language Development (ELD), particularly in academic English—the vocabulary, syntax, genres, and conversation that are essential for more abstract, formal, and demanding academic discussions. And ELLs also need academic content. Content knowledge is essential for reading comprehension and general academic success (Goldenberg, 2011). Again and again, we see that the most efficient and effective way to deliver both is through wide, extensive reading with engaging, content-rich books. In this way, all children, including ELLs, become better readers, plus they easily acquire a robust vocabulary, an understanding of English grammar, and writing and spelling skills.

The thematically organized *Comprehension Clubs* units of study showcase age-appropriate content that appeals to all students. *Comprehension Clubs* is also organized around a spiral of increasing difficulty—which provides challenge and support for students new to English.

Talk and Interactive Tools for Your English Language Learners

Embedding the books in rich text talk for your ELLs is more important than ever. Your ELLs may come to you with an extensive background of understanding and experience, but not yet have the labels in English for what they know. And then, too, those students who are recent arrivals to this country may not be familiar with United States culture and may find its idioms and certain cultural expressions particularly confusing. The more texts these students read—surrounded by the meaningful talk of the interactive read-alouds and book clubs—the faster they are able to absorb our language and culture.

The interactive read-aloud is a particularly powerful learning context for English learners because children can just listen to the story—they don't need to track the print, decode words or attempt to decipher the range of punctuation they encounter. Additionally, when you're reading aloud, you can pace yourself, slowing down to aid comprehension, stopping to explain unknown words in context, and then stopping and inviting your students to predict and fill in the words that might come next. This is often easiest to do with folktales and fairy tales, many of which have predictable, repeated refrains. Be sure your students can hear and understand the separate words embedded in the phrases they are repeating. Be aware of idioms, similes, and other unique American expressions that may stump them. Our rule of thumb: don't wait until after reading to find out if they understood the text. Continually monitor and check as you are reading aloud to make sure that they are following and comprehending the story.

Consider using graphic organizers, story maps, time lines, or co-constructing charts using shared or interactive writing to lend additional support. Just remember that simply filling these in is not the point and is not nearly as helpful as working on them together—what matters is the language you use that surrounds the charts and graphic organizers as you think together about how to fill them in. True learning occurs during conversations in which you scaffold your students' thinking and help them express their ideas. Additionally, invite your students to use their readers' notebooks; if they are more comfortable taking notes or writing a response to the story in their primary language, that's okay. Language is language, and either the primary or target language can be used to make meaning.

Your lesson cards, of course, will help you prepare for your teaching interaction—but you also know the unique needs of your students. The greater the extent to which you can respond to their specific challenges, the better.

And don't forget the audiobooks—listening to books again and again while following along in the book will work wonders for your ELLs. Fluency and comprehension go hand in hand as ELLs acquire both the sounds and sense of English.

Again, keeping in mind the importance of helping your ELLs develop their English vocabulary, you'll want to pay special attention to opportunities to help them learn new words. Here are some tips you might try to help your students develop their vocabulary:

- Always help your students believe in themselves as competent, capable learners.

- Don't hesitate, also, to find language partners for your ELLs. Reach out to families, newcomer centers in your community, community colleges, universities, and the like for native speakers of your students' primary language, who may be willing to partner with your students to provide additional support. Partners can read, write, and converse in your students' home language while also providing the support that enables them to move into the academic English they need for school success.

Dear Family:

Comprehension Clubs is a unique program that allows our whole class to explore challenging literature and informational texts together, meeting the highest standards of effective reading instruction. The program includes units of study on important themes or topics. In each unit of study, five books are read aloud and discussed by the whole class. Students also choose books to read on their own and then discuss in a book club.

Your child may do book club reading in school, with the option of reading along with an audio version of the book. In addition, your child may bring home the book club books to prepare for our classroom book club discussions. Here are some suggestions for helping your child before, during, and after reading:

Before: Ask your child why he or she chose this book and discuss what the book may be about.

During: Your child may wish to use his or her reader's notebook to make notes or write a question.

After: Encourage your child to talk with you about what he or she might want to share in the book club discussion.

Have fun reading and discussing books together, and your child will have fun, too!

Sincerely,

Your Child's Teacher

Estimada familia:

Nuestra clase está utilizando el programa de lectura *Comprehension Clubs* (Club de comprensión) en el que exploramos obras de literatura y textos informativos, cumpliendo con los más altos objetivos y estándares para la instrucción de la lectura. El programa *Comprehension Clubs* incluye varias unidades de estudio sobre temas importantes. En cada unidad se leen cinco libros en voz alta y se intercambian opiniones entre los miembros de la clase. Los alumnos también seleccionan libros para leer por su cuenta y comentarlos en un club de lectura.

Su hijo/a puede participar en el club de lectura de la escuela, donde tiene la opción de leer simultáneamente mientras escucha el libro en audio. Además, puede llevar a casa los libros del club de lectura para prepararse para las sesiones del club. A continuación, algunas sugerencias para ayudar a su hijo/a antes, durante y después de la lectura:

Antes: Pregúntele a su hijo/a por qué seleccionó el libro y hablen sobre lo que puede tratar el libro.

Durante: Le puede gustar a su hijo/a utilizar la libreta de notas del lector para escribir notas o preguntas sobre la lectura.

Después: Anime a su hijo/a a hablarle sobre lo que querrá discutir en el club de lectura.

Disfrute mientras lee y comenta los libros con su hijo/a, y él o ella también los disfrutará.

Atentamente,

El maestro/La maestra

Sample Student Book Club Cycles and Pacing Charts

Let's see how one primary teacher organizes her first-grade book clubs around the picture book explorations.

Sample Primary Book Club Cycle

One theme cycle takes 2–3 weeks. Week 1 includes reading the read-alouds, introducing the student book club books, and allowing students to begin reading their selections.

Week 1, Day 2	Week 2	End of Week 2– End of Week 3
• Book-talk four book club titles. • Students choose book club books by ballot. • Teacher forms groups. • Students may take books home in plastic bag with parent letter (see previous page) to share with families. • Students may share inquiry projects they developed this week.	• Students have time to read book club book with peers, older students, adult volunteers, or their parents, or they can read along with the streaming audio. • Teacher meets with two book clubs per day for discussion and written response in readers' notebooks. • Students who aren't meeting with teacher select from menu of literacy activities (e.g., phonics practice, listening center, writing related to previous book or inquiry project, and so forth).	• Teacher and students meet in final book club to record and share closing reflections about the book, their discussions, comparisons to other books, and final thoughts about what they have learned. • If selected, students share their theme projects.

This primary teacher relies on supportive families to help her young students read the book. If similar support isn't possible in your community, find ways to provide the extra support needed yourself or enlist the help of classroom aides, parent volunteers, or responsible cross-age tutors.

Week 1, Day 2: Morning

I book-talk and introduce each of the four new titles for our next round of book clubs. Children rate the books from 1–3, with a 1 indicating their first choice. I let my students know that not everyone will get their first choice, but they will read their favorite book sometime during the book club cycle.

Week 1, Day 2: Afternoon

My book clubs work best when I involve my students' families, so on Tuesday afternoon, I send home the books and sometimes one to three sticky notes in large plastic bags. I always include a letter to parents explaining what to do. The letter explains the objectives of book clubs: to read, discuss, write about, and respond to a book in a way that is meaningful to the child. I also make some suggestions about open-ended questions family members could ask as prompts for their child's thinking. I ask students to mark pages they really liked with the sticky notes or paper, and to talk with their families about the story.

Week 2, Day 1

The books are returned to school. During our reading and writing workshop, I conduct mini-lessons on reading and writing strategies such as identifying unknown words, making predictions, using capitalization in writing, or citing textual evidence from a story in their readers' notebooks. These mini-lessons provide instruction in how to read and write more effectively. In addition, we will spend time rereading the books. This is important for those children who were not able to read at home. Some of my students are already fairly adept readers; they reread their books either on their own or with a partner. For others, this is the time when I will tailor my guided reading instruction to those skills and strategies needed to read the book club book. I also make sure that all my challenged readers and English Language Learners have multiple opportunities to listen to and read along with the books on audio.

I will meet with two book club groups during reading and writing time today. We sit in a cozy corner of my room surrounded by bookcases and snuggle on our shaggy rug. This helps us concentrate on the discussion but leaves me free to observe what is going on with the rest of the students. We use the comprehension framework to guide our discussions: thinking within, beyond, and about the text. I record on chart paper what my students share.

Week 2, Day 2

I meet with the other two book clubs and repeat the process. As a class, we discuss possible extension projects. At the beginning of the year, when students are gaining strength as readers and writers, I may invite them to demonstrate their growing comprehension in more visual or dramatic ways through posters, readers theater, and the like. Later in the year, as they become more competent readers and writers, it's easier for them to handle book critiques, research reports, and projects that demand more written work.

Discussion and Reader's Notebook. *Because book clubs are one component of our reading workshop, students participate in discussion and reader's notebook writing at varying times. Some of them will come to the discussion first and then write in their notebooks, capturing their memory of what was discussed in the club; others will bring their notebooks to the discussion and take notes during the discussion. I find this works really well for first graders—some children need to talk about what they've read before they're ready to write, and just the opposite for others.*

We begin the year with journal prompts to help students focus their thinking about books. I provide short sentence starters, model my own journal entry, and talk about what makes a good entry. I use the following prompts: I think . . . I wonder . . . I noticed . . . I would like to know more about . . . Each of these helps first graders gradually move beyond, "I like the story. It was funny."

Week 2, Day 3

All four book clubs meet on their own for further discussion and wrap-up work; I circulate, checking in with each one, taking notes, making sure each group is on track and centered on the text.

Week 2, Day 4

This is our day of reflection. . . . We may come together as a whole group to share our thinking collectively about our book club experience: What did we learn? What do we still question? What connections do we see across the books? What conceptual information are we absorbing from the unit of study? The students who are working on book extension projects have time to complete these and prepare to share them the next day.

Week 2, Day 5

Children share their extension projects with the class. And we begin the book club cycle again: I use the students' rating lists to organize them into new clubs. I remind them that they will get to read their first-choice book at some point during the book club cycle—and if, for some reason, that doesn't happen, I'm always happy to make the book available to them for independent reading on their own time. (See the facing page for an example of a letter that the primary teacher sends home to her students' families.)

Dear Family,

Student book clubs are a wonderful part of our reading program. Just as in the adult book clubs you may be familiar with, children come together in small groups to read, discuss, and write about engaging, high-quality books, both fiction and informational texts. On Tuesday, I will introduce the book choices. Students will then select the book they want to read and bring it home to share with you and read over the weekend. The next week, the book clubs will meet on Monday, Tuesday, Wednesday, and Thursday, and it is essential that students arrive having read the book and being prepared to discuss it. I will, of course, also provide time for them to read at school. Students will sometimes write about their books in their readers' notebooks. In addition, our literacy centers may feature projects the students can do based on the books they are reading and discussing.

Your child has selected a book from several choices related by theme, topic, and/or genre. Because your child has self-selected the book, it may not be at his or her appropriate level for independent reading. This means that your child can listen to an audio version or to someone reading the book aloud. Then your child will be able to think and talk about the book at our meeting.

Here are ways to read and discuss the books together in preparation for book clubs:

❏ Talk about the book after reading it.

❏ Read the book a second time and note favorite passages. Remind your child to record the page numbers in his or her reader's notebook that he or she would like to share and to use sticky notes to mark places in the book he or she wants to talk about.

❏ Your child should be prepared to direct the group to the selected part(s) he or she marked. By the end of the year, we want to make sure that all students understand how to do a close reading of every book we read and how to cite examples from the text to explain his or her thoughts, questions, and opinions about the book.

❏ Send the book back to school on Monday with sticky notes adhered to the pages and passages your child has selected to discuss.

Thank you for your support and assistance! The students and I look forward to many stimulating book discussions this year to extend and refine our love of reading.

Sincerely,

Your Child's Teacher

Let's see how one intermediate teacher organizes her Grade 5 book clubs around chapter book explorations.

Sample Intermediate Book Club Cycle

Week 1	Week 2	Week 2 Wrap
• On the second day of Read-Aloud instruction, introduce book through booktalks.	• Teacher provides mini-lesson on reading skills and processing strategies on an as-needed basis.	• Clubs meet at least one more time, wrap up their discussion, and come to final conclusions.
• Students rate books on rating list.	• Students continue to read chapter book at school during independent reading time and at home.	• Students record final reflections about the book and their discussion in their reader's notebooks.
• Teacher forms groups and either assigns or negotiates with students the date by which they must finish reading their book.	• Students record notes and analysis for discussion and written response in readers' notebooks.	• Teacher suggests possible extension projects—or responds to students' ideas—as needed or desired.
• Students take books home, possibly in plastic bag with sticky notes and parent letter and begin reading, ideally, using their readers' notebooks to keep track of how many pages they read each day.	• Struggling students can listen to their selections on streaming audio. • Clubs meet for the first time.	

The intermediate teacher explains her process for organizing and implementing book clubs with her fifth-grade students:

Selecting the Books

At the start of the year, I read aloud many books and engage the students in thinking and talking about them. The students learn what it means to read closely and analyze text through a collaborative book discussion. Typically, after several weeks of daily interactive read-alouds, my students understand how to read, discuss, and analyze literature. We're ready to begin our book clubs. We typically participate in a two-week cycle but can extend into three weeks as needed, especially for more complex and demanding books.

Book-Talking the Books

At the start of each round of book clubs, I book-talk all four titles—only to pique students' interest, being careful to avoid giving away any of the important information that students should be encouraged to discover on their own. After the booktalks, I give students a chance to look at the books; then they vote for their top three choices. From their votes (and my knowledge of how they work best together) I organize them into groups of approximately six students per book. The groups' first task is to create a reading schedule. I tell them when the book needs to be finished and which days they will be discussing it. The reading schedule tells the students how much they need to read each day before their first meeting. I give the students a calendar, which they keep in their reader's notebook, with the discussion days marked; they can use the calendar to record and keep track of their independent reading time, too.

Weekly Schedule
Each book club cycle lasts approximately two weeks, from first read (when students crack open their books and start reading) to final discussion. The cycle may stretch to another week if we include theme projects.

Daily Schedule
Each book club meeting has a similar structure. Before the clubs meet, the students read their book and mark with sticky notes sections that they want to discuss or share; they may jot notes or page numbers in their readers' notebooks. (I study the lesson cards in advance to help me be ready to support the discussion as needed.) Then, the students begin discussing the book, sharing parts that they found interesting, asking open-ended questions of each other about the text, and sharing their opinions. They cite evidence from the text to back up their stance, connecting parts of the story to our overarching theme, building connections between the books, and sharing their notebook entries. On some days, I also give students a specific topic or question to include in their discussion.

After discussing the reading, students sometimes write in their readers' notebooks in response to a prompt or in answer to a question. They may also respond to something that arose in their group discussion, allowing for some choice in what they are writing about.

The end of each session is the most important. We debrief as a class: What went well in your discussions? What can you do better next time? I give examples of things that I noticed while I was monitoring the groups. During this process we refer to the criteria we established early in the year for what makes a good discussion. It is very important to have the students reflect and set goals for the future because this is where I see the most progress in their discussion abilities.

Final Project
We may end our round of book clubs with a unit theme project. The type of project students create varies with each book. I offer students a choice of projects and I show them examples when available. We create evaluation criteria as a class so they know the expectations up front. (See unit project suggestions and project rubrics, pp. 86–105.) For each project, students create a rough draft that I check off before they start the final copy. At the end of the project, the students evaluate their own project based on the criteria we created together.

Suggested Planning and Pacing Guide #1

WEEK 1

Day 1	Day 2	Day 3
Introduce the Unit Whole-Class Interactive Read-Aloud (20 Minutes)	Whole-Class Interactive Read-Aloud (20 Minutes) Booktalks* (Introduce Book Club books)	Whole-Class Interactive Read-Aloud (20 Minutes) Students read and prepare for Book Clubs

WEEK 2

Students read and prepare for Book Clubs	Book Clubs meet**	Book Clubs meet

WEEK 3

Discussion of Unit Theme ———————————————————————

Optional Unit Theme Projects—Complete and Review ——————————

WEEK 4

Optional Wrap-up ——————————————————————————————

* **Booktalk** Introduce each of the student book selections with a brief booktalk.

** **Book Clubs** Clubs typically meet for 20–30 minutes, though initially the time should be shorter. Younger children will have shorter Book Clubs (10–15 minutes). Allow time for students to summarize and evaluate at the end of their meetings. You can vary the scheduling and monitoring of Book Clubs.

Day 4	Day 5
Whole-Class Interactive Read-Aloud (20 Minutes) **Students read and prepare for Book Clubs**	**Whole-Class Interactive Read-Aloud (20 Minutes)** **Students read and prepare for Book Clubs**
Book Clubs meet	**Book Clubs meet**

Suggested Planning and Pacing Guide #2

WEEK 1

Day 1	Day 2	Day 3
Introduce the Unit Whole-Class Interactive Read-Aloud (20 Minutes)	Booktalks* (Introduce Book Club books)	Whole-Class Interactive Read-Aloud (20 Minutes)

WEEK 2

	Whole-Class Interactive Read-Aloud (20 Minutes)	

WEEK 3

Students read and prepare for Book Clubs		Students read and prepare for Book Clubs

WEEK 4

Students read and prepare for Book Clubs	Book Clubs meet**	Book Clubs meet

WEEK 5

Discussion of Unit Theme ─────────────────────────────

Optional Unit Theme Projects—Complete and Review ─────────

* **Booktalk** Introduce each of the student book selections with a brief booktalk.

Day 4	Day 5
Students read and prepare for Book Clubs	Whole-Class Interactive Read-Aloud (20 Minutes)
Whole-Class Interactive Read-Aloud (20 Minutes)	Whole-Class Interactive Read-Aloud (20 Minutes)
	Students read and prepare for Book Clubs
Book Clubs meet	Book Clubs meet

** **Book Clubs** Clubs typically meet for 20–30 minutes, though initially the time should be shorter. Younger children will have shorter Book Clubs (10–15 minutes). Allow time for students to summarize and evaluate at the end of their meetings. You can vary the scheduling and monitoring of Book Clubs.

Unit Project Overview and Rubric

Unit or theme projects invite students to continue the conversation about books they love and want to revisit, as well as demonstrate what they have learned as the result of exploring the theme or unit of study. As Katherine Schlick Noe writes, "a good project lures the students back into the book[s] to cement, enhance, and even reinvent what they gained from their first visit" (2004).

Unit projects offer all readers a way to sum up their learning and to gain a sense of accomplishment. Collaborative projects provide additional layers of meaning and support. Inviting students to present in another format or medium what they've learned from their reading gives them a way to shape and express their evolving understandings. Thus, unit projects can be helpful for the developing reader, challenged reader, or reader for whom English is a target language.

Selecting Options That Suit Your Needs

Unit projects are flexible and entirely optional; in other words, you'll know what makes the most sense for your students. A project shaped and driven by a student's passionate interest is always the best kind! On the following pages, you will find suggestions to sum up and extend your work with each unit of study. These include general discussion questions and options for three easy-to-implement projects. You may elect to use one of these options per unit, create your own projects based on your students' interests, or simply move on without doing any projects at all. The choice is yours!

Options for each grade may be found on the following pages in this guide:

Kindergarten . . . . pp. 88–90	Grade 3 . . . . pp. 97–99
Grade 1 . . . . pp. 91–93	Grade 4 . . . . pp. 100–102
Grade 2 . . . . pp. 94–96	Grade 5 . . . . pp. 103–105

What About Evaluations?

Unit projects offer numerous opportunities for assessment; simply observing your students while they are at work on their projects will yield invaluable information about their comprehension, interpretation, use of resources, and ability to collaborate with and learn from their peers.

We've included a possible rubric; feel free to adapt in ways that work best for you and your students or create something new that fits your own needs and interests. For example, select goals that you think are especially appropriate for the option or options you worked with or are important for specific students.

Comprehension Clubs

Name _____ **Date** _____

Unit/Option/Book(s) _____

Rubric for Assessing Student Progress on Unit Projects

Behaviors to Notice (Select goals appropriate for the option.)	Notes	Rating 1 (Limited Evidence) 2 (Consistent Evidence) 3 (Very Strong Evidence) N/A (Doesn't Apply to This Option)
Talks about texts in a way that shows deeper understanding.		
Talks about texts in a way that shows awareness of the author's craft.		
Notices and expresses connections between texts.		
Infers and expresses the larger ideas or lessons from texts.		
Comes up with ideas based on information from texts.		
Refers to texts as resources for further discussion, activity, or creative projects.		
Uses drawing, writing, or other creative activity to reflect and extend the meaning of texts.		
Draws from and expresses personal connections to texts and opinions about them.		
Works well with others (partners and team members).		
Reports or summarizes activity and/or what was learned in a clear way.		
Other		
TOTAL SCORE/HIGHEST POSSIBLE SCORE (Number of Applicable Goals X 3)		

Kindergarten: Unit Projects

Being a Friend

It's nice to have friends to play with, but friends are important in more ways than that. *What is being a friend all about?*

You may wish to choose from the options below to offer students the opportunity to sum up their key understandings about this unit.

Discuss

- What does it mean to be a good friend? What did you learn about friendship from these stories?

- What did the writers do to help you understand what it means to be a good friend?

Friendship Wish List Ask children to think about the characters from this unit. Which of these characters would they want as a friend? Why?

A Little Help, Please Friends help each other. Invite children to match these problems with characters from the books they have read.

- You are feeling sad or shy. Who would try and help you feel better?

- You want to make a new neighbor feel welcome. Who would know how to help?

- You want to find a lost stuffed animal. Who could help you think of a plan?

- You want a great pet. Who can give you advice?

Act It Out Invite children to work in pairs or groups to select their favorite books from this unit and act out the story.

Telling Tales

Animals that talk? Events that repeat? Told and retold in different ways? That's just some of the fun! *What makes a folktale a special kind of story?*

You may wish to choose from the options below to offer students the opportunity to sum up their key understandings about this unit.

Discuss

- What animal characters did you meet in these stories? What lessons did they learn?

- What things did the writers repeat that made each story so much fun to read?

Thinking in "Threes" Remind children that authors of folktales often include things in threes, such as three bears, three bowls, and three chairs. Talk about the "threes" found in the tales. Then ask children to choose a set(s) of threes to draw.

Old Tales, New Ways Show the two Little Red Hen books. Point out that different authors may choose to retell the same folktale. Talk about how these two books are alike and different. Ask children to draw the things that were alike in the two tales.

Who Am I? Invite children to use the following sentence frames and play a guessing game.

I _____.
I _____.
Who am I?

Use the following example as a model.

I thought the sky was falling.
I told my friends.
Who am I?

Trees & Other Plants

From the tallest tree to the tiniest flower, plants are an important part of our world. *How do writers help you care about trees and plants?*

You may wish to choose from the options below to offer students the opportunity to sum up their key understandings about this unit.

Discuss

- What do plants need to live and grow?

- Why do you think these writers thought it was important to write about plants?

Yummy Plants! Help children recall the names of the plants they read about that were fruits or vegetables people eat. Provide colored paper and have children draw and cut out pictures of fruits and vegetables. Help children label their plants. Use their cutouts to make a Vegetables chart and a Fruits chart for display.

Be a Gardener Ask children to imagine they have been given a little land to use for a garden. Then ask: *What are the tools and materials you would need to start your garden?* Invite children to draw and label pictures of all the tools and materials they would need.

Favorite Facts Ask children to share what they thought was the one most interesting fact they now know about plants. Then help them write the facts on index cards. Collect the cards and make a fact file to share.

Feelings

Are you happy? Sad? Angry? Thankful? *How does understanding your own feelings and the feelings of others help you in everyday life?*

You may wish to choose from the options below to offer students the opportunity to sum up their key understandings about this unit.

Discuss

- What are some of the different feelings that people have? When do their feelings change?

- How did the writers help you understand what it means to be thankful? Grumpy? Happy?

Spin and Say Feelings Use a paper circle to make a spinner divided into eight spaces. Label spaces with the following feelings: *grumpy, happy, sad, surprised, sorry, angry, shy,* and *glad.* Have children take turns spinning and telling about the feeling they land on. For example, *I feel grumpy when I hurt my knee.*

Tell a Story Recall with children that they listened to two different stories about Bird. Then ask them to work in a group to create a new story about Bird. Remind children to make up a beginning, middle, and ending for their story.

Sing Out! Invite children to make up new lyrics to the song "If You're Happy." Instead of *clap your hands,* sing *make a face* and have children show a happy face. Continue by replacing *happy* with different adjectives that describe feelings and showing that face.

All Kinds of Jobs

Jobs, jobs, jobs! *Where do people work and what jobs do they do?*

You may wish to choose from the options below to offer students the opportunity to sum up their key understandings about this unit.

Discuss

- What kinds of jobs did you learn about in these books?

- How did the illustrations help you learn about the different kinds of work that people do?

What's My Job? Invite children to use the following sentence frames and play a guessing game.

> I work in (at) _____.
> At work, I _____.
> What's my job?

Use the following example as a model.

> *I work in a hospital.*
> *At work, I see patients.*
> *What's my job?*

Cool Tools Ask children to think about one of the workers they read about. Have them name the worker and use that to label the top of a page. Have children draw pictures to show the tools and materials the person uses at work. Use a firefighter as an example.

Usual and Unusual Jobs Give children a paper divided in half. Ask them to draw a person at work at a usual job, a job that is very familiar. Then ask children to draw a picture to show someone at work at an unusual job. Help them label their drawings and then share them.

 ## Concept Books

Colors. Letters. Numbers. Days of the week. Lots of books are written about these things! *How do writers make concept books fun to read?*

You may wish to choose from the options below to offer students the opportunity to sum up their key understandings about this unit.

Discuss

- Why is it important to learn the names of colors? Letters? Numbers? Days of the week?

- How do books help you learn about numbers? Colors? Letters? Days of the week?

Author! Author! Display pairs of books by the same author (Donald Crews, Eric Carle, Audrey Wood). Have children take turns telling how each author's two books are alike. Help compare characters, settings, and story events.

If . . . ? Display the nine books in this unit of study. Invite children to match these concepts to the books that focus on them.

- Which book would I look at if I wanted to learn about . . .

  ❏ colors?

  ❏ numbers?

  ❏ the names of the days of the week?

  ❏ the letters of the alphabet?

Make Concept Cards Invite pairs or groups to make flash-card sets to show colors, numbers, letters, or days of the week. Have children draw pictures, write labels, illustrate events, or represent the sound of a letter. Display the sets for center use.

Grade 1: Unit Projects

 ## My Family & Me

Moms, dads, sisters, brothers, aunts, uncles, cousins, and grandparents, too! *How do people in a family help each other and have fun together?*

You may wish to choose from the options below to offer students the opportunity to sum up their key understandings about this unit.

Discuss

- How did the authors writing for this unit make the characters seem real?

- How did the setting, where and when the story took place, help the story seem like something that could happen in real life?

Family Time Fun Ask children to choose one story from the unit and draw a picture that shows two or more people in the family. Ask children to show the family members cooperating and doing something together for "family time fun."

Family Word Wall Talk about how the different family members were important to each family in the books they read. Point out that there are many words that name the people in a family. Then ask children to help you name those people. Write their suggestions on cards and display them. You might begin with *Mother, Father, Mom, Dad, Mommy,* and *Daddy.* After the cards are completed, have children take turns choosing a card and reading it aloud.

Who Helps? Have children work in pairs or in a group to create a list, or series of pictures, to show what the characters did to help their families.

 ## Stories With a Moral

Sometimes writers want you to learn from how their characters behave. *How can folktales teach people how to act in real life?*

You may wish to choose from the options below to offer students the opportunity to sum up their key understandings about this unit.

Discuss

- Why is a folktale a good way to teach readers a lesson?

- How did the illustrations help you understand where and when the story took place?

Message From an Author Display the unit books. Write or say the messages below and ask children to match each with a unit book.

- It's important to tell the truth.

- You can't play for two teams at the same time.

- Sharing makes everyone richer.

- Don't talk to strangers.

- Slow and steady wins the race.

The Best Character Establish with children that great characters help make these stories well liked and worthy of repeated retelling. Using children's suggestions, list great characters from this unit. Then have children choose and vote on their favorite. After tallying results, have children draw and write about what makes that character memorable.

Put on a Show Invite pairs or groups to act out a scene from the story or the entire story. Help children assign the different roles and choose a narrator to tell the story.

Strong & Healthy

Everyone wants to be healthy and strong! *How do writers help you find out about healthy habits?*

You may wish to choose from the options below to offer students the opportunity to sum up their key understandings about this unit.

Discuss

- What healthy habits did you learn about?
- How did the illustrations help you understand what it means to be strong and healthy?

Labels and Captions Invite children to work with partners and look through books in this unit for places where the author used captions or labels to tell about the pictures. Have children read the captions or labels with their partners.

Interview an "Author" Pair children and assign one child the role of interviewer and the other the role of author. Explain that the interviewer will ask the author a question about how to stay healthy and the author will answer. Children may find it helpful to focus on questions that relate to one book at a time.

Make a "Healthy Salad" Invite children to work in pairs or groups to write or draw on small pieces of paper ideas for staying healthy, based on the things they learned from the books in this unit. Then put all the ideas in a bowl for a "healthy salad." Have children take turns choosing a paper from the bowl and reading or telling about what it says.

 ## What I Can Do

Trying something new can be hard. But it also can make you feel good. *How do you know what you can do—unless you try?*

You may wish to choose from the options below to offer students the opportunity to sum up their key understandings about this unit.

Discuss

- What does it mean to try as hard as you can?
- Why do you think the authors thought readers would be interested in stories about children who try hard?

Who Is It? Ask children to think about the characters from this unit. Have children take turns describing a character from one of the stories, without mentioning the character's name. Then ask the other children to guess which character is being described.

Book Review Explain to children that sometimes people decide if they want to buy a book by reading a review. Tell children that a review tells about the book and then tells why the writer of the review liked or did not like the book. Have children choose from the books in this unit and help them write book reviews. Suggest that one sentence tell about the book and another tell why children did or did not like the book.

Retell a Story Invite children to work in pairs or groups to select their favorite book in this unit and draw a series of pictures from the story. Then have them take turns using the pictures to retell the story to their partners or to the group.

It Happened to Me

Sometimes, authors use their own experiences in the books they write. *What do you learn from authors who write about their own lives?*

You may wish to choose from the options below to offer students the opportunity to sum up their key understandings about this unit.

Discuss

- What happy childhood memories did you read about in these stories?

- Why do you think these authors chose to write about their own lives? Which authors used humor to tell their stories? Why?

You're Invited Have children decide which character from all the books in the unit they would most like to meet. Then together, write an invitation asking the character to come to the class for a book party. Have children explain in their letter why they want the character to come and why they think it would be fun to talk about his or her story.

My Story Remind children that the authors wrote these stories based on their own childhood memories. Ask children to remember something that happened to them recently or when they were little. Then invite them to make up a story based on that experience and draw and write about it. Invite children to share their stories.

Advice From Freckleface Strawberry! Review the two books by author Julianne Moore with the children. Ask: *Based on her stories, what advice do you think the main character would give us if she were here in our classroom?* Record their answers on chart paper.

 Animal Stories

Bears and frogs don't talk in real life. But they sometimes do in stories! *How—and why—do writers create animal characters that act like people?*

You may wish to choose from the options below to offer students the opportunity to sum up their key understandings about this unit.

Discuss

- How did the problems the animal characters faced in these books remind you of the kinds of problems that people have in real life?

- Why do you think the writers used animal characters instead of people?

Just Like You and Me Remind children that in fantasy animal stories, writers make animals act like people. Ask children to work in pairs or small groups and choose one animal character from these stories. Have children work together to make a list of the ways in which the animals acted like a real person.

Where and When? Recall with children that the stories in this unit had different settings, showing where and when the story took place. Have each child choose one of the stories and draw and label a picture to show the setting of the story.

Problems! Problems! Just like in stories about real children, animal characters sometimes have problems. Ask children to choose one story, draw a picture of an animal character from the story, and write a sentence that tells what problem the character had.

Grade 2: Unit Projects

It Happened in School

What happens in school? A lot! *How do people in school learn from each new experience—and from each other?*

You may wish to choose from the options below to offer students the opportunity to sum up their key understandings about this unit.

Discuss
- How did the authors in this unit make the schools they wrote about or their characters' reactions to school events seem real? Can you think of examples?
- Almost all of the books in the unit include some humor. Which of the funny incidents in these stories remind you, at least in some way, of things that could happen at your school?

School Rules Invite children to work in groups to come up with a list of rules inspired by the books in this unit. Challenge children to come up with a rule to go with every book they have read.

How Do You Define Friendship? In many of these stories, the idea of finding or being a friend is important. Using events from one or more of these books as examples, ask children to explain in writing what it means to be a friend.

Worries From the Black Lagoon Briefly revisit the two Black Lagoon books. How do the author and illustrator show that people sometimes worry more than they need to? Which of the other authors in this unit express a similar idea in their books?

Wishes & Promises

An old saying warns, "Be careful what you wish for!" *How can a wish or a promise change someone's life?*

You may wish to choose from the options below to offer students the opportunity to sum up their key understandings about this unit.

Discuss
- Why is a folktale a good kind of text to help people learn lessons?
- In a number of these stories, people who are poor become wealthy. Why do you think this detail is often found in folktales?

Let Me Try Again Invite children to think about a big mistake that a character made in one of these stories. Speaking or writing as that character, have children try and persuade the class why he or she deserves another chance to do things right.

It's Magic! In folktales, magical beings and objects can create big changes. Ask children to work in pairs or small groups to pick one magical being or object from these stories and together write about what they would do with that object or being if they could have its help for one day.

Favorite Folktale Take a class poll. Which stories in the unit did children like most and why? Create and post a chart to show the results.

Search & Survive

Surviving in the wild is not easy! *How do animals find food—and avoid becoming another creature's dinner?*

You may wish to choose from the options below to offer students the opportunity to sum up their key understandings about this unit.

Discuss
- How did these writers show you what animals need to do to survive? Did you see some similarities across the books? Can you think of some examples?
- Think about the ways in which these writers presented information. Which book or books were the most fun to read? Why?

Survival Guide Invite children to work on their own or in small groups to create a survival guide for one of the animals they read about. Remind them to consider what the animal has to do to find food and what it has to do to avoid becoming someone else's food.

Picture This Ask children to work in pairs to consider how the photos and art in the books they have read added information. Then ask them to tell or write about which book has the best visuals and why.

Who Eats What? Invite children to work in pairs to make a game that matches predators and prey from the reading. Have them use 12 index cards to draw and label six different predators and their prey. When the cards are ready, children can place them facedown and invite other children to turn cards over and make matches.

 Like No One Else

No two people are exactly alike. How do authors get readers to think about this question: *What makes you—and others—unique?*

You may wish to choose from the options below to offer students the opportunity to sum up their key understandings about this unit.

Discuss
- What was the big idea, or message, you got from all of these books?
- Which book do you think expressed this message in the most memorable way? Why?

Good Advice Invite children to choose one character from their readings and, speaking or writing as that character, use examples from the book to explain why it is important to respect yourself and others and to appreciate what makes you—and others—unique.

It's All in the Details The authors of these books wanted to create characters who were like no one else. Survey children to find out which character or characters children think are the most unique and why. Post the completed survey for all to share.

A Can-Do Attitude No one is good at everything. But a positive attitude can help you succeed when you face challenges. Invite children to select one character and explain how a positive attitude helped him or her overcome a big challenge.

Animal Watch

Sometimes, animals can surprise you. *What have people discovered by watching and caring for animals?*

You may wish to choose from the options below to offer students the opportunity to sum up their key understandings about this unit.

Discuss

- How did these writers show you how important it is to observe very closely?

- How did reading these books help you learn more about how scientists make discoveries and share information?

Wow! Point out that these books contain some surprising facts. Invite children to select their favorite book from the unit and write about and illustrate something surprising they learned from it. Compile children's responses to make a class book called "Wow! Amazing Animal Facts."

Ask a Scientist As a class, compile a list of questions that children might ask a scientist about the animals from these readings. While your class may not have a scientist around to provide answers, discuss how children might also find answers using print or online resources in the library. If time permits, help children research answers to their questions and add an answer column to your list.

Hero Award Invite children to work in groups to discuss how people helped animals—or animals helped others—in many of these books. Have each group select one person or animal they read about and create an award certificate that explains why this person or animal deserves to be called a hero.

 # Realistic Fiction

Some of the best fiction stories seem very, very real! *How do authors make the characters and situations they create seem so true to life?*

You may wish to choose from the options below to offer students the opportunity to sum up their key understandings about this unit.

Discuss

- How did the problems characters faced in these books remind you of the kinds of problems people face in real life? Why do you think the authors chose to write about these kinds of problems?

- How did characters in this unit learn from their mistakes? Why do you think the authors chose to have the characters make mistakes to begin with?

Believe It or Not! When authors create realistic fiction, they try to make their settings seem like places that you could see in real life. Invite children to discuss which settings seem the most like places they know—or places they'd like to visit—and why.

If It's Realistic Fiction Have children work in small groups to make a list of what must happen in a story in order for it to be realistic, citing examples from the books they have read.

Author Study In this unit, children had the opportunity to read two books by Gary Soto and three by Nikki Grimes. Invite children to work in groups and choose one of these authors and revisit his or her books. Have children list their findings. What does each book by that author seem to have in common with the others?

Grade 3: Unit Projects

Brothers & Sisters

They argue—but not all of the time! *Why do brothers and sisters often clash? How can they get along?*

You may wish to choose from the options below to offer students the opportunity to sum up their key understandings about this unit.

Discuss

- Each author in this unit chose to write from one character's point of view. What can be tricky about reading—and writing—this kind of story?

- Which of these narrators (or their siblings) seem like people you would want to know? Why?

Another Point of View Invite students to work in pairs to pick a favorite book from the unit and explain the events from the point of view of the sibling who did not narrate the story.

Family Rules Using the characters from these books as examples, have students work in groups to create a list of dos and don'ts for brothers and sisters.

Sibling Awards Invite students to argue orally or in writing which character from their readings deserves to be crowned the best or the worst sibling ever!

Trickster Tales

Tricksters may not always be big and strong, but they're always clever! *What lessons can you learn from trickster tales?*

You may wish to choose from the options below to offer students the opportunity to sum up their key understandings about this unit.

Discuss

- How do these tales show that someone smaller or weaker can win over someone bigger and stronger?

- What similarities did you notice about the ways in which these stories begin and end? What patterns do you see?

Lessons Learned Ask students to work in groups to list life lessons, linking each lesson to one or more books in this unit. Then have students write and illustrate these lessons using different kinds of colorful lettering and paper or by creating artwork on the computer. Share finished pieces with the rest of the class.

Fair or Unfair? Invite students to select one book from this unit and, writing from the point of view of one of the characters, explain why he or she was treated fairly or unfairly. Have volunteers perform monologues for the class, based on what they wrote.

No Need for Greed Characters get into trouble in these tales for being too greedy. Have pairs of students select one villain they have read about and write a letter, offering their advice about what the villain could do differently to avoid getting into trouble.

Life Depends on Water

Yes, ocean animals need water—but they're not the only ones. *Why is water so important to all living things?*

You may wish to choose from the options below to offer students the opportunity to sum up their key understandings about this unit.

Discuss

- How has reading these books changed the way in which you think about the ocean and ocean life?

- How has your reading changed your ideas about how water is used by people and animals that live on land?

Mission Accomplished Each author in this unit set out with the same basic goals: to share factual information about water and help readers appreciate why all living things need that vital substance. Take a class poll. Which author did the best job of conveying these goals? What about that author's approach made his or her book stand out?

Information, Please Invite students to select a topic from their reading that they'd like to know more about. Have students share with the class their topics and their questions about it. Together, brainstorm kinds of sources students could use to find answers to their questions. If time permits, have students conduct research and report their findings.

Picture It Ask: *How did the art and photos in each book help you appreciate the text?* Then invite students to each select one book and write a review emphasizing the role of the photos or illustrations in setting a mood and conveying information.

 ## Courage

What happens when people face their fears and accomplish something they feared they could not do? *What does it take to have courage?*

You may wish to choose from the options below to offer students the opportunity to sum up their key understandings about this unit.

Discuss

- What did you notice about the way problems got solved in each of these books?

- How did the main characters in these books benefit from acting courageously?

Being Courageous As these books demonstrate, there are different ways to be brave. Ask students to select a character, describe what he or she was afraid of, and explain how and why that character decided to face his or her fears. Build a chart to summarize students' observations.

Brave Words As a class, briefly revisit the books in this unit and brainstorm a list of words that describe how the main characters felt about facing their fears. For example: Who was cautious? Determined? Bold? Nervous? Challenge students to find at least one descriptor for each character.

Keep Trying Invite students to select a character and, writing or speaking from that character's point of view, explain why courage often includes the willingness to try again and again to reach a goal.

Sports Stars

There's more to being a successful athlete than scoring points. *What makes an athlete great, both on and off the playing field?*

You may wish to choose from the options below to offer students the opportunity to sum up their key understandings about this unit.

Discuss

- What qualities do you think a sports star must have to succeed at his or her chosen sport? Which of these same qualities helps people succeed in things other than sports?
- Think about the books you enjoyed most. How did the author's approach contribute to your enjoyment? How much did your interest in the sport affect your choice?

Hall of Fame Nominees Have students, in groups or independently, write or present an oral argument for why one person they read about deserves to be in a hall of fame, based on achievements and personal qualities. Discuss these nominations as a class and then vote on which seems most deserving.

Unsung Heroes Many of these books reveal how other people helped the athlete face challenges. Have small groups select a person whose encouragement helped one of the athletes profiled. Ask students to write thank-you notes to that person. Have the notes read aloud or displayed with the related books.

Game Changers Some of the sports stars profiled here proved that gender, race, or even size need not keep someone from playing a sport. In doing so they influenced people's attitudes in ways that went beyond sports. Have students pick two "game changers" to compare by writing about how each brought about change.

 Mystery

It's fun to read a mystery and to challenge yourself to try to solve it. *What are the elements that make a mystery story work?*

You may wish to choose from the options below to offer students the opportunity to sum up their key understandings about this unit.

Discuss

- What common elements did you notice in the plots of each of these books? How did each author build suspense?
- How did the setting of each story affect the kinds of mysteries the detectives solved?

Detective Profiles Invite groups of students to write content for a Web page or print ad about detectives for hire. Ask students to include the detective's name, where he or she lives, and the kind of cases he or she is good at solving. Before students create their profiles, have them discuss what made each detective from their reading unique.

Genre Debate: Fantasy vs. Reality Some of the mysteries in this unit star talking animals. One detective is even an egg! Others, like the books by author Ron Roy, feature children who seem like real people and solve mysteries by working together. Invite students to use examples from the books to debate which kind of mystery story is more fun or more challenging to read.

Details, Details In a good mystery story, the author leaves clues for readers to follow. Invite students, as a class, to create a list of tips to help future readers notice clues and other details to get the most out of reading mysteries.

Grade 4: Unit Projects

 Boys vs. Girls

Boys and girls often find reasons NOT to get along. *What can you learn from the way characters clash and resolve differences?*

You may wish to choose from the options below to offer students the opportunity to sum up their key understandings about this unit.

Discuss

- Why do you think many of these authors used humor to address this topic?

- Which books reflected behavior that seemed realistic? What did the authors do to make their characters and situations seem real?

Class Survey Have students come up with a short survey about the books in the unit, asking questions such as, *Which book was your favorite?* and *Which character was your favorite?* After students fill out the surveys, collect the girls' in one pile and boys' in another. As a class, tally and discuss results.

Character Mix-Up! Divide the class into pairs of one boy and one girl. Write the names of each of the female characters on separate slips of paper, put them in a hat, and have each girl in the class choose a slip of paper. Repeat with the names of the male characters for the boys in the class. Have each pair write a scene for their characters, introducing a problem and solution, using what they know about the characters from the books. (Note: If students choose a character from a book they did not read, they can choose again.)

What Are They Thinking? Have students write an "autobiography" from the perspective of one of the characters. Encourage students to include background information or anything else the character might wish other people knew about him or her.

 Cinderella Tales

Cinderella stories have been told in many cultures and in many different ways. *What are the essential elements in a Cinderella tale?*

You may wish to choose from the options below to offer students the opportunity to sum up their key understandings about this unit.

Discuss

- What do all of these stories have in common? How are the characters alike? The plots?

- The tale of Cinderella has been told and retold in various cultures for many, many years. Why do you think people continue to want to share this story?

Popularity Poll Have students choose their favorite Cinderella tale from the unit reading. Go around the class and have each student tell which version they picked and why.

Write Your Own Have students write their own retellings of Cinderella. Combine all the stories into a class book of Cinderella tales, or post them on your class website.

Cinderella Ad Assign students to small groups and have them create an advertisement for all the different Cinderella books they have read, emphasizing what is unique about each tale. When they are finished, invite groups to share their ads with the class.

Amazing Animals

Scientists are not the only ones fascinated by animal behavior! *What do authors do to show that animals are amazing?*

You may wish to choose from the options below to offer students the opportunity to sum up their key understandings about this unit.

Discuss

- Why do you think animals are such a popular topic for writers? Which authors seemed especially well qualified to write about their subjects? Why?

- What were some of the most surprising facts you learned about animals from your reading? What do you consider "amazing" about these facts?

Introduce It Yourself! Revisit with students several of the introductions or author's notes from the books in this unit. Then, have students write their own similar introductions for the whole unit of readings. Students can describe the books, give background information, or petition readers to take action.

Design a Web Page Invite students to design the opening screen for a website about saving endangered animals. Encourage students to include text, pictures, links, drop-down menus, and anything else that might appear on such a page. For reference, students can visit websites included in some of the books.

Photographs or Pictures? All the books in the unit are informational, but some have photographs and others have illustrations. Have students work in pairs to compare the photos and illustrations in the books, then write about the images they think provided the most information and those they found most interesting visually.

 # Taking Responsibility

How do you decide what you should and should not do? *How can you take action to help yourself and others?*

You may wish to choose from the options below to offer students the opportunity to sum up their key understandings about this unit.

Discuss

- Do you think some of these authors were writing about experiences drawn from their own lives or the lives of other real people? What makes you think that?

- Why do you think it took some of the main characters so long to decide what action to take? Did this indecision make the book more interesting to read? Why or why not?

Act It Out As a class, discuss mistakes made by characters in the readings. Then, think of a scenario in which someone makes a poor decision—for example, someone teases a new student or fails to do an assignment. Create four groups of students to perform four skits—one group to act out the cause of the poor decision, one group to act out making the mistake, one group to act out the effect of the ill-advised action, and one group to demonstrate the person taking responsibility.

Can I Help You? Discuss with students the characters who go out of their way to help others. Then, have students give a short speech to the class about a way they could do the same to help others or the environment.

Ripple Effect Invite students to think of an event in one of the books that was affected by the main character's actions—in either a positive or a negative way. Have them write a letter to that character, explaining how that action in turn affected the reader.

Grade 4: Unit Projects (continued)

 The Artist's Eye

Through their skill, artists may lead us to a new understanding of things. *How do artists help others experience the world in a new way?*

You may wish to choose from the options below to offer students the opportunity to sum up their key understandings about this unit.

Discuss

- What do you think each author wants you to remember about these artists?

- What do you think is the most challenging thing about being an artist? Can you give some examples from your readings to support your ideas?

Cartoons Galore! Revisit the three books by Mike Venezia and remind students that he uses cartoons to supplement the text and add humor to the story. Have students draw a cartoon for a different book in the unit.

An Artist Is . . . Point out that several different kinds of artists are featured in this unit. Have students write a paragraph that answers the question, What makes a person an artist? Encourage students to think about the qualities that make someone an artist and to use examples from the books.

Try It Yourself Use the two books about Frida Kahlo to show that two authors can tell about the same artist in different ways. Have students write and design a page about one of the artists featured in this unit and present their pages to the class. Classmates can compare a student's page to the book about the same artist. Combine all of the pages into a class book.

 Fantasy

Amazing characters? Incredible places? Events unlike anything that happens in real life? *What makes a fantasy story exciting and fun to read?*

You may wish to choose from the options below to offer students the opportunity to sum up their key understandings about this unit.

Discuss

- Why is the setting an author selects for a fantasy story so important? Can you give some examples of how the settings in your readings affect the events that occur?

- How do authors of fantasies combine the incredible with the ordinary to make their characters interesting? Cite examples from your reading to help explain your answers.

Fantasy Features Revisit the books and list their fantasy elements, including magic, animals that talk, and sometimes a search or quest. Then have students write their own fantasies, incorporating some of the elements you discussed.

Author Study Divide the class into groups and have each group discuss and compare the Kathryn Lasky books in this unit. Have students vote on which book they prefer and then report back to the class which title won the vote and why students preferred it to the other books by the same author.

Fantasy Charades On slips of paper, write the names of characters from the books. Invite students to take turns picking names out of a hat and pantomiming an action typical of the character. The classmate who guesses the character first gets the next turn. (Note: If a student chooses a character not familiar to him or her, he or she can choose again.)

Grade 5: Unit Projects

 Better Together

Some problems are so complicated that they seem impossible to solve. But the consequences of not solving them are too great to ignore. *How can people work together to reach their goals?*

You may wish to choose from the options below to offer students the opportunity to sum up their key understandings about this unit.

Discuss

- How did the events these writers described help you understand the power of cooperation?

- Which of the examples of teamwork described in these books has the most relevance for our lives today? Why?

Motivational Review Most of the authors in this unit crafted stories inspired by actual events. Ask students to work in groups to consider which author best succeeded in explaining why people banded together to take the action they did. Have them then write a brief review explaining how that author made the characters' motivation come alive.

Investigate Invite students to brainstorm, in groups, something they would like to investigate further about one of the topics in the unit. Have students use other books or the Internet to learn more about their topic. Invite groups to present their findings to the class. .

Chain of Events In these books, what chains of events led to the resolution of certain problems? Which events were characters able to control? Which were out of their control? Ask students to diagram the chain of events in one of the books, labeling the problem and resolution. Discuss: *Were some events in the chain more significant than others? How so?*

 Watch Out!

A shiver of suspense is often found in folklore as well as other kinds of writing that these tales have inspired. *How do authors use a sense of danger to shape stories?*

You may wish to choose from the options below to offer students the opportunity to sum up their key understandings about this unit.

Discuss

- Which authors included some kind of warning or hints of looming danger in their stories? Why do you think they did so?

- Some of these books blend humor and suspense. Others are pure drama. Which kind of story did you find more effective? Why?

Screenplay Suspense Invite students to work in groups to choose a suspenseful section from one of the books to adapt as a scene for a screenplay. Encourage students to mimic suspense-building techniques the authors used and to insert stage directions to enhance the suspense of the plot. Have volunteers film their scenes and/or act them out for the class.

Once Upon a Time Work together as a class to list common elements found in folklore. Then, discuss how those elements were applied in the books in the unit.

Illustrate the Mood Revisit one of the picture books and discuss how the illustrations build suspense or set a mood. Then, invite students to choose a book to re-illustrate, or create illustrations for a unit book that has none. Have students present their illustrations to the class and explain the mood or moods they wanted to convey, based on their interpretation of the text, and the techniques they used— such as color, shape, or design.

Under the Surface

It's more complex and marvelous than any machine. *What tools and techniques help scientists study the human body?*

You may wish to choose from the options below to offer students the opportunity to sum up their key understandings about this unit.

Discuss

• What are the most impressive facts you have learned about the inner workings of the human body and the tools and techniques used to study these functions?

• How do the illustrations in these books help you appreciate the details the authors shared? Why are having photos and illustrations so important for this topic?

Talk About It Invite students to give a short speech on the subject they found the most interesting in this unit, using facts from the books to support their opinions.

Text Features Divide the class into groups and assign each group one or two books from the unit. Have groups identify text features used to present information in their book(s) and show the class specific examples. Then have groups redesign a section from their book, incorporating a text feature that was described by a different group.

Tools and Techniques The books in the 24/7 series list additional resources such as professional organizations, websites, books, and movies. Have small groups each check some of the resources from one of the 24/7 books. Have each group create a fact book based on their research.

 # Dealing With Change

Some people fear change. Others embrace it. *How do books reflect the kinds of changes people face in real life?*

You may wish to choose from the options below to offer students the opportunity to sum up their key understandings about this unit.

Discuss

• What did you learn from all of these books about dealing with change?

• Which characters' reactions to change seemed the most realistic? Why?

Dialogue In pairs, have students write dialogue that reveals something interesting about two characters from the reading and how they deal with change. Invite the pairs to perform their scenes for the class.

What If? Write down the names of characters from the books and put the names into a hat. Describe for students a scenario that involves change or a challenging situation. Then, have students each pick a name out of the hat and write a paragraph about how the character they chose would react to the scenario you described.

Try This Book Point out that the blurb found on the back of a book is designed to entice readers. Ask students to write new book blurbs for the book of their choice, emphasizing the role of dealing with change, in a way designed to make the book sound like a must-read. Invite students to read their blurbs aloud or post them on your website to help other students decide which books they would like to read.

It Takes a Leader

Throughout history, there have been people who have led the way—changing the way others think and live. *What makes a great leader, and how do leaders effect change?*

You may wish to choose from the options below to offer students the opportunity to sum up their key understandings about this unit.

Discuss

- What are some of the strengths that different leaders from this unit had in common with each other?

- How did the authors humanize their subjects—to show them as imperfect people, with flaws and fears?

Now Is the Time All of the characters in this unit were passionate about making a difference. If they lived in current times, which of today's issues would be important to them? As a class, make a list.

Quality Counts Have each student work with a partner. Each will write down the one quality he or she thinks is most important for a leader to have, based on their unit reading. Then have students trade papers with their partners and write a brief analysis of how a character or characters from the unit demonstrated the quality their partner selected. Partners should discuss with each other what they wrote, and then present their ideas to the class.

Debate Hold a debate to consider which character from the unit contributed the most to society. Split the class into four groups and have each group choose a different character to champion. Then have groups pair up to present their arguments.

 ## Historical Fiction

Yes, it takes research, imagination, and creativity! *How do authors use actual events from history to create memorable fiction?*

You may wish to choose from the options below to offer students the opportunity to sum up their key understandings about this unit.

Discuss

- What techniques did the authors in this unit use to help you get to know their characters? How did this help you appreciate what life was like at other times in history?

- How were you able to distinguish factual and fictional details in your reading? What problems did the characters face that could have occurred only during certain times in history?

Genre Swap! How are historical fiction and informational text similar? How are they different? Have students do more research about a historical event in one of the stories and rewrite that story, or a section of that story, as informational text.

Author Study Divide the class into two groups—in one, students who have read one of the two books by Pam Muñoz Ryan, and in the other, students who have read one of the Christopher Paul Curtis books. Have each group discuss the common threads in their books and the techniques the author uses to keep readers interested. Then have the group share their findings with the other group.

Act It Out Divide the class into groups and have each group make a skit that re-creates a problem from one of the books. Students can present their completed skits to the class.

Characteristics of Units by Theme: Grades K–2

K Being a Friend

Characteristics of Text

In this unit, children explore a variety of picture book texts: some with just a few words to help develop a sense of print and others with richer language to build vocabulary. All the books support the themes of friendship and cooperation. The texts also invite discussion of how authors use words and pictures to show what their characters are like.

Behaviors to Notice and Support

- **Recognizes** how the words characters say make them seem like real people

- **Understands** that authors use the events in their stories to show characters' personalities and how characters approach and solve problems

- **Uses** information from a story to predict what a character is likely to do

- **Has** opinions about the characters' actions and what the author wants readers to know about the characters

- **Offers** examples based upon reading and discussion in response to the unit focus question: *What is being a friend all about?*

Community & Relationships

As children progress through the grades, they use a variety of text types and genres to explore friendships, family dynamics, and school situations.

GRADE 1 — My Family & Me

Characteristics of Text

Each book in this unit has something to say about families. In each case, photos or illustrations support the author's message. Children are asked to compare books about families, searching for the key ideas and supporting details that the authors want to share about family life and the love and support family members provide.

Behaviors to Notice and Support

- **Recognizes** how authors use narration and dialogue to show what characters think and feel

- **Interprets** how illustrations and photos add information

- **Notices** how the themes of sharing and cooperation are expressed in these books

- **Identifies** how authors choose specific words and details to help readers focus on important ideas

- **Offers** examples based upon reading and discussion in response to the unit focus question: *How do people in a family help each other and have fun together?*

GRADE 2 — It Happened in School

Characteristics of Text

The books in this unit use good humor and both believable and exaggerated situations that reflect common experiences. Throughout, details in the text and illustrations highlight school settings and how characters react to situations in school.

Behaviors to Notice and Support

- **Realizes** that authors carefully choose the settings for their stories and that what happens to characters in a story is affected by the setting

- **Identifies** how authors use details to reveal interesting and significant information about setting and character

- **Notices** how exaggeration in text descriptions and art can add humor

- **Uses** details from a story to interpret characters' feelings and relationships

- **Understands** the problems in the story and uses story details to predict how the problems will be solved

- **Offers** examples based upon reading and discussion in response to the unit focus question: *How do people in school learn from each new experience—and from each other?*

Folklore & Literary Traditions

As children advance, they gain familiarity with well-known characters, predictable text patterns such as the "rule of three," talking animals, and magical wishes and promises.

GRADE K — Telling Tales

Characteristics of Text

This unit includes conceptually appropriate picture-book retellings of favorite tales from a variety of cultural traditions. The patterns in the text are notable, and children are supported in recognizing the patterns as well as other elements often found in folktales. These elements include talking animal characters and the ways in which characters deal with problems or learn lessons.

Behaviors to Notice and Support

- **Notices** how authors use repetition or patterns to structure their folktale retellings

- **Follows** the events and patterns in a story and uses them to predict what might happen next

- **Compares** versions of the same tale, noticing how authors may use different details to retell a traditional story

- **Identifies** how the text and the pictures work together to provide information about the characters, setting, and problem in a story

- **Notices** how descriptive language and dialogue add information about characters and that animals that talk and act like people are found in some stories, but not in real life

- **Offers** examples based upon reading and discussion in response to the unit focus question: *What makes a folktale a special kind of story?*

GRADE 1 — Stories With a Moral

Characteristics of Text

The folklore retellings in this unit use entertaining artwork, memorable characters, and predictable story patterns to guide children toward the moral or lesson the authors state or imply at the end.

Behaviors to Notice and Support

- **Notices** how authors use a pattern of events to make the problems characters face easy to understand

- **Makes connections** between the stories and discusses similarities and differences

- **Understands** how authors use what happens to characters to teach a lesson

- **Realizes** that authors can use description, dialogue, and humor to make their characters and stories interesting

- **Notices** that some authors may change an old story to teach a different lesson

- **Offers** examples based upon reading and discussion in response to the unit focus question: *How can folktales teach people how to act in real life?*

GRADE 2 — Wishes & Promises

Characteristics of Text

The texts in this unit are all retellings of folktales that clearly present a sequence of events and teach a lesson about how to behave. In these tales, characters find that their actions have consequences, either good or bad, that are often quite unexpected.

Behaviors to Notice and Support

- **Recognizes** how authors use repetition and patterns in folktale retellings

- **Identifies** how an author's choice of words helps build suspense and reveal characters and settings

- **Understands** the cause-and-effect chains that lead to specific consequences and teach specific lessons in these folktales

- **Distinguishes** fantasy elements from reality and recognizes that the consequences in these stories are different from things that happen in real life

- **Notices** how the illustrations in a story help establish the setting and provide more information about the characters

- **Offers** examples based upon reading and discussion in response to the unit focus question: *How can a wish or a promise change someone's life?*

GRADE K — Trees & Other Plants

Characteristics of Text

These simple and engaging informational texts vary in format but all include important information in the text and the illustrations about how plants grow, the diversity of plant life, and why plants are an important part of our world.

Living Things

As children continue through the grades, they build knowledge and technical vocabulary about life science, spiraling from an exploration of plants as living things to wellness, to how animals survive in the wild.

Behaviors to Notice and Support

- **Notices** different ways in which authors share information about plants

- **Recognizes** how photographs and illustrations provide information that supports and extends the texts

- **Notices** how authors use sequence words and specialized vocabulary to explain how plants grow

- **Recognizes** how authors help readers visualize important information

- **Expresses** opinions about interesting plant facts in a text

- **Offers** examples based upon reading and discussion in response to the unit focus question: *How do writers help you care about trees and plants?*

GRADE 1 — Strong & Healthy

Characteristics of Text

These age-appropriate informational texts use a variety of techniques and formats including diagrams, photos with captions, teaching stories, and even rhyming texts. But all the authors share a similar purpose: to provide important ideas about health and wellness and to persuade children to value their own health.

Behaviors to Notice and Support

- **Notices** the different techniques authors use to get readers interested in healthy habits

- **Connects** health information in the texts with real-life experiences

- **Recognizes** how some authors use humor to make a point about healthy habits

- **Understands** how illustrations, photographs, and diagrams support the texts

- **Notices** the ways in which authors organize information and the specialized vocabulary they use to explain healthy habits

- **Offers** examples based upon reading and discussion in response to the unit focus question: *How do writers help you find out about healthy habits?*

GRADE 2 — Search & Survive

Characteristics of Text

The informational texts in this unit use a variety of formats and types of photos and illustrations to present information about animal adaptations and how animals search for food and find ways to evade predators.

Behaviors to Notice and Support

- **Recognizes** how an author begins a book in order to grab a reader's interest

- **Notices** how authors organize information and use specialized vocabulary to show a sequence of events and convey important ideas about animals and food chains

- **Understands** how cause and effect are explained in these texts to express the interdependence of living things

- **Identifies** similarities and differences among different texts in how the authors approach the topic

- **Notices** the connections between the illustrations or art in the book and the information in the text

- **Offers** examples based upon reading and discussion in response to the unit focus question: *How do animals find food—and avoid becoming another creature's dinner?*

Feelings

Characteristics of Text

A hallmark of the books in this unit is the use of precise vocabulary and supportive illustrations and photos to help children learn more about emotions and self-control.

A Sense of Self

Children begin by using their reading to build vocabulary that names and describes feelings and progress to exploring stories that focus on how characters recognize their abilities and build confidence.

Behaviors to Notice and Support

- **Notices** the specific words authors use to describe feelings and how these words relate to what their characters do and say

- **Recognizes** how the feeling words authors use, in both fiction and informational texts, relate to the facial expressions and body language depicted in illustrations or photographs

- **Tells** why characters' emotions relate to the problem in a story and to how that problem is solved

- **Understands** how other characters' actions or specific events affect someone's feelings

- **Offers examples** based upon their reading and discussion in response to the unit focus question: *How does understanding your own feelings and the feelings of others help you in everyday life?*

GRADE 1 · What I Can Do

Characteristics of Text

Each picture book or simple chapter book in this unit shows how characters find ways to solve problems and gain pride in their own abilities.

Behaviors to Notice and Support

- **Identifies** the main problem in a story and the sequence of events that leads to the solution of the problem

- **Discusses** how authors reveal a character's personality and abilities

- **Recognizes** that a character's personality and abilities affect the way the character approaches a problem and how the problem gets solved

- **Notices** how authors convey a character's sense of accomplishment when a problem has been solved

- **Talks** about how characters change after reaching their goals and predicts what characters might do after the story ends

- **Offers examples** based upon their reading and discussion in response to the unit focus question: *How do you know what you can do—unless you try?*

GRADE 2 · Like No One Else

Characteristics of Text

The authors in this unit share a similar purpose: to communicate a message of respecting yourself and others for everyone's unique qualities. Each book club choice is a chapter book, so children can see how a message can build across a longer text.

Behaviors to Notice and Support

- **Notices** how authors craft realistic fiction, fantasy, and biography to explore important themes and convey a message

- **Understands** that some authors use humor to help get their messages across

- **Identifies** descriptive details, plot points, and illustrations that help readers connect to an author's message

- **Recognizes** the importance of respecting others for who they are

- **Understands** that different individuals have different strengths and goals

- **Offers** examples based upon their reading and discussion in response to the unit focus question: *What makes you—and others—unique?*

GRADE K — All Kinds of Jobs

Characteristics of Text

While these books vary in format, all serve a similar purpose: to introduce children to the variety of jobs people do, the steps people follow to accomplish their jobs, and how all kinds of workers contribute to the community.

Inspired by True Stories

Beginning with an overview of jobs, children go on to read autobiographical stories from favorite authors who use their own experiences to shape the books they write. In Grade 2, children explore how caring for and observing animals have changed people's lives.

Behaviors to Notice and Support

- **Notices** how authors use different types of text to inform readers about what it takes to do a job

- **Realizes** how the organization of the text helps readers take in information

- **Recognizes** how authors explain the meaning of important job-related words

- **Follows** the steps in a process it may take to complete a job, as explained in the text and supported by the photos or art in a book

- **Notices** how authors include the themes of teamwork and helping others as they explain jobs

- **Offers** examples based upon reading and discussion in response to the unit focus question: *Where do people work and what jobs do they do?*

It Happened to Me

Characteristics of Text

In this unit, children are introduced to ways in which authors use their own experiences in the stories they write. Children will take note of the kinds of childhood experiences the authors chose to share and of how problems get solved in these stories.

Behaviors to Notice and Support

- **Understands** that an author wrote each book using his or her own real-life experiences as inspiration

- **Notices** how illustrations help establish settings and add information about the characters

- **Makes predictions** about what characters will do and uses evidence from the text to support these predictions

- **Notices** similarities and differences among these autobiographical books

- **Compares** the memories the authors share with what life is like for children today

- **Offers** examples based upon reading and discussion in response to the unit focus question: *What do you learn from authors who write about their own lives?*

GRADE
2

Animal Watch

Characteristics of Text

The informational texts in this unit vary in format and style to present information about what real people have learned and the problems they were able to solve by studying animals and caring for them.

Behaviors to Notice and Support

- **Recognizes** that information can be presented in a variety of formats

- **Notices** how authors use specific events and details to explain important ideas about animals and the people who study or take care of them

- **Understands** that the authors did research or used their personal experiences with animals as the basis for their informational texts

- **Notices** and derives information from photographs and illustrations

- **Understands** how the authors' curiosity about nature has led them to discover new information about animals

- **Offers** examples based upon reading and discussion in response to the unit focus question: *What have people discovered by watching and caring for animals?*

Genre Study

The genres highlighted as children progress from kindergarten to Grade 2 are concept books, animal stories, and realistic fiction.

GRADE K   Concept Books

Characteristics of Text

These playful books challenge children to explore the alphabet, counting, colors, and days of the week, through simple text that is perfectly matched with vibrant illustrations. This unit includes several books by Donald Crews, Eric Carle, and Audrey and Bruce Wood, to offer opportunities for author/ illustrator studies.

Behaviors to Notice and Support

- **Notices** and understands texts that are based on established categories, such as colors, numbers, the alphabet, or days of the week

- **Recognizes** that authors may present more than one kind of concept in a book

- **Understands** that the purpose of a concept book is to find an entertaining way to get readers thinking about a concept such as the alphabet, colors, numbers, or days of the week

- **Notices** when authors include rhyme or predictable patterns in concept books

- **Interprets** the way in which illustrations support and extend ideas in the text

- **Notices** the similarities between texts that were written or illustrated by the same person

- **Offers** examples based upon reading and discussion in response to the unit focus question: *How do writers make concept books fun to read?*

GRADE 1 — Animal Stories

Characteristics of Text

Each story in this unit features animal characters that, in some ways, act like people. Children are invited to look for fantasy elements in each of these stories. This unit includes several books by Karma Wilson and two by Arnold Lobel, to offer opportunities for author studies.

Behaviors to Notice and Support

- **Notices** how the authors make their animal characters act like people in some ways

- **Notices** how authors make their animal characters seem like real animals

- **Expresses** opinions about how animal characters are described and the problems they face in a story

- **Understands** and identifies the elements in these fantasy stories about animals that are unlike things that could happen in real life

- **Notices** how authors add humor in text and in art to make their stories memorable

- **Discusses** similarities and differences among texts by the same author

- **Offers** examples based upon reading and discussion in response to the unit focus question: *How—and why—do writers create animal characters that act like people?*

GRADE 2 — Realistic Fiction

Characteristics of Text

Each picture book or chapter book in this unit features realistic characters, plots, and settings. This unit includes three books by Nikki Grimes and two by Gary Soto, to offer opportunities for author studies.

Behaviors to Notice and Support

- **Notices** the problem in a story and evaluates what is realistic about the problem and how it is solved

- **Infers** characters' intentions, feelings, and motivations from what they say and do

- **Shares** examples of details the authors use to make their characters seem believable as people

- **Understands** realistic fiction as stories that could happen in real life

- **Predicts** what will happen to the characters after the story ends

- **Discusses** similarities and differences among the texts, especially those that were written by the same author

- **Offers** examples based upon reading and discussion in response to the unit focus question: *How do authors make the characters and situations they create seem so true to life?*

Community & Relationships

As students progress from Grade 3 to Grade 5, they explore sibling rivalries, misunderstandings and assumptions that can complicate relationships between girls and boys, and ways in which people can team up to accomplish important goals.

GRADE 3 — Brothers & Sisters

Characteristics of Text

Each memoir, realistic story, or poem in this unit uses a first-person narrative to reveal the thoughts and feelings of its main character and to invite readers to consider other points of view about sibling relationships.

Behaviors to Notice and Support

- **Understands** that the narrator's point of view affects the way in which the story is told

- **Discusses** sibling relationships and the attributes and actions that help in understanding character development

- **Uses** first-person narratives to hypothesize about underlying motivations of other characters that are not stated

- **Understands** how an author's own experiences are reflected in his or her writing

- **Notices** ways in which an author makes characters and their conflicts seem real

- **Indicates** awareness of the author's underlying messages and purpose

- **Offers** examples based on reading and discussion in response to the unit focus question: *Why do brothers and sisters often clash? How can they get along?*

GRADE 4 Boys vs. Girls

Characteristics of Text

Through clever dialogue and description, authors reveal how characters' attitudes and perceptions affect their abilities to understand and resolve conflicts.

Behaviors to Notice and Support

- **Understands** how authors reveal conflict through dialogue and description to show the logical progression of events

- **Recognizes** how authors indicate multiple points of view within the same book

- **Infers** characters' feelings and motivations from description, what they do or say, and what others think about them

- **Recognizes** how authors use humor to make their plots entertaining

- **Makes predictions** based on information in the text as to what will happen, what characters are likely to do, and how the book will end

- **Compares** the way in which conflicts are resolved in the texts with the way in which people negotiate relationships in real life

- **Offers** examples based on reading and discussion in response to the unit focus question: *What can you learn from the way characters clash and resolve differences?*

GRADE 5 Better Together

Characteristics of Text

The authors in this unit have drawn on many real-life experiences to create both informational texts and works of fiction that reflect the power of collaboration and creative problem solving.

Behaviors to Notice and Support

- **Considers** the influence of setting and events on characters' decisions and on how goals are achieved

- **Recognizes** how authors use historical and other factual details to help readers understand the choices characters make in their books

- **Notices** how authors reveal the underlying messages or the theme of teamwork (through a character, through plot and events)

- **Follows** the series of challenges that need to be overcome before the main problem in the story can be resolved

- **Identifies** and discusses how authors use literary devices such as foreshadowing, figurative language, and symbolism to build suspense and appeal to readers' emotions

- **Offers** examples based on reading and discussion in response to the unit focus question: *How can people work together to reach their goals?*

Characteristics of Units by Theme: Grades 3–5

Folklore & Literary Traditions

As students advance through the exploration of folklore, they become familiar with classic tricksters, variations on Cinderella, the significance of warnings, and how folklore provides a foundation for contemporary fantasy.

Characteristics of Text

The traditional tales retold in this unit feature tricksters drawn from a variety of cultural traditions. The patterns of events that advance the plots, the characteristics of a trickster, lessons learned, and the use of humor are features these stories share.

Behaviors to Notice and Support

- **Follows** the events and patterns in a trickster story and uses them to predict what might happen next

- **Compares** versions of the same trickster tale, noticing how authors may use different details to retell a traditional story

- **Identifies** how the text and the pictures work together to provide information about the characters, setting, and problem in a story

- **Notices** how descriptive language and dialogue add information about the characters and their personality traits

- **Understands** how an author can use humor, exaggeration, or suspense to support the message of a trickster tale

- **Offers** examples based upon reading and discussion in response to the unit focus question: *What lessons can you learn from trickster tales?*

GRADE 4 Cinderella Tales

Characteristics of Text

Both traditional and contemporary variations of this fairy tale reveal the decisions authors make when they choose to tell a story their own way. Students will note common details relating to plot, character, and magical events.

Behaviors to Notice and Support

- **Notices** how authors use setting and symbols to reflect a specific culture or to make their Cinderella retellings unique

- **Identifies** how the author makes a Cinderella character seem likeable and deserving of good fortune

- **Makes connections** among different Cinderella tales and discusses similarities and differences

- **Understands** how illustrations help establish the tone of the retelling and support the text by revealing information about the characters and the setting

- **Realizes** that authors can use description, dialogue, and humor to make their characters and fairy-tale retellings interesting

- **Notices** that some authors may change an old story to teach a different lesson

- **Offers** examples based upon reading and discussion in response to the unit focus question: *What are the essential elements in a Cinderella tale?*

GRADE 5 Watch Out!

Characteristics of Text

Using atmospheric descriptions, both the folktales and the longer works of fantasy inspired by folklore motifs use suspense to keep students reading and thinking about the lessons in the stories in this unit.

Behaviors to Notice and Support

- **Identifies** how an author uses story events to build suspense and reveal characters and settings

- **Recognizes** how authors use imagery and symbols to set the mood and reinforce the meaning of characters' actions

- **Understands** the cause-and-effect chains that lead to specific consequences and reinforce the author's message

- **Notices** how the illustrations in a story help establish the setting and the mood

- **Notices** folklore motifs and characters in longer works of fantasy and how these familiar elements are used to shape an original work

- **Offers** examples based upon reading and discussion in response to the unit focus question: *How do authors use a sense of danger to shape stories?*

Characteristics of Units by Theme: Grades 3–5

Living Things

As students continue through the grades, they build knowledge and technical vocabulary about life science, spiraling from the life-sustaining importance of water, to an analysis of animal behavior, to a look at the tools and techniques scientists use for learning about the human body.

GRADE 3 · Life Depends on Water

Characteristics of Text

Each author whose work is included here has a distinctive way of presenting facts and sharing his or her opinions about water and the interconnectedness of all life on Earth.

Behaviors to Notice and Support

- **Notices** how authors balance their presentations of facts and of opinions as they write about living things

- **Follows** a sequence of events presented in the text and understands how changing one event in a sequence could lead to a different outcome

- **Critically examines** how authors balance facts and opinions as they write about the effect of water on living things

- **Understands** how authors organize their texts to help readers focus on certain ideas

- **Compares and contrasts** the ways in which different authors present information on the same topic, noting techniques the authors use to make their books entertaining as well as informative

- **Notices** how photographs or illustrations support the mood the author sets as well as add information

- **Offers** examples based upon reading and discussion in response to the unit focus question: *Why is water so important to all living things?*

GRADE 4 — Amazing Animals

Characteristics of Text

The informational texts in this unit show how different authors organize information to present what they consider the most important ideas about animals.

Behaviors to Notice and Support

- **Notices** how authors organize and present information about animals in informational text—for example, through use of categories, comparisons, or sequence

- **Understands** and discusses how scientific terms explained in context and photos, illustrations, and maps enhance the information in the text

- **Distinguishes** between more important and less important information about animals and cites textual evidence to explain why some details are more important than others

- **Describes** how factual information and the author's opinions are combined in the text

- **Uses** scientific terms from the texts to demonstrate understanding of the relationships among habitat, an animal's physical characteristics, and behaviors that help animals survive

- **Offers** examples based upon reading and discussion in response to the unit focus question: *What do authors do to show that animals are amazing?*

GRADE 5 — Under the Surface

Characteristics of Text

A variety of informational text formats supported by eye-catching photos and illustrations are used to explain essential body systems and how science and technology help you better understand the inner workings of the human body.

Behaviors to Notice and Support

- **Understands** that authors organize their texts in specific ways to help readers absorb technical information

- **Notices** that some authors use humor to make learning facts appealing and to get their message across

- **Identifies** how diagrams, illustrations, and photographs with captions provide information to support the text and to help readers grasp scientific methods and discoveries

- **Notices** the sequence words and the technical and descriptive language an author uses to make the steps in a scientific process easy to understand

- **Understands** how persuasive language and facts can be used to create persuasive arguments about healthy habits

- **Recognizes** that descriptive details as well as photographs and illustrations help readers visualize the inner working of the human body

- **Offers** examples based upon reading and discussion in response to the unit focus question: *What tools and techniques help scientists study the human body?*

Characteristics of Text

Each of the books in this unit shows how characters struggle with problems and find the courage to respond to them.

A Sense of Self

Students explore books that mirror their maturing world view, focusing on how characters gain the confidence to face their fears, take responsibility for their actions, and deal with change.

Behaviors to Notice and Support

- Notices and discusses how authors make characters and their fears and concerns seem believable

- Uses evidence from the text to explain how authors build plots that convey the importance of determination and resilience

- Explains how the dialogue authors create reflects how people speak and behave in real life

- Understands how authors use humor or suspense to help make a point about determination

- Offers examples based upon reading and discussion in response to the unit focus question: *What does it take to have courage?*

GRADE 4 — Taking Responsibility

Characteristics of Text

The authors in this unit have crafted complex characters whose actions support their books' themes and show the importance of taking responsibility for fixing mistakes and helping others.

Behaviors to Notice and Support

- **Notices** how authors make readers aware of the book's themes or big ideas

- **Discusses** how authors reveal a character's personality and abilities through dialogue and description

- **Recognizes** how authors use characters' attempts at problem solving to reveal their personalities and levels of self-awareness

- **Appreciates** why taking the correct action is often not easy—in books or in life

- **Talks** about how characters change after taking responsibility and predicts what characters might do after the story ends

- **Offers** examples based upon reading and discussion in response to the unit focus question: *How can you take action to help yourself and others?*

GRADE 5 — Dealing With Change

Characteristics of Text

The authors whose works are represented here are skilled in creating narratives that reveal their characters' thoughts and emotions and help readers consider how the characters grow and change as they respond to challenges.

Behaviors to Notice and Support

- **Notices** how authors craft realistic fiction, fantasy, and biography to explore important themes about dealing with change

- **Understands** that some authors use humor to help convey their messages

- **Identifies** descriptive details, plot points, and illustrations that help readers connect to the characters and to the author's message

- **Recognizes** the importance of respecting others for who they are

- **Understands** that different individuals have different strengths and goals

- **Offers** examples based upon reading and discussion in response to the unit focus question: *How do books reflect the kinds of changes people face in real life?*

Characteristics of Text

Each sports star's personality and accomplishments are revealed through description and quoted dialogue in these memoirs and biographical picture books.

Inspired by True Stories

In Grades 3–5, students study biographies that explore the qualities that allowed certain individuals to excel in sports, in the arts, and as leaders.

Behaviors to Notice and Support

- **Understands** how authors use details and dialogue to convey a person's values and character

- **Recognizes** the differences between biography, fictionalized biography, and memoir and the different kinds of challenges involved with each kind of text

- **Notices** how authors convey the meaning of sports-related terminology in context

- **Understands** the roles other people played in encouraging an athlete to succeed

- **Notices** how authors include in their texts the themes of determination and overcoming obstacles

- **Offers** examples based upon reading and discussion in response to the unit focus question: *What makes an athlete great, both on and off the playing field?*

GRADE 4 — The Artist's Eye

Characteristics of Text

The biographical and autobiographical works in this unit use a variety of techniques to talk not just about an artist's life but also about the process these artists followed to create the artwork or music for which they are remembered.

Behaviors to Notice and Support

- **Notices** how authors select events in an artist's life to convey the obstacles and inspirations that affected the artwork created

- **Compares** the ways in which different authors guide readers to appreciate what artists have accomplished

- **Discusses** how illustrators use their own artwork to convey another artist's experiences and intentions, help establish settings, and add information about the subject

- **Thinks critically** about the quality of writing and accuracy in the text, as well as what else a reader would want to know about each artist

- **Notices** similarities and differences among the artists profiled in this unit

- **Offers** examples based upon reading and discussion in response to the unit focus question: *How do artists help others experience the world in a new way?*

GRADE 5 — It Takes a Leader

Characteristics of Text

The well-researched biographical works in this unit invite students to look back at different times in history to explore the qualities that make a leader successful—or unsuccessful.

Behaviors to Notice and Support

- **Recognizes** that biographical information can be presented in a variety of formats

- **Notices** how authors use specific historical events and details to reveal their subject's character

- **Understands** that the authors did research and that dialogue and events used in biographies are derived from that research

- **Notices** and derives information from photographs and illustrations about a specific person, time, or place, and realizes that the illustrations or photos support the tone of the book

- **Understands** how an author's attitude about the subject is reflected in the facts the author chooses to include and that the author's purpose may be to persuade readers to form a certain opinion about the subject

- **Offers** examples based upon reading and discussion in response to the unit focus question: *What makes a great leader, and how do leaders effect change?*

Genre Study

The three genres highlighted as students progress from grade to grade are fiction genres that make specific demands on readers—mystery, fantasy, and historical fiction.

Characteristics of Text

Students read well-plotted, suspenseful, and sometimes silly mystery stories that feature detectives as main characters who use logic and some luck to solve mysteries. Two books by Ron Roy are included to encourage readers to consider how authors build successful mystery series.

Behaviors to Notice and Support

- **Understands** the role of the detective as a character in a mystery story

- **Identifies** how authors build suspense in a mystery story and how they share clues as the plot unfolds

- **Explains** how an author reveals a detective's personality and case-solving process

- **Interprets** the way in which illustrations support and extend significant details in the text that concern characters, setting, and plot

- **Notices** the similarities among mystery stories, especially those that were written by the same author

- **Offers** examples based upon reading and discussion in response to the unit focus question: *What are the elements that make a mystery story work?*

GRADE 4 Fantasy

Characteristics of Text

The books in this unit offer adventures that embody the classic elements of fantasy: events, characters, or settings that could never occur in real life. Three works by Kathryn Lasky are included to allow for an author study.

Behaviors to Notice and Support

- **Analyzes** ways in which authors of fantasy make the impossible seem believable

- **Discusses** similarities and differences among works of fantasy, especially those that were written by the same author

- **Describes** how illustrations enhance the setting and mood of a fantasy

- **Identifies** descriptions and figurative language that help readers visualize a fantasy setting and character

- **Notices** how authors add humor in text and in art to make their stories entertaining

- **Offers** examples based upon reading and discussion in response to the unit focus question: *What makes a fantasy story exciting and fun to read?*

GRADE 5 Historical Fiction

Characteristics of Text

Students explore this genre, noting how authors blend authentic details about the setting, events, and people from the past with fictional details. Two books by Pam Muñoz Ryan and two books by Christopher Paul Curtis are included to allow for the option of author studies.

Behaviors to Notice and Support

- **Notices** how authors make historical settings and plot points seem authentic

- **Infers** characters' intentions, feelings, and motivation from what they say and do as well as the historical context authors provide

- **Shares** examples of details the authors use to make the problems of historical characters seem relevant to life today

- **Understands** the differences between historical fiction and informational text that do not include fictional details

- **Discusses** similarities and differences among works of historical fiction, especially those that were written by the same author

- **Offers** examples based upon reading and discussion in response to the unit focus question: *How do authors use actual events from history to create memorable fiction?*

Assessment

The most effective teaching is *responsive*—possible only when we know our students so well that we can respond instructionally, at the exact moment of need, to their immediate learning challenge. Knowing our students as learners arises most reliably from observing them in class in the midst of learning— listening to them converse with others, talking with them ourselves, and watching over their shoulders as they orchestrate the skills, strategies, and understandings necessary for successful reading. Teaching and assessing are part of a continuous learning loop—ideally, for both the teacher and student. Literacy researcher Peter Afflerbach (2007) outlines the challenge:

> **"Reading assessment is central to knowing students' reading progress and achievement. Reading assessment helps teachers construct understanding of how students are developing as readers. In doing so, reading assessment provides critical information to make important instructional decisions. The relationship between reading assessment, teaching, and student progress in reading could not be more important. "**

Why and What We Assess

The primary reason to assess is to determine what our students know and what they need to know in order to move forward in their literacy development. Although we can't peer directly into our students' minds and know exactly what they are thinking about each text, we can hypothesize what they are processing and understanding based on 1) their *actions* as they are reading and 2) their *responses* to text through their talk, writing, or other means of self-expression such as drawing, dramatic performance, and the like. You'll want to gather as many different kinds of evidence of your students' comprehension and problem solving as possible—what you collect both systematically, during assigned grading periods with specific assessment tools, as well as spontaneously, during the daily flow of classroom life as you observe and interact with your students on a moment-by-moment basis.

What we assess also reflects our theoretical understandings of what literacy is— how it develops and what we can do as teachers to support that process. What's more, our assessments also reflect what we value about literacy (Fountas & Pinnell, 2006). If we regard reading as the development of a complex processing system, we will want to be sure that we are monitoring and documenting our students' control of this complete system of strategic actions.

Assessment Tools

In the succeeding pages, you'll find a range of assessment tools: checklists, rubrics, self-evaluation prompts for students, and so forth. You'll know which tools make the most sense for you and your students and how best to use them in ways that maximize learning for all. Of every form or rubric you choose to use you might ask: "Does this assessment help me understand what my students know and what they need to know—and does it show me what I can do to help students acquire the additional strategic actions and understandings they need to develop as proficient readers?"

Note that both you and your students can use some of the same forms for either the interactive read-aloud or book clubs. Also, some of the forms overlap; we share a sampling of forms so that you can pick and choose, rethink and revise, in ways that work best for you and your class.

Student Tools

Here are quick descriptions of some self-reflection and tracking tools that students in grades 2–5 can use to guide and monitor their own reading, writing, book conversations, and thinking. Each completed form will provide you with invaluable insights into your students' developing understandings, attitudes, strategic actions, and reading habits.

Reading Log A reading list in a reader's notebook is a record-keeping tool for individual students—and an assessment tool for you and them. It encourages students to keep track of, monitor, and document their independent reading so that both you and the students can see how many books they are reading and how much time it is taking them to read each one. You might ask students to staple this log to the inside of their readers' notebooks. (p. 134)

Close Reading & Text Evidence This form encourages close reading and citing text evidence. It's an easy way to encourage your students to back up their opinions with concrete evidence from the text and it reminds students to follow a line of thinking across the text—thinking within, beyond, and about—recording evidence not once but multiple times. (p. 135)

Quotations & Responses Encourages students to play close attention to beautiful literary language, intriguing twists in the plot, or surprising facts and details. Paying close attention to text will not only bolster their contribution in discussions, but also extend their own vocabulary and language repertoire. (p. 136)

Student Book Club Discussion Tracker This form tracks a student's journey through a book club discussion—from reading the book and preparing to discuss it, to the book club meeting(s) and discussions with peers, to an analysis of the meeting(s) once the club has ended. The Book Club Discussion Tracker helps students meet deadlines and stay on course throughout the process and helps you track their progress, making sure they are engaging with each book in a meaningful, insightful way. (pp. 137–138) You may wish to use this form in conjunction with the Book Club Self-Assessment forms on pages 45–46.

Teacher Tools

The tools below are meant for you to monitor, document, and assess your students' progress and, perhaps most importantly, plan next steps for instruction. The Units of Study Projects section of this guide and the section on Characteristics of Units by Theme also include options for supporting assessment.

Comprehension Clubs **Literacy Development Across the Year** Across the year— at the beginning, middle, and end—you can monitor whether your students are emerging, developing, and achieving proficient status as readers and writers. You'll be able to collect the information through daily observation and through conversations with your students: What do they regard as their personal reading and writing strengths? What do they regard as their challenges? How do they aim to achieve their goals? (p. 139)

Book Club Log/Teacher Observation Form This form will help you keep track of each individual student's contribution in book club meetings as well as the book club as a whole—what was discussed, what needs were revealed, and what you might do instructionally to support further development. (p. 140)

Book Club Teacher's Assessment Checklist This checklist is a quick and easy way for you to document each student's participation in the book club. Did they arrive prepared with evidence of close reading and deep thinking in their reader's notebook? Do their comments reflect understanding of the book? Are they engaged and thoughtful participants in the discussion, demonstrating an ability to extend and refine the comments of others? (p. 141)

Thinking Across Texts Within a Unit of Study This form enables you to track how students' key understandings build across texts and within a unit's discussion. (p. 142)

Reader's Notebook Rubric Used properly, students' readers' notebooks showcase their reading lives: the books they've read, reading times, how they engaged with each book; what they learned and questioned; the connections they made to other books. The notebook also invites thoughtful analysis, an opportunity for students to marshal the full power of writing as a tool to dig deep and make sense of text— thinking within, beyond, and about the text. (p. 143)

Reading Log

	Book Title	Author	Genre/Unit	Date Started	Date Finished
1					
2					
3					
4					
5					
6					
7					
8					
9					
10					

Name _____ **Date** _____

Book Title _____

Close Reading & Text Evidence

My opinion is . . .	My opinion is . . .
Text Evidence	**Text Evidence**

Comprehension Clubs

Student Name _____

Book Title _____

Book Club _____ Date _____

Quotations & Responses

1. While you're reading, mark or note passages or quotations that strike you as provocative, inspiring, puzzling, game-changing, and so on.

2. Choose three or four of the most striking passages or quotations you've marked and then explain why you chose each one.

Passage or Quotation	Page	Response

Comprehension Clubs

Student Name _____ **Date** _____

Book Title _____ **Book Club** _____

Student Book Club Discussion Tracker

Part 1: Preparing for Book Club Discussion (Reference page numbers when you cite text.)	
My first reaction is . . .	
I predict . . .	
This part makes me think . . .	
I'm uncertain about this part because . . .	
I'm drawn to this phrase, passage, scene, detail, graphic, character, setting, plot, facts because . . .	
I could use help with the words . . .	
I wonder about . . .	
This textual detail is a standout because . . .	
I'm eager to find out more about . . .	
I really need help with . . .	

Student Name _____ Date _____

Book Title _____ Book Club _____

Student Book Club Discussion Tracker (continued)

Part 2: Summing Up After the Book Club Discussion	
My thoughts about _____ changed as the result of our discussion because . . .	
We all agreed that . . .	
We were surprised when . . .	
We disagreed about . . .	
The highlight was . . .	
What I think worked well about our discussion was . . .	
What didn't work as well was . . .	
Additional Comments:	

 **Comprehension Clubs**

Student Name _____ Date _____

Comprehension Clubs Literacy Development Across the Year

Student Year _____

Key: **E** (Emerging) **D** (Developing) **P** (Proficient)

Capacities	Beginning	Middle	End
Reads familiar texts smoothly (fluency)			
Reads independently for 30–45 minutes (stamina)			
Reads at home independently for 20–30 minutes			
Participates in and sustains booktalk			
Selects books according to self-awareness of reading interests and tastes			
Demonstrates ability to assume a reading stance and back it up with evidence from the text			
Writes independently for 30-plus minutes (stamina)			
Writes at home independently			
Sustains selected writing piece/unit theme project over three or more days (stamina)			
Rereads own writing to add on, delete, revise, edit			
Reads and interprets texts in a variety of genres			
Defines characteristics of different genres			
Writes in a variety of genres			

Identity as a Reader & Writer	Beginning	Middle	End
Works effectively within the daily routines			
Approaches book club with reader's notebook and prepared notes, comments, questions, text evidence			
Exhibits active decision making and accountability for his or her outcomes during independent practice			
Actively and independently contributes new writing to his or her reader's notebook			
Articulates personal reading strengths			
Articulates personal reading challenges			
Articulates personal writing challenges			
Sets realistic and appropriate writing goals			
Achieves writing goals			
Recognizes and uses the perspective of others to revise or deepen the understanding of text			
Stays on topic			
Strong collaborator; participates fully			
Asks questions to clarify understanding			
Engages in close reading and rereads in search of text evidence to support thinking			
Recognizes and uses the perspective of others to help revise writing/ theme project work			

Comprehension Clubs

Club _____

Book Title _____

Book Club Log/Teacher Observation Form

	Observations	Needed Follow-up
Student 1		
Student 2		
Student 3		
Student 4		
Student 5		
Student 6		
Student 7		
Student 8		
Student 9		
Student 10		

Comprehension Clubs

Student _____ Unit _____

Book Title _____

Book Club _____ Date _____

Book Club Teacher's Assessment Checklist

Preparation	☐ Read assigned pages ☐ Listed comments and questions for discussion in reader's notebook ☐ Identified text evidence to back up opinions and comments
Participation: Process	☐ Arrived prepared and ready to participate ☐ Followed conversational turn-taking conventions ☐ Listened attentively and respectfully to each speaker ☐ Built on comments of others ☐ Asked for clarification as needed
Participation: Content	☐ Shared on-target comments, opinions, and questions ☐ Cited related textual evidence ☐ Demonstrated literal understanding of text ☐ Demonstrated inferential understanding ☐ Identified literary elements ☐ Identified structural components of text ☐ Provided evidence of analytical thinking ☐ Used the comprehension framework to structure thinking within the text, beyond the text, and about the text ☐ Noticed aspects of the text such as language, structure, or writer's craft
Assessment	☐ Understands the nature of a productive discussion ☐ Identified challenges and framed needed improvements ☐ Provided an on-target assessment of self as participant
Next Steps for the Reader	Student's Thoughts
	Teacher's Thoughts

Thinking Across Texts Within a Unit of Study

Reinforce thinking across texts with questions like these. See also the unit-specific questions in the Unit Projects section of this guide.

Genre/Text Type	How does the book [title] compare with other books of the same genre?	How are the picture books in this unit alike? How are they different?	Which authors in this unit do you think would also be successful writing in a form such as plays, essays, or poetry? Why?
Author's Purpose or Message	Which two books in this unit are most alike in terms of the authors' messages?	Do you think all the authors in this unit had the same purpose? Why or why not?	Which author's message did you find most convincing or most memorable? Why?
Illustrations or Photos	Which two books are the most different in how they used photos or illustrations? Explain.	Which book or books in this unit most need the support of photos or art that add information to the text?	Which book in this unit would you like to see re-illustrated? What kinds of illustrations would you like to see?
Organization and Style	Which text features or terms did you see again and again?	Which books were organized in similar ways? Give some examples.	Which authors' approaches would you want to try and follow in your own writing? Why?
Characters, Plot, and Setting	Which characters in this unit have similar problems? Compare how their problems get solved.	Which books have the most details about the setting? How did these details affect you as a reader?	Which characters would you like to read more about? Why?
Facts and Authenticity	How did the facts in one book support the facts in another?	Which authors were able to use their life experiences to add authenticity to their writing?	How was the way this author told you about the topic different from the way the other authors did?

How would you finish these sentences?

1. The two authors whose work seems most alike are _____ and _____, because . . . .

2. The most important thing someone should know before reading the books in this unit is . . . .

Comprehension Clubs

Reader's Name _____ Date _____

Reader's Notebook Rubric

The Reader . . .	Emerging	Proficient	Outstanding
keeps track of books and reading times in his/her reading log.			
includes thorough notes on each assigned book.			
identifies accurately the genre for each book recorded.			
is reading in a range of genres.			
demonstrates evidence of thinking within, beyond, and about text; includes page numbers and text citations.			
demonstrates growing ability to write in response to reading.			
draws connections among books and themes; compares and contrasts.			
creates a refined written response or theme project that demonstrates thorough knowledge of the book.			
Next Instructional Steps/ Needed Follow-up:			

Comprehension Clubs Streaming Audio and Other Resources

Comprehension Clubs provides technology resources to support both educators and students at *http://www.comprehensionclubs.scholastic.com*. Here you will find audio versions of book club books, as well as resources to support planning, teaching, and assessment.

Audiobooks

Visit *http://www.comprehensionclubs.scholastic.com* to access streaming audio versions of all book club choices in *Comprehension Clubs*. These audiobooks are available as read-along support for students who otherwise may not be able to access the text in print form. Enter the user name "hear" and the password "books," then follow directions on the site to select the specific audios you would like to access.

Book-Specific Internet Resources

Each *Comprehension Clubs* teaching card includes suggestions for Internet sites to visit for more information related to the book being read and discussed. These sites are hosted by a variety of educational institutions, children's book authors, and scientific organizations.

Additional Internet Resources

Explore *www.scholastic.com* for numerous teacher, student, and parent resources related to books and to researching topics of interest. You may wish to use these for independent or group extension activities.

Comprehension Clubs and the Common Core State Standards

As Sue Pimentel, one of the primary architects of the English language arts Common Core State Standards, reminds us, we should center our instructional efforts on "texts worth reading and questions worth answering" (2012). High-quality, complex text, by its very nature, automatically prompts dynamic, provocative, intriguing discussions. Truly compelling titles, often linked together under an overarching theme, leave us longing to discuss them with other readers. The theme is so striking, the content so intriguing, the lessons so transformative, and our engagement with each book so deep that our need to discuss and make sense with others may feel urgent. This, in a nutshell, summarizes what we hope to accomplish through our *Comprehension Club* interactive read-aloud and student book club discussions.

The Common Core State Standards, spearheaded by the Council of Chief State School Officers and the National Governors Association, are a response to the call by the states to "create the next generation of K–12 standards in order to help ensure that all students are college- and career-ready in literacy no later than the end of high school" (CCSS, 2010, p. 3). The Common Core State Standards (CCSS), built on research and international models, draw information and inspiration from numerous sources, including state departments of education, professional organizations, scholars, educators from kindergarten through college, parents, and concerned citizens. As a result, the Standards meet the criteria listed below.

The CCSS are

- research- and evidence-based
- aligned with college and work expectations
- rigorous
- internationally benchmarked

Matched Goals: The CCSS and *Comprehension Clubs*

Everything the Common Core English Language Arts Standards require can be easily accomplished through *Comprehension Clubs*. Sue Pimentel (2012) created the chart below, which shows what's in—and what's out. You'll notice that everything that's "in" characterizes *Comprehension Clubs*.

What's In and What's Out		
	IN	**OUT**
1.	Daily encounters with complex texts	Leveled texts (only)
2.	Texts worthy of close attention	Reading any ol' text
3.	Balance of literary and informational texts	Focus only on literature
4.	Coherent sequence of texts	Collection of unrelated texts
5.	Mostly text-dependent questions	Mostly text-to-self questions
6.	Evidence-based analyses	Personal opinions about issues
7.	Accent on academic vocabulary	Accent on literary terminology
8.	Emphasis on reading and rereading	Emphasis on prereading
9.	Reading strategies at point of need	Overemphasis on reading strategies
10.	Pre-mediation	(Just) remediation

> *"The Common Core State Standards call for reading across a wide range of increasingly complex texts. And, in perfect alignment with the CCSS, Comprehension Clubs teachers strive to help students read and comprehend increasingly complex literary and informational texts independently and proficiently."*

In addition to supporting CCSS reading standards, *Comprehension Clubs* also supports CCSS standards for writing, through the writing prompts included on the teaching cards and the unit projects included in this guide. Speaking and listening standards are addressed by the interactive read-alouds and book club sessions.

Developing Literate Capacities

Both the Common Core State Standards and *Comprehension Clubs* aim to produce students who advance through the grades developing as fully literate, curious, independent learners. In the overview of the CCSS (2010), a student who has mastered the standards in reading, writing, speaking, listening, and language is able to "exhibit with increasing fullness and regularity" seven "capacities of the literate individual" or what might also be regarded as seven essential habits of mind. Teachers who adopt the strategic, exemplary instructional practices of *Comprehension Clubs* find it creates confident learners who can read critically, ask essential questions that relate to the text under review, follow a line of inquiry, articulate their own ideas, and, in general, enjoy the life of the mind that robust literacy makes possible. As outlined by the Common Core State Standards and achievable through *Comprehension Clubs*, students develop the literate capacities outlined below.

Demonstrate Independence Students are able to comprehend and critique a wide range of complex text types and genres, pinpoint the key message, request clarification, and ask relevant questions. As they engage in lively, content-rich discussions, we see evidence of their growing academic vocabularies, control over Standard English, and ability to build on others' ideas while articulating their own. Ultimately, they become self-directed learners, obtaining support from teachers, peers, authorities, and other resources—print, digital, and multimedia—that they need for their own learning.

Build Strong Content Knowledge Students engage with complex texts of quality that are a "rich repository of ideas" (Pimentel, 2012) and therefore also replete with academic vocabulary. In the process, students learn to read purposefully, often led by their own essential questions. They hone their general knowledge while they gain content-specific vocabulary and information. They also learn how the meanings of words vary with context. Ultimately, students learn how to extend and refine their evolving understandings across a spiralling continuum of text and conceptual complexity.

Respond to Varying Demands of Audience Students become text- and audience-sensitive, understanding that different texts arrive in different formats and serve different purposes (consider the audience for a recipe versus a poem or the delivery of an advertising jingle versus a persuasive essay). As students are immersed in multiple examples of text types, exploring their form and function, they soon learn to control the various texts themselves, adjusting their purpose for reading, writing, and speaking in ways that align with the task at hand.

Comprehend As Well As Critique In this era of print and multimedia bombardment, teachers recognize that their ultimate aim is to help their students become critical readers, so they not only understand the message but also can question its assumptions, relevance, and validity. Learning how to be thoughtfully discerning is a key skill in 21st-century learning—and in Common Core-aligned *Comprehension Club* classrooms, where every day, students are engaged in "substantive academic discussions that ask students to draw on textual evidence" (Pimentel, 2012).

Value Evidence Again, with the explosion of new information, students need to learn how to back up what they say and write with evidence—beginning with reading texts that are "worthy of close attention" (Pimentel, 2012). The ability to articulate what we believe and why—citing relevant evidence to make key points—and expecting the same of others is, today, a standard skill and expectation. Pimentel (2012) suggests that a significant percentage (80%–90%) of the questions students ask and discuss should be "text dependent." What's more, students need extensive practice with writing to analyze sources (arguments and writing to inform) and short research projects.

Use Technology and Digital Media Strategically and Capably Technology offers a universe of learning, but students need guidance in how to conduct efficient, productive online searches and then integrate what they learn into other media. Students also need to have a sense of what technology can and cannot do. What are its limitations? What technical tool is the best fit for a task? Such decisions demand the critical thinking students acquire through the close reading and text analysis that *Comprehension Clubs* provides. The extension projects, which include online research and integrate reading, writing, talking, and listening, also help build the thoughtful, critical literacy that's become more important than ever.

Come to Understand Other Perspectives and Cultures Reading in general and literature in particular have always offered opportunities to experience other lives, universes, and emotional frameworks. A kaleidoscope of culture, language, human values, opinions, and perspectives comes into brilliant focus through reading, and helps to shape the awareness, sensitivity, and appreciation of a literate person. The Common Core urges teachers to provide "works of exceptional craft that span eras, cultures, and genres" (Pimentel, 2012).

How *Comprehension Clubs* Helps Students Develop the Literate Capacities the CCSS Promote

Literate capacities begin with understanding. In order to crack open and comprehend a text, our students need to engage in all the important aspects of literal, inferential, and critical thinking.

These mental acts of processing happen simultaneously and largely unconsciously; indeed, as we have explained in *Teaching for Comprehending and Fluency* (2006), our goal, as teachers, is to "enable readers to assimilate, apply, and coordinate systems of strategic actions without being fully aware that they are doing so" (p. 45). But it is engagement with text, most successfully learned within the context of *Comprehension Clubs* and its two talk structures—the interactive read-aloud and book clubs—that enables the habits of mind or literate capacities promoted by the CCSS.

Thinking Within the Text

Key Ideas and Details

- Read closely to determine what the text says explicitly and make logical inferences from it; cite specific textual evidence when writing or speaking to support conclusions drawn from the text.

- Determine central ideas or themes of a text and analyze their development; summarize key supporting details and ideas.

- Analyze how and why individuals and ideas develop and events take place over the course of a text.

Thinking Beyond the Text

Integration of Knowledge and Ideas

- Integrate and evaluate content presented in diverse media and formats, taking into account the validity of the reasoning as well as the relevance and sufficiency of the evidence.

- Delineate and evaluate the argument and specific claims in a text, including the validity of the reasoning as well as the relevance and sufficiency of the evidence.

- Analyze how two or more texts address similar themes or topics in order to build knowledge or to compare the approaches the authors take.

Thinking About the Text

Craft and Structure

- Interpret words and phrases as they are used in a text, including determining technical, connotative, and figurative meanings, and analyze how specific word choices shape meaning or tone.

- Analyze the structure of a text, including how specific sentences, paragraphs, and portions of the text, such as a section, chapter, scene, or stanza, relate to each other and the whole.

- Assess how point of view or purpose shapes the content and style of a text.

Closing Thoughts

We want our students to develop powerful individual reading identities. To this end, students need ample opportunity to read, write about, and discuss content-rich, intriguing, complex texts. In this way, they begin to discover themselves as readers with preferences, passions, and pursuits. *Comprehension Clubs*, drawing from the Common Core as well as deep theoretical understandings about language and literacy development, honors all students as worthy of analyzing and assimilating challenging material. At the same time, however, we celebrate the diversity within every classroom. We encourage our students to reflect on their strengths and needs as readers, and help them establish and work toward personal literacy goals. Fully realized, proficient reading is within their reach in the Common Core–aligned *Comprehension Clubs* classroom.

Comprehension Clubs Units at a Glance

Title	Author	Genre	Text Type	Themes/Ideas	Author's Craft	Vocabulary	Writing Options	Technology
Kindergarten								
Strand: Community & Relationships								
				Unit: Being a Friend	**Unit Focus: What is being a friend all about?**			
RA 1 — Yo! Yes?	Chris Raschka	Realistic Fiction	Picture Book	being open to friendship; overcoming differences; understanding the feelings of others	dialogue with few words; use of special typeface, and punctuation to convey meaning; use of illustrations to develop characters and create a message	friends, Oh, Well?, Yes?, Yo!, communicate, different, shy	sentence frame (narrative)	www.care2.com/cards/writeups/inthello.html
RA 2 — My Friend Is Sad	Mo Willems	Fantasy	Series Picture Book	caring for friends; sharing experiences; misunderstandings between friends	animal characters used to relate a message; illustrations and dialogue to develop the characters and plot and make the story humorous	happy, robot, sorry, affection, enjoyment, misunderstand, worry	speech balloon (narrative)	www.pigeonpresents.com
RA 3 — Not Norman	Kelly Bennett	Realistic Fiction	Picture Book	how pets provide friendship; changing one's mind; unexpected outcomes	first-person narration used to develop the main character and his point of view; descriptive language and dialogue that develop story themes	goldfish, keep, trade, disappointment, qualities	favorite scene (narrative)	http://kellybennett.com
RA 4 — Chester's Way	Kevin Henkes	Fantasy	Picture Book	appreciating individual differences; learning from others; forming new friendships	animal characters used to relate a message; humor in text and illustrations used to communicate central themes	always, disguises, exactly, neighborhood, acceptance, habit, identical, similar	letter (expository)	www.kidsarespecial.org/index.php?page=the-more-we-get-together
RA 5 — Knuffle Bunny Too	Mo Willems	Realistic Fiction	Picture Book	special bonds; sharing feelings; resolving conflict	combination of photographs and art to depict setting, characters, and events; a story with a message; dialogue in speech balloons that adds to character development and drama	arrangements, exchange, excited, realized, identical, identify, mistaken, special, unique	story (narrative)	www.readingrockets.org/books/interviews
BC 1 — My Friends	Taro Gomi	Fantasy	Picture Book	friendship all around us; appreciating what we learn from others; learning about the world through observation	mix of fantasy, first-person narration, and everyday activities that helps show appreciation for others; concepts made accessible through organization; illustrations that provide context and support vocabulary	explore, from, learned, appreciate, imaginary, world	readers' notebooks	www.animalfactguide.com
BC 2 — Lost and Found	Oliver Jeffers	Fantasy	Picture Book	having compassion and using persistence to help others; understanding loneliness and the importance of companionship; being a friend	fantasy used to tell a tale about loneliness and companionship; problem-solution story structure used to develop characters; illustrations that mix realism with fantasy	lonely, mistake, row, searched, adventure, companionship, compassion, persistent	readers' notebooks	http://kidzone.ws/animals/penguins/index.htm
BC 3 — Margarita and Margarita y Margarita	Lynn Reiser	Realistic Fiction	Picture Book	communicating in different languages; appreciating differences and finding commonalities; taking risks to make new friends	dialogue in Spanish and English that tells a story about forming a friendship; illustrations and colored font that make bilingual text accessible	meet, speak, Sweet dreams!, communication, conversation, language	readers' notebooks	http://pbskids.org/noah/index.html
BC 4 — Just a Little Bit	Ann Tompert	Fantasy	Picture Book	friends using teamwork can solve problems; every effort helps, no matter how small	fantasy and a problem-solution story structure that deliver a message; predictability and repetition used to advance the plot	seesaw, strength, urged, cooperation, succeed, weight	readers' notebooks	http://pbskids.org/sid/games.html
Kindergarten								
Strand: Folklore & Literary Traditions								
				Unit: Telling Tales	**Unit Focus: What makes a folktale a special kind of story?**			
RA 1 — Chicken Little	Rebecca & Ed Emberley	Folktale	Picture Book	thinking before you act; the importance of staying calm	use of repetitive plot structure; twist ending that creates a modern feel; lively dialogue and onomatopoeic words	anxious, foolishness, plan, witless, calm, consequence, prepare	illustration (expository)	http://us.macmillan.com/chickenlittle/RebeccaEmberley
RA 2 — The Three Bears	Paul Galdone	Folktale	Picture Book	respecting others' belongings; making mischief; thinking before acting; having good manners; asking permission	traditional plot structure; type size formatted to imitate three sizes of the Bears; illustrations that reflect characters' feelings	harm, peeked, trusting, intrude, mischief, permission	description (persuasive)	http://pbskids.org/video/?category=Clifford the Big Red Dog&pid=CxcBP5NTG_2CS2_AI2kxXlhZl_Camov5
RA 3 — This Is the House That Jack Built	Simms Taback	Folktale	Picture Book	connections among people and things; creation of art	use of a cumulative story structure with repeating plot elements and characters; traditional rhyme transformed; detailed pictures that provide extra information	crumpled, forlorn, shorn, tattered, worried, connection, cumulative, relationship	illustration (narrative)	www.simmstaback.com
RA 4 — The Little Red Hen	Lucinda McQueen	Folktale	Picture Book	importance of hard work; earning a reward; responsibility	detailed pictures and descriptive text that provide information about each character; plot pattern with repeated events; steps in a process	gossip, sprout, thresh, vain, harvest, responsibility	illustrative description (narrative)	http://pbskids.org/video
RA 5 — The Little Red Hen (Makes a Pizza)	Philemon Sturges	Folktale	Picture Book	cooperation; responsibility; benefits of hard work; sharing	plot pattern with repeated events; steps in a process; updated plot and setting; revised moral	dough, fetch, grated, kneaded, rummaged, generous, repay	illustration (expository)	www.sproutonline.com
BC 1 — The Mitten	Jan Brett	Folktale	Picture Book	being responsible; seeking shelter; animal relationships; sharing	cumulative story structure; realistic details about animals in the illustrations and text	bulged, burrowed, commotion, jostled, lumbered, careless, neighborly	readers' notebooks	www.janbrett.com
BC 2 — Goldilocks and the Three Bears	Caralyn Buehner	Folktale	Picture Book	respect and consideration for others; thinking before you act; behaving appropriately	plot structure that repeats events in threes; character built through story details and dialogue; plot advanced through use of rhymes	appetite, disturbed, porridge, sputtered, wee, consideration, respect, rude	readers' notebooks	www.sesamestreet.org/videos

	Title	Author	Genre	Text Type	Themes/Ideas	Author's Craft	Vocabulary	Writing Options	Technology
Kindergarten									
Strand: Folklore & Literary Traditions									
Unit: Telling Tales (cont'd.)									
Unit Focus: What makes a folktale a special kind of story?									
BC 3	Let's Play in the Forest	Claudia Rueda	Folktale	Picture Book	playing games; being careful; getting ready for the day	use of a call-and-response story structure; humor and a plot twist that engages readers; colorful illustrations that support the text	around, favorite, forest, routine, surprise, suspense	readers' notebooks	www.claudiarueda.com/p/lets-play-in-forest.html
BC 4	The Three Billy-Goats Gruff	Ellen Appleby	Folktale	Picture Book	standing up for yourself; cleverness; bullying	suspense built through repetition; varying type size used to show emphasis; pictures that support story events	gobble, poker, tramping, tripping, bully, defend, threaten	readers' notebooks	www.northrup.org/photos/goat
Kindergarten									
Strand: Living Things									
Unit: Trees & Other Plants									
Unit Focus: How do writers help you care about trees and plants?									
RA 1	Are Trees Alive?	Debbie S. Miller	Informational Text	Picture Book	trees are living things; each part of a living thing does a unique job; comparing people and trees; appreciating different forms of life	Introduction that states the book's purpose; comparisons of trees and people; variety of settings	alive, gather, limbs, protects, support, bark, trunk, veins	poster (expository)	www.arborday.org/kids/carly/lifeofatree
RA 2	The Surprise Garden	Zoe Hall	Informational Text	Picture Book	planting and growing a garden; vegetables look different and grow differently; vegetables are picked when they are ripe	sequential presentation of events; child's point of view; basic factual information about different fruits and vegetables; summary chart	loosen, poke, ripens, surprise, food, tools	food fact card (expository)	www.foodchamps.org
RA 3	Up, Down, and Around	Katherine Ayres	Informational Text	Picture Book	learning about direction; growing vegetables	use of rhyme to tell a story; pattern of repeated words that teaches readers about direction	around, dirt, fresh, grow, row, tasty, garden, wind	chart (expository)	www.hhmi.org/coolscience/forkids
RA 4	Flip, Float, Fly: Seeds on the Move	JoAnn Early Macken	Informational Text	Picture Book	how seeds move; the interdependence of living things	use of descriptive language to present factual information; similes; action words that indicate movement	clusters, explodes, glide, soaring, twirl, breeze, cling, scatter	draw and write a sentence (narrative)	http://dnr.wi.gov/org/caer/ce/eek/cool
RA 5	A Dandelion's Life	John Himmelman	Informational Text	Picture Book	the life cycle of a dandelion; the seasons of the year; the interaction of plants and animals	use of text and illustrations to provide factual information; temporal sequential order; realistic style of illustration to depict nature	thirsty, dozens, fuzzy, withers, seasons, insects	diagram (expository)	http://jch.homestead.com/home.html
BC 1	From Seed to Dandelion	Ellen Weiss	Informational Text	Picture Book	the life cycle of a plant; identifying the parts of a plant	events presented sequentially; different text features used to provide information and help readers keep track of it	dandelion, fluff, petals, seed, blooms, weed, yard	readers' notebooks	www.absurdintellectual.com
BC 2	Flower Garden	Eve Bunting	Realistic Fiction	Picture Book	planting a flower garden; bringing nature to the city; surprising loved ones; lifting people's spirits	rhymes used to tell a story; setting revealed through details; girl's point of view used to tell a story	garden, mix, potting, stairs, birthday, colorful	readers' notebooks	http://chicagobotanic.org/kidssite
BC 3	From Bulb to Daffodil	Ellen Weiss	Informational Text	Picture Book	the life cycle of a plant; identifying parts of a flower; tracing the life of a flower	events presented sequentially; different text features that provide information and help readers keep track of it	buds, bulbs, daffodil, roots, gardeners, stored	readers' notebooks	www.rhs.org.uk/Children/For-families/Plants-to-grow-with-kids/Bulbs
BC 4	Wonderful Worms	Linda Glaser	Informational Text	Picture Book	appreciating small creatures; understanding interactions in nature	factual information given from a child's viewpoint; descriptive language; sensory details; cause and effect; first-person narration by child	burrows, passageways, tunnel, worms, helpful, underground	readers' notebooks	http://urbanext.illinois.edu/worms
Kindergarten									
Strand: A Sense of Self									
Unit: Feelings									
Unit Focus: How does understanding your own feelings and the feelings of others help you in everyday life?									
RA 1	How Are You Peeling? Foods With Moods	Saxton Freymann & Joost Elffers	Informational Text	Picture Book	we all experience many moods and emotions; facial expressions and body language can reveal feelings; we can name our feelings	photographs of fun food sculptures that illustrate human emotions; rhyme that engages the reader in an understanding of feelings	ashamed, bold, jealous, secure, amused, confused, frustrated	sentence stem (expository)	www.amnh.org/ology/features/expressyourself
RA 2	Grumpy Bird	Jeremy Tankard	Fantasy	Picture Book	a bad mood can overshadow everything else; good friends can help us cheer up	use of repetitive plot structure and humorous illustrations to emphasize the main character's feelings; use of dialogue	company, nice, snapped, mood, upset	draw and label (expository)	www.scholastic.com/parents/play&grumpybird
RA 3	Ruthie and the (Not So) Teeny Tiny Lie	Laura Rankin	Fantasy	Picture Book	feelings of guilt can be overwhelming; sharing feelings is often more helpful than hiding them; honesty; considering others	conflict and its effects on characters shown through illustrations; use of dialogue and precise language	absolutely, click, courage, expression, guilt	draw and label (expository)	www.storyarts.org/library/aesops/stories/boy.html
RA 4	Boo Hoo Bird	Jeremy Tankard	Fantasy	Picture Book	getting hurt can be upsetting; there are many different ways to feel better; pain can go away long before our feelings heal	use of a problem-and-solution story structure that leads to the story's climax; use of dialogue, actions, and humor to convey feelings	cry, help, hurt, sorry, wounded, injury, problem, solution	predict next scene (narrative)	www.jeremytankard.com/index.html
RA 5	Feeling Thankful	Shelly Rotner & Sheila Kelly	Informational Text	Picture Book	feeling grateful for good things in life; finding pleasure in small details	use of repetition to reinforce the theme of feeling gratitude; photographs that illustrate all the things children can feel thankful for	family, thankful, grateful, appreciate	sentence stem (expository)	www.shelleyrotner.com/portraits
BC 1	Maybe a Bear Ate It!	Robie H. Harris	Fantasy	Picture Book	exaggerating small problems; letting your imagination run wild can make a problem feel worse	use of first-person point of view to have character share feelings of anxiety and worry; use of different-sized type and different fonts to convey emphasis	anywhere, nowhere, stomped, lose, worry	readers' notebooks	http://www.michaelemberley.com/questions/
BC 2	Sometimes I'm Bombaloo	Rachel Vail	Realistic Fiction	Picture Book	losing your temper can turn you into a different person; quiet time can help you calm down; it's important to have someone who understands you	first-person point of view articulates shifts in mood and confusing emotions; language and story details show a character's traits and the ways in which feelings are expressed and how they are controlled	fierce, hate, smile, sometimes, sorry, blow up, calm, temper	readers' notebooks	http://www.jacketflap.com/yumi-heo/162034
BC 3	Katie Loves the Kittens	John Himmelman	Fantasy	Picture Book	the importance of knowing how to control our feelings; our feelings and actions can be misunderstood by others	development of characters (Katie the dog) through illustrations, narration, and actions; plot that unfolds in a series of events	control, excited, frightened, missed, sweet, confused, pest, trust	readers' notebooks	http://jch.homestead.com/home.html

Code	Title	Author	Genre	Type	Unit/Theme	Teaching Point	Vocabulary	Activity	URL
BC 4	If You're Happy and You Know It	James Warhola	Fantasy	Picture Book	expressing joy; using your imagination is fun	use of a familiar song with new lyrics to express feelings of joy; playful setting that unleashes children's imagination	blink, clap, flap, roar, dance, song	readers' notebooks	http://www.worthingtonlibraries.org/interact/av/2008-3/if-youre-happy-and-you-know-it

Kindergarten

Strand: Inspired by True Stories

Unit: All Kinds of Jobs

Unit Focus: Where do people work and what jobs do they do?

Code	Title	Author	Genre	Type	Unit/Theme	Teaching Point	Vocabulary	Activity	URL
RA 1	Lola at the Library	Anna McQuinn	Realistic Fiction	Picture Book	the wonder of libraries; the enjoyment of reading books; being responsible; family love; being part of a community	character's perspective created through simple, childlike language; character used to develop story themes and ideas	borrowed, chooses, important, library, community, enjoyable, subject	draw and write a caption (expository)	http://pbskids.org/lions/videos
RA 2	My Mom Is a Firefighter	Lois G. Grambling	Realistic Fiction	Picture Book	teamwork; firefighting; fire safety; different kinds of families	first-person narration; use of words and actions to develop the main character	dangers, rig, team, brave, responsible, task	describe a day (narrative)	www.sparky.org/firetruck
RA 3	ABC of Jobs	Roger Priddy	Informational Text	Picture Book	variety of jobs; special skills needed for some jobs; training; some workers require equipment	one profession and job description for each of the 26 letters of the alphabet; first-person accounts of working	emergency, medicine, protective, uniform, profession, skill, service	draw and label (expository)	http://pbskids.org/curiousgeorge/games
RA 4	All About Things People Do	Melanie & Chris Rice	Informational Text	Picture Book	different kinds of jobs from around the world; cooperation; understanding steps in a process	grouping of jobs by type of work or setting; emphasis on steps in a process and cooperation to achieve goals	factory, goods, mining, services, cooperate, manufacture	draw and write a caption (expository)	http://pbskids.org/sid/scientist.html
RA 5	Bones, Bones, Dinosaur Bones	Byron Barton	Informational Text	Picture Book	working together; the study of dinosaurs and dinosaur bones	first-person plural voice; use of simple language and illustrations to inform readers; use of rhythmic language and repetition to structure text; bright illustrations	bones, load, pack, wrap, skeleton, tool, paleontologist	describe a task (expository)	http://www.amnh.org/explore/ology/paleontology
BC 1	Road Builders	B. G. Hennessy	Informational Fiction	Picture Book	building roads with specialized trucks and teamwork; the importance of roads; jobs for everyone	introducing road-building trucks and the people who use them to show that everything and everyone has an important job to do	cement, gravel, scoops, worker, process, specialized, teamwork	readers' notebooks	www.bghennessy.com/funstuff.html
BC 2	Miss Bindergarten Gets Ready for Kindergarten	Joseph Slate	Fantasy	Picture Book	preparing for the first day of school; doing a good job benefits everyone; fantasy makes reading and learning fun	fantasy and rhyme; alphabet sequence used to introduce animal characters as kindergartners	marches, rushes, sneaks, prepare, welcome	readers' notebooks	www.hbofamily.com
BC 3	The Wheels on the Truck!	Steve Metzger	Informational Fiction	Picture Book	specialized machinery and skilled people work together to build a house; work follows a process; making a home	rhythm and musicality used to tell about the process of building a house; each verse used to inform about the job of a truck or a worker	earth, frames, house, site, construction, job, special	readers' notebooks	www.bobthebuilder.com/usa/projects.asp
BC 4	Kindergarten ABC	Jacqueline Rogers	Informational Fiction	Picture Book	use the alphabet to structure a story; learn about "work" kindergarteners and their teacher do; find words that begin alike	girl as narrator of story about kindergarten; specialized font used to introduce letters of the alphabet; story structure follows the alphabet	build, day, learn, pretend, activity, alphabetical order, letter	readers' notebooks	www.sesamestreet.org

Kindergarten

Strand: Genre Study

Unit: Concept Books

Unit Focus: How do writers make concept books fun to read?

Code	Title	Author	Genre	Type	Unit/Theme	Teaching Point	Vocabulary	Activity	URL
RA 1	More Than One	Miriam Schlein	Concept Book	Picture Book	counting; thinking about numbers in new ways; the concept that one can represent many	text features that teach number concepts; questions that engage readers	crowd, dozen, flock, pair, grains, grouping	draw and label (expository)	www.scholastic.com/clifford/games.asp
RA 2	The Very Hungry Caterpillar	Eric Carle	Concept Book	Picture Book	days of the week; counting to five; stages of a caterpillar's life cycle	use of a predictable story structure to teach multiple concepts; colorful and engaging illustrations that connect to the text	cocoon, nibbled, through, nutrition, stages	show stages (expository)	http://bcove.me/02dndkew
RA 3	Ten Little Fish	Audrey Wood	Concept Book	Picture Book	counting backward; subtracting one from a number	use of rhymes to teach counting backward from 10; use of patterned text; challenging word choice for rhymes	crate, shore, survive, adding, school, subtracting	practice counting (expository)	http://pbskids.org/curiousgeorge/games
RA 4	Alphabet Adventure	Audrey Wood	Concept Book	Picture Book	the letters of the alphabet; the importance of lowercase letters and capitals; teamwork	use of a fantasy adventure to teach the letters of the alphabet; asking a question to involve readers; use of problem and solution	canals, proper, rescued, searching, mystery, teamwork	alphabet cards (expository)	http://pbskids.org/video/
RA 5	Freight Train	Donald Crews	Concept Book	Picture Book	colors; parts of a train; places where trains travel	simple, descriptive words that teach about train cars and colors; large simple illustrations that connect to the book's concepts; font colors that support text	engine, freight, steam, track, trestles, goods, transportation	extend the book (narrative)	www.thomasandfriends.com
BC 1	Today Is Monday	Eric Carle	Concept Book	Picture Book	learning the days of the week; sharing food; community	cumulative story structure that teaches the days of the week; colorful illustrations that connect to the text	fresh, roast, string beans, feast, pattern, repetition	readers' notebooks	www.learninggamesforkids.com/educational_videos/
BC 2	The Deep Blue Sea	Audrey Wood	Concept Book	Picture Book	colors; nature; weather	cumulative story structure; rhythm and rhyme; text features that connect to the story's concepts and ideas	middle, parrot, shines, nature, rainbow, weather	readers' notebooks	http://pbskids.org/video/
BC 3	K Is for Kissing a Cool Kangaroo	Giles Andreae	Concept Book	Picture Book	learning the alphabet; letter sounds; rhyming words	alphabet and letter sounds taught in an imaginative way; text features used to clarify concepts	mighty, mischievous, naughty, shudder, creative, discover	readers' notebooks	www.britishcouncil.org/kids-songs-alphabet-popup.htm
BC 4	Ten Black Dots	Donald Crews	Concept Book	Picture Book	counting; using your imagination; discovering shapes in everyday objects	illustrations used to teach about numbers and counting; rhymes used to engage readers	portholes, rank, stringing, counting, imagination	readers' notebooks	http://pbskids.org/curiousgeorge/busyday

	Title	Author	Genre	Text Type	Themes/Ideas	Author's Craft	Vocabulary	Writing Options	Technology
Grade 1		**Strand: Community & Relationships**			**Unit: My Family & Me**	**Unit Focus: How do people in a family help each other and have fun together?**			
RA 1	*You and Me Together*	Barbara Kerley	Informational Text	Photo Essay	family interactions; cultural diversity; parent-child bond	use of photographs to present information and cultural diversity; use of rhythm, rhyme, and repetition; incorporation of different lettering to emphasize important words	forever, together, world, affection, bond, customs	picture (expository)	www.poetryfoundation.org/features/video/191
RA 2	*Bunny Cakes*	Rosemary Wells	Fantasy	Picture Book	sibling dynamics; solving problems; doing things for others	characters are revealed by their words and actions; detailed illustrations enhance the text	grocer, iced, list, thrilled, bossy, clumsy, frustrated, persistent	descriptive chart (expository)	http://rosemarywells.com
RA 3	*Daddy Calls Me Man*	Angela Johnson	Poetry	Picture Book	family love; longing to be grown up; accepting a new sibling	book that is organized through a series of rhythmic, rhyming poems; theme and character revealed through first-person narration	glowing, share, swirl, twirl, twist, affection, artist, relationship	description (expository)	http://solarsystem.nasa.gov/planets
RA 4	*Let's Eat!*	Ana Zamorano	Realistic Fiction	Picture Book	portraying members of an extended family; showing the importance of the family circle; working together	use of actions and dialogue to reveal realistic characters; use of repetition and a pattern; Spanish words that make the story more authentic	pity, sighs, wriggling, excuse, feast, tradition	riddle (expository)	http://pbskids.org/buster/recipes/index.html
RA 5	*The Relatives Came*	Cynthia Rylant	Realistic Fiction	Picture Book	importance of family; family bonds; spending time together and helping each other	use of imagery to show details and the passage of time; use of sensory details to describe how things look, feel, and sound	particular, relatives, traveled, anticipate, memories, reunion	letter (expository)	http://statesymbolsusa.org/index.html
BC 1	*A Chair for My Mother*	Vera B. Williams	Realistic Fiction	Picture Book	saving money; working toward a goal; family love and support; community support	plot and character revealed through first-person narration and organization; watercolors that support the text	armchair, exchanged, spoiled, tips, goal, sacrifice, save	readers' notebooks	www.practicalmoneyskills.com/games
BC 2	*What Aunts/Uncles Do Best*	Laura Numeroff	Fantasy	Picture Book	spending time together; enjoying everyday moments; family love	two stories combined in one book; repetition and simple language used to tell each story; familiar activities used as narrative content in both versions	clubhouse, prize, silly, affection, enjoyment, nephew, niece	readers' notebooks	http://lauranumeroff.com/books/my_books.htm
BC 3	*Noisy Nora*	Rosemary Wells	Fantasy	Picture Book	being a middle child; feeling left out; sibling rivalry; family routines; solving family problem	using animal characters and rhyming verse to engage readers and develop story themes and ideas; illustrations add details and humor	banged, felled, filthy, slammed, routines, siblings	readers' notebooks	www.rosemarywells.com
BC 4	*Peter's Chair*	Ezra Jack Keats	Realistic Fiction	Picture Book	family displacement; sibling rivalry; accepting change	story events told in sequence; credible dialogue that moves the story along; vivid verbs that show how Peter is feeling; illustrations used to support character	cradle, fussing, muttered, attention, jealousy, sharing	readers' notebooks	www.ezra-jack-keats.org/fun-games
Grade 1		**Strand: Folklore & Literary Traditions**			**Unit: Stories With a Moral**	**Unit Focus: How can folktales teach people how to act in real life?**			
RA 1	*Caps for Sale*	Esphyr Slobodkina	Folktale	Picture Book	expressing frustration; actions have consequences	patterned plot; repetitive events and phrases; detailed illustrations that support text	peddler, refreshed, upset, wares, examine, imitate, temper	graphic sequence (expository)	http://pbskids.org/berenstainbears
RA 2	*The Little Boy Who Cried Wolf*	Darice Bailer	Folktale	Picture Book	value of honesty; treating others with respect	plot pattern using repetition; dialogue and narration to advance the story and ultimately teach a lesson	blame, lonely, longing, protect, threatening, consequences, responsibility, trustworthy	letter (persuasive)	www.pbskids.org/noah/videogames_tab.html
RA 3	*The Rabbit and the Turtle*	Eric Carle	Folktale	Picture Book	be true to who you are; respect; kindness; fairness	lively dialogue and vivid illustrations that capture important moments in the story; one-sentence morals at the end of each tale; book organized into several two-page tales	imitate, outwit, proud, steady, volunteer, moral, self-centered	illustration description (narrative)	www.eric-carle.com/q-makepic.html
RA 4	*The Hatseller and the Monkeys*	Baba Wagué Diakité	Folktale	Picture Book	helping yourself when you can; perseverance; learning from mistakes	detailed illustrations and a pattern of events and words; problem/solution story structure; lyrical language and West African words	curious, goodwill, imitated, satchel, success, concentrate, instructive	understanding allegory (expository)	www.africancrafts.com
RA 5	*Stone Soup*	Jon J Muth	Folktale	Picture Book	sharing with others brings happiness; kindness and generosity; learning from new experiences	use of soup as a metaphor for a communal effort; detailed illustrations	banquet, generous, suspicious, community, donate	recipe (expository)	www.starfall.com/h/level-c/folk-tales/
BC 1	*Anansi the Spider*	Gerald McDermott	Folktale	Picture Book	being fair; sharing and cooperation; family loyalty; helping others being more important than receiving a reward	art elements and language patterns inspired by Ashanti culture; repetitive text structure; pourquoi tale	argue, decide, deserve, globe, prize, cooperation, fair, oral storytelling	readers' notebooks	http://pbskids.org/africa/tale/index.html
BC 2	*City Mouse-Country Mouse*	John Wallner	Folktale	Picture Book	peace of mind is more important than fine things; appreciation for what others can do for you; ideas are useless without action	story events told with a problem/solution structure; animal characters who act like people; use of descriptive language; detailed illustrations that portray plot events and characters' emotions	fine, gnawed, grand, plain, discontented, impractical, underestimate	readers' notebooks	www.nationalzoo.si.edu/animals/ecard
BC 3	*Bat's Big Game*	Margaret Read MacDonald	Folktale	Picture Book	loyalty; being a good team player does not always mean winning the game	plot pattern of repeated events; lively dialogue	mistake, snatched, sticks with, switch, loyalty, scrawny, selfishness, team spirit	readers' notebooks	www.nationalgeographic.com/video/kids/animals-pets-kids/mammals-kids/bat-flying-fox-kids/
BC 4	*Red Riding Hood*	James Marshall	Folktale	Picture Book	better safe than sorry; listen to advice from those older and wiser than you; watch out for tricks	detailed and funny pictures; dialogue that establishes characters and gives plot information; retelling of classic tale in author's own visual and narrative style	charming, clever, considerate, escort, gobbled, advice, cautious, disguise, trusting	readers' notebooks	http://www.usm.edu/media/english/fairytales/lrrh/lrrhqi.htm
Grade 1		**Strand: Living Things**			**Unit: Strong & Healthy**	**Unit Focus: How do writers help you find out about healthy habits?**			
RA 1	*The Busy Body Book*	Lizzy Rockwell	Informational Text	Picture Book	staying fit and healthy; understanding how different body systems work	use of text and illustrations to present facts; information presented by body systems; conversational tone; second-person point of view	energy, healthy, oxygen, strong, active, exercise	exercise poster (expository)	http://teamnutrition.usda.gov/Resources/eatsmartactivitysheets.html

Code	Title	Author	Genre	Format	Unit / Theme	Description	Vocabulary	Writing	URL
RA 2	Animal Action ABC	Karen Pandell	Poetry	Picture Book	body movements; the world of animals in action; similarities between the way humans and animals move	use of alphabetical organization; use of poetry to relate information; comparison of animal and human movements	arch, balance, flex, stretch, muscle, imitate, movement	alphabetical illustration (expository)	www.scholastic.com/teachers
RA 3	Growing Vegetable Soup	Lois Ehlert	Informational Text	Picture Book	growing nutritious food; gardening; cooking	use of bright colors and shapes; a sequential order that tells about a process; first-person point of view; labeled illustrations	grow, soup, tools, vegetable, garden, harvest	garden diagram (expository)	http://urbanext.illinois.edu/firstgarden
RA 4	Gregory, the Terrible Eater	Mitchell Sharmat	Fantasy	Picture Book	making food choices; nutritious foods; trying new foods; eating enough to stay healthy	problem and solution story format; use of humor to create a lighthearted tone; character revealed through actions, thoughts, and dialogue	fussy, junk, meal, picky, choices, refuse, wise	illustrative excerpt (persuasive)	www.nourishinteractive.com/kids
RA 5	Eating the Alphabet	Lois Ehlert	Informational Text	Picture Book	learning about fruits and vegetables; eating foods that are good for you	use of rhyme to engage readers; alphabet format; interweaving of unfamiliar with familiar content; large, colorful illustrations; Glossary	alphabet, fruits, vegetables, familiar, food, unfamiliar	counting book (expository)	www.foodchamps.org
BC 1	Healthy Me	Melvin & Gilda Berger	Informational Text	Picture Book	following healthy habits; taking responsibility	opening question to motivate readers about topic; cause-and-effect organization of information; additional facts in inset boxes; glossary	body, helmet, safe, wash, clean, reason, sports	readers' notebooks	http://pbskids.org/video
BC 2	Hippo and Rabbit in Three Short Tales	Jeff Mack	Fantasy	Easy Chapter Book	eating healthy foods; getting exercise; the importance of rest; friendship	comic strip format; humor through words and images; contrasting characters that demonstrate theme or convey message	breakfast, salad, smart, differences, friendship, support	readers' notebooks	http://pbskids.org/zoom/activities/games
BC 3	Let's Talk Tae Kwon Do	Laine Falk	Informational Text	Easy Chapter Book	fitness; movement; physical skill	sequential presentation of events; first-person point of view; variety of text features that provide information and help readers keep track of information	practice, protect, stretch, benefit, skill	readers' notebooks	http://pbskids.org/hooper/coach-hooper
BC 4	How Do Dinosaurs Get Well Soon?	Jane Yolen	Fantasy	Picture Book	sickness; wellness; cooperation; acting responsibly	question-and-answer format; rhyme; contrast and humor used to communicate a message	doctor, medicine, rest, well, ill, recover	readers' notebooks	www.readingrockets.org/books/interviews
Grade 1		**Strand: A Sense of Self**			**Unit: What I Can Do**	**Unit Focus: How do you know what you can do—unless you try?**			
RA 1	How You Got So Smart	David Milgrim	Poetry	Picture Book	being persistent; using your imagination; creative problem solving	playful illustrations that support and enhance the text; humor; use of rhyme to create patterned text	challenged, courageous, wondered, accomplish, achieve, persist	story (narrative)	www.davidmilgrim.com
RA 2	A Birthday Basket for Tía	Pat Mora	Realistic Fiction	Picture Book	thoughtfulness toward someone special; creativity in solving a problem; pride in one's accomplishment	revealing Cecilia's character through the choices she makes; conveying the pride Cecilia feels in her accomplishment; using Spanish to relate to Cecilia's culture	collect, decorate, musicians, accomplishment, creative, generous, thoughtful	description (narrative)	www.patmora.com/childrens_books.htm
RA 3	A Color of His Own	Leo Lionni	Fantasy	Picture Book	looking at a problem in a new way; friendship	use of animal characters to relate a message; simple but effective dialogue; illustrations that emphasize the role of color in the story	cheerfully, except, remain, wiser, advice, encourage	description (narrative)	www.pbs.org/edens/madagascar/creature3.htm www.sandiegozoo.org/animalbytes/t-chameleon.html
RA 4	What Should I Make?	Nandini Nayar	Realistic Fiction	Picture Book	creativity; quick thinking; pride and satisfaction in one's work	demonstrating the power of imagination to answer a question; entertaining readers by sparking their imaginations; conveying the satisfaction Neeraj feels after making his own bread	dough, kneading, squeezed, imagination, satisfaction	recipe (expository)	www.scholastic.com/teachers/lesson-plan/homemade-play-dough
RA 5	Lilly's Purple Plastic Purse	Kevin Henkes	Fantasy	Picture Book	knowing appropriate behavior; the joys of a creative environment; expressing one's creativity	revealing Lilly's character by showing her reactions to situations; use of illustrations to portray the characters; pictures drawn by Lilly to convey her feelings	considerate, disturb, expressed, uncooperative, appropriate, control	description (narrative)	www.kevinhenkes.com
BC 1	Houndsley and Catina and the Quiet Time	James Howe	Fantasy	Chapter Book	making the most of a situation; encouraging a friend to see things differently; using your imagination	humorous dialogue used to reveal characters' personalities; descriptive language that appeals to the senses; using chapters to allow the story to build	audience, fret, island, lingered, appreciate, attitude, daydream	readers' notebooks	www.dsokids.com/listen/instrumentist.aspx
BC 2	I Can't Take a Bath!	Irene Smalls	Humorous Fiction	Picture Book	using imagination to solve a problem; avoiding something that has to be done; looking at a situation in a new way	use of rhyme to tell the story; humor; story character narrates from first-person point of view	crime, disease, doom, serpent, submarine, avoid, exaggerate, excuses	readers' notebooks	www.kidsonthenet.com/motel
BC 3	Inch by Inch	Leo Lionni	Fantasy	Picture Book	using imagination and skills to solve a problem; not giving up	dialogue that advances the plot; using fantasy to teach a lesson; colorful illustrations that emphasize size of the characters	emerald, gobble, measure, useful, fable, inventive, predator, prey	readers' notebooks	http://nationalzoo.si.edu/Animals/Birds/Facts/
BC 4	Hi! Fly Guy	Tedd Arnold	Fantasy	Picture Book	using quick, creative thinking to solve a problem; making the best of a situation; friendship	dialogue and simple, direct language used to tell the story; expressive illustrations; humor	amazed, award, dived, judges, pests, slimy, friendship, helpful	readers' notebooks	www.teddarnoldbooks.com/drawing.html
Grade 1		**Strand: Inspired by True Stories**			**Unit: It Happened to Me**	**Unit Focus: What do you learn from authors who write about their own lives?**			
RA 1	The Art Lesson	Tomie dePaola	Memoir	Picture Book	the importance of dedication and practice; pursuing dreams	use of third-person narration; illustrations that help tell a real-life story and convey setting	collected, smock, turquoise, unfinished, dedication, overcome, practice	letter (expository)	www.readingrockets.org/books/interviews
RA 2	David Gets in Trouble	David Shannon	Humorous Fiction	Series Picture Book	learning right from wrong; learning to apologize; loving your family	words and illustrations that create humor; use of first-person narration; childlike style of writing and illustration	accident, fault, slipped, consequence, excuse, mischief	describe favorite scene (expository)	http://bcove.me/i55cdpzn
RA 3	Freckleface Strawberry	Julianne Moore	Realistic Fiction	Series Picture Book	being teased; accepting who you are; the value of friendship	use of narration and dialogue to present events, develop characters, and reveal theme; use of humor to portray a character's problem	everybody, lonely, nobody, accept, alike, difference, unique	descriptive list (expository)	www.readingrockets.org/books/interviews
RA 4	The Ugly Vegetables	Grace Lin	Realistic Fiction	Picture Book	respecting different cultures; being part of a community; sharing	first-person point of view; language that appeals to the senses; time-order words and illustrations that move the plot	aroma, blooming, different, recipe, culture, tradition, unusual	procedural steps (expository)	www.readingrockets.org/books/interviews

	Title	Author	Genre	Text Type	Themes/Ideas	Author's Craft	Vocabulary	Writing Options	Technology
Grade 1									
					Strand: Inspired by True Stories				
RA 5	*Bigmama's*	Donald Crews	Memoir	Picture Book	**Unit: It Happened to Me (cont'd)**	**Unit Focus: What do you learn from authors who write about their own lives?**			
					the importance of family; looking back on childhood	descriptions and illustrations that reveal setting; use of specific details; strong mood	friendly, plenty, summer, carefree, memories, vacation	describe favorite place (expository)	www.scholastic.com/play/prestates.htm
BC 1	*Freckleface Strawberry and the Dodgeball Bully*	Julianne Moore	Realistic Fiction	Series Picture Book	overcoming fears; understanding bullies; building friendships	sound words and language patterns used to establish conflict and build suspense; childhood experiences used to teach a lesson	bully, imaginary, monster, notice, pretending, face, suspense	readers' notebooks	http://pbskids.org/arthur/games/aboutface
BC 2	*David Goes to School*	David Shannon	Humorous Fiction	Series Picture Book	appropriate school behavior; purpose of rules; being considerate; facing consequences; praise is more rewarding than punishment	use of direct address and illustrations to create a humorous story with a message	pay attention, tardy, yelling, misbehave, punish	readers' notebooks	www.readingrockets.org/books/interviews
BC 3	*Knuffle Bunny: A Cautionary Tale*	Mo Willems	Realistic Fiction	Series Picture Book	a favorite toy; places in the city; communicating	words and artwork used to create humor and convey story details; conflict used to create story tension	bawled, fussy, Laundromat, machine, communicate, frustration, tantrum	readers' notebooks	www.pigeonpresents.com/video-mohistory.aspx
BC 4	*I Lost My Tooth in Africa*	Penda Diakité	Memoir	Picture Book	cultural traditions; caring for animals; visiting family in another country	first-person point of view used to tell a story in the present tense; temporal words used to signal order of events; Malian cultural details	cluster, compound, gourd, responsible, traditions	readers' notebooks	http://ada.org/3230.aspx
Grade 1									
					Strand: Genre Study				
RA 1	*Bear Snores On*	Karma Wilson	Fantasy	Rhyming Picture Book	**Unit: Animal Stories**	**Unit Focus: How—and why—do writers create animal characters that act like people?**			
					cooperation and teamwork; friendship; sharing; looks can be deceiving; hibernation	repetitive story pattern; repetitive refrain; rhyme; onomatopoeia; creation of animal characters with both animal and human characteristics	blubbers, dank, lair, slumbering, snores, whimpers, cooperate, hibernate	invitation (expository)	www.nwf.org/Kids/Ranger-Rick/Animals.aspx
RA 2	*Bear's New Friend*	Karma Wilson	Fantasy	Rhyming Picture Book	friendship; persistence; encouragement	use of rhyme; use of a repetitive story pattern; animal characters with both animal and human characteristics	bashful, clatter, dare, trembling, encourage, season	describe summer activities (expository)	www.desertmuseum.org/center/edu
RA 3	*Julius, the Baby of the World*	Kevin Henkes	Fantasy	Picture Book	dealing with change; sibling relationships; jealousy	dialogue; repetition of text; use of fantasy characters to reflect everyday human situations; illustrations that give more information about the characters	admired, disgusting, germ, insulting, uncooperative, adapt, expectation, jealous	extend the story (narrative)	www.kevinhenkes.com/?page_id=161
RA 4	*Always In Trouble*	Corinne Demas	Fantasy	Picture Book	learning to change; understanding that some things do not change	humor; time-order organization; dog with both animal and human characteristics	attention, behaved, diploma, training, command, obedient	flyer (persuasive)	www.corinnedemas.com/books/trouble.html
RA 5	*Frog and Toad Are Friends*	Arnold Lobel	Fantasy	Illustrated Short Stories	friendship and companionship; encouragement; kindness; patience	dialogue; illustrations that support the text; creation of a fantasy world with animal characters that have human characteristics	lonely, meadows, perhaps, porch, shiver, companion, optimistic	letter (persuasive/expository)	www.kidzone.ws/lw/frogs/facts8.htm
BC 1	*Bear Wants More*	Karma Wilson	Fantasy	Rhyming Picture Book	helping friends; solving problems; bear behavior	use of rhyming and rhythmic text; repeating plot pattern; animal characters with human characteristics	feast, pries, roots, shoots, wedged, forage, satisfied	readers' notebooks	http://pbskids.org/lunchlab/#games
BC 2	*Days With Frog and Toad*	Arnold Lobel	Fantasy	Picture Book	friendship; cooperation and teamwork; encouragement	dialogue and illustration as narrative tools; animal characters with human characteristics	climbed, junk, thud, pessimistic, wise	readers' notebooks	www.youtube.com/user/OurCoastVideo
BC 3	*The Great Gracie Chase: Stop That Dog!*	Cynthia Rylant	Fantasy	Picture Book	wanting things to remain the same; dealing with change; laughing at things animals, and people, do	patterned sequence of plot events; humor in dog's viewpoint	arrived, clangy, except, realized, suddenly, neighborhood, routine	readers' notebooks	www.bowwow.com.au
BC 4	*Sheila Ray, the Brave*	Kevin Henkes	Fantasy	Picture Book	bravery; encouragement; imagination	repetition; dialogue; animal characters with human characteristics	brave, convince, familiar, fearless, boast, support	readers' notebooks	www.kevinhenkes.com/?page_id=161
Grade 2									
					Strand: Community & Relationships				
RA 1	*Louder, Lili*	Gennifer Choldenko	Realistic Fiction	Picture Book	**Unit: It Happened in School**	**Unit Focus: How do people in school learn from each new experience—and from each other?**			
					overcoming fear; taking responsibility for others; finding one's own voice; making friends	elements of fantasy and descriptive details that set a humorous tone; use of dialogue to reveal characters' traits	bossy, laryngitis, speak up, voice, assertive, defend, shy	compare (expository)	www.humanesociety.org/animals/guinea_pigs
RA 2	*The Secret Shortcut*	Mark Teague	Humorous Fiction	Picture Book	solving problems at school; using your imagination to create excitement; balancing fantasy and reality	illustrations that depict what characters imagine and their point of view; use of fantasy to create humor and develop characters	excuses, secret, shortcut, warned, adventure, imagination, pretend	adventure story (narrative)	www.poetry4kids.com/poem-349.html
RA 3	*Those Shoes*	Maribeth Boelts	Realistic Fiction	Picture Book	not always getting what we want; fitting in at school; the power of fads and advertising; concern for others	use of first-person narration to show the inner struggles of a character; story events that develop character and themes	dreams, need, price, thrift shop, advertisement, envy, fad	list (expository)	http://pbskids.org/mayaandmiguel
RA 4	*Crazy Hair Day*	Barney Saltzberg	Humorous Fiction	Picture Book	building a community by valuing all of its members; providing support when others need it; dealing with embarrassment	humorous characters and situations that deliver a message; use of dialogue and illustration to develop character and themes; repetition that adds structure to the story	celebrating, nervous, teasing, weirdo, belonging, embarrassment	dialogue (narrative)	www.barneysaltzberg.com/crazyhair/
RA 5	*The Class From the Black Lagoon*	Mike Thaler	Humorous Fiction	Series Picture Book	the power of anxiety; the effect of rumors; finding that things are not as bad as they seemed	use of exaggeration and wordplay to create humor; character and themes that are revealed through first-person point of view	contagious, expertise, ghouls, virtuosos, anxiety, exaggeration, rumor	letter (narrative/persuasive)	http://bcove.me/znaepqb3
BC 1	*Ruby the Copycat*	Peggy Rathmann	Realistic Fiction	Picture Book	dealing with insecurity; fitting in at a new school; individuality	character whose actions reflect story themes; dialogue and events used to further develop those themes; illustrations that give details about characters' responses to story events	coincidence, copycat, loyal, modeled, whispered, individuality, insecure, resent	readers' notebooks	http://bblocks.samhsa.gov

Code	Title	Author	Genre	Format	Theme	Unit Focus / Skills	Vocabulary	Writing	Website
BC 2	The Best Seat in Second Grade	Katherine Kenah	Realistic Fiction	Chapter Book	care and concern for pets; following rules; solving problems; showing support	chapter organization used to build suspense; setting used to build character and plot	dashed, hamster, sneezed, subject, trembled, concern, suspense	readers' notebooks	www.buzzle.com/articles/hamster-facts.html
BC 3	Make Way for Dyamonde Daniel	Nikki Grimes	Realistic Fiction	Chapter Book	coping with change; making new friends; speaking out and defending others	humor, insight, and believable dialogue used to develop characters and themes; chapters and settings used to develop characters and their relationship with each other	figured, odd, rude, solid, acceptance, attitude, communication	readers' notebooks	http://kidshealth.org/kid
BC 4	The Gym Teacher From the Black Lagoon	Mike Thaler	Humorous Fiction	Series Picture Book	the power of imagination; the effect of rumors	a boy's fantastic imagination and first-person narration used to tell a story; exaggeration and wordplay used to create humor	donated, gymnastics, posture, semester, misunderstand, relief	readers' notebooks	www.jaredlee.com
Grade 2	**Strand: Folklore & Literary Traditions**				**Unit: Wishes & Promises**	**Unit Focus: How can a wish or a promise change someone's life?**			
RA 1	Mouse & Lion	Rand Burkert	Fable	Picture Book	being brave and loyal; appreciating small things as well as big things; understanding that help can come from many sources	use of narration and dialogue to depict characters' motives and thoughts; depiction of a strong relationship between characters	brave, humor, liberty, loyal, appreciate, depend	summary (expository)	www.biodiversityexplorer.org
RA 2	The Talking Eggs	Robert D. San Souci	Folktale	Picture Book	keeping a promise; the importance of kindness toward others; good vs. evil	idioms and figurative language that describe characters; use of repeated plot events to contrast how characters react in similar situations; lesson that is typical of folktales	contrary, cross, kind, deserve, trustworthy	bumper sticker (persuasive)	www.jerrypinkneystudio.com
RA 3	Two of Everything	Lily Toy Hong	Folktale	Picture Book	solving a problem; learning to make the best of a bad situation	plot structure and lesson common to many folktales; illustrations that enhance readers' involvement and establish setting	clever, double, identical, plentiful, positive, solution	math word problems (expository)	http://kakooma.com
RA 4	The Twelve Dancing Princesses	Rachel Isadora	Fairy Tale	Picture Book	following useful advice; staying focused on a goal	use of story elements common to many folktales; colorful illustrations that bring the setting and characters to life	confessed, discovered, grove, worn through, advice, concealed	extend the story (narrative)	http://www.pbs.org/wonders/Kids/kids.htm
RA 5	The Mud Pony	Caron Lee Cohen	Folktale	Picture Book	listening to others; facing fears; persistence; relationship between humans and nature	plot with a strong narrative voice that is commonly used in folktales; use of characters' words and actions to develop theme	guide, victory, weary, worn, bravery, persistent	character description (expository)	http://shontogallery.com/wp/
BC 1	The Magic Fish	Freya Littledale	Fairy Tale	Picture Book	gratitude; being greedy can have bad effects; appreciating what you have	repetition used to build the plot structure; character traits revealed through dialogue and narration	begs, hut, throne, demand, greedy	readers' notebooks	http://ohia.org/ohia/roadshows/ocean/fishermen/fisherhome.htm
BC 2	Strega Nona	Tomie dePaola	Folktale	Picture Book	keeping a promise; learning not to show off	adaptation of existing story; story elements common to many folktales; detailed illustrations that bring characters and setting to life	barricade, overflow, simmer down, boast, irresponsible	readers' notebooks	www.tomie.com
BC 3	The Runaway Wok	Ying Chang Compestine	Folktale	Picture Book	sharing; selfishness; Chinese New Year; receiving rewards	repeated pattern of events used to build plot structure; trickster character common to many folktales; simple rhyming verse that highlights important actions in the story	celebration, cheated, feast, misfortune, distribute, fair	readers' notebooks	http://pbskids.org/sagwa
BC 4	The Frog Prince	Edith H. Tarcov	Fairy Tale	Picture Book	keeping a promise; helping others	adaptation of an existing story; character traits revealed through dialogue and narration; humor used to engage readers; theme explicitly stated	court, nasty, promise, reluctant, truthful	readers' notebooks	www.exploratorium.edu/frogs
Grade 2	**Strand: Living Things**				**Unit: Search & Survive**	**Unit Focus: How do animals find food—and avoid becoming another creature's dinner?**			
RA 1	Chameleon!	Joy Cowley	Informational Fiction	Photo Essay	survival; interdependence of living things; communication; animal relationships	use of storytelling techniques to provide information about animal behavior and the natural world; factual end note	creeps, dangerous, insect, peaceful, poisonous, behavior, communicate, instinct	description (expository)	www.nationalgeographic.com
RA 2	Animal Snackers	Betsy Lewin	Informational Poetry	Picture Book	diversity of animal life and diet	use of rhyming verse, figurative language, and illustrations to describe the dietary habits of animals; a humorous tone that appeals to a child	carnivorous, indigestion, odd, snack on, comparison, diet, habit, tone	description (expository)	http://pbskids.org/video
RA 3	A House Spider's Life	John Himmelman	Informational Fiction	Picture Book	stages of development; life cycle; survival; struggles in nature; interrelationship of humans and animals	use of a story to provide information about the natural world; realistic illustrations and descriptions of a spider and its activities; glossary	battle, escapes, weaves, capture, develop, survive	outline (expository)	www.howstuffworks.com
RA 4	Bugs for Lunch	Margery Facklam	Informational Poetry	Picture Book	insects as a food source; diversity in eating habits of living things	use of rhyming verse to present factually accurate information about the natural world; organizational structure that supports the author's message and engages readers	cruises, prey on, searching, trapping, depend, riddle	riddle (expository)	http://video.pbs.org
RA 5	Who Eats What?	Patricia Lauber	Informational Text	Science Picture Book	interdependence of living things; interconnectedness of food chains; effects of humans on nature; caring for Earth's environments	specific examples that explain scientific concepts and incorporate children's experiences; text is organized to support graphics	energy, food chain, food web, linked, diagram, nourishment	food chain (expository)	www.sheppardsoftware.com
BC 1	Plants That Eat Animals	Allan Fowler	Informational Text	Science Picture Book	basic needs; adaptability; natural processes; interdependence in nature	key ideas and supporting details that tell what, when, how, why, and where; descriptive text that expands on and clarifies information contained in photographs	attracts, breaks down, liquid, consume, process	readers' notebooks	www.nationalgeographic.com
BC 2	A Salamander's Life	John Himmelman	Informational Fiction	Picture Book	cycles and seasons of life; threats to survival; adaptations	storytelling used to give information about the natural world; detailed, engaging illustrations that are scientifically accurate	hunts, journey, return, environment, season	readers' notebooks	http://animaldiversity.ummz.umich.edu

	Title	Author	Genre	Text Type	Themes/Ideas	Author's Craft	Vocabulary	Writing Options	Technology
Grade 2									
	Strand: Living Things								
	Unit: Search & Survive (cont'd.) — Unit Focus: How do animals find food—and avoid becoming another creature's dinner?								
BC 3	The Emperor's Egg	Martin Jenkins	Informational Fiction	Picture Book	animal behavior and survival; life cycles; habitat and adaptations; cooperation; dependence of young on parents	humor and storytelling used to inform about the natural world; problem and solution; additional facts; talking to the reader (direct address)	gobbles, hatch, huddle, meal, adaptation, protect, provide	readers' notebooks	http://kids.nationalgeographic.com/kids
BC 4	Dangerous Animals	Melvin & Gilda Berger	Informational Text	Picture Book of Facts	predators and prey; finding food; adaptations for survival; interactions between humans and animals	true-or-false, question-and-answer format that presents facts about the natural world; graphic features and figurative language	avoid, charge, poison, scavengers, amazing, predator	readers' notebooks	http://animal.discovery.com
Grade 2									
	Strand: A Sense of Self								
	Unit: Like No One Else — Unit Focus: What makes you—and others—unique?								
RA 1	Two Eyes, a Nose, and a Mouth	Roberta Grobel Intrater	Informational Text	Photo Essay	differences among people; what makes people interesting or special	use of photographs and simple rhyme to convey a message; inviting reader participation	amazing, feature, variety, facial, unique	description (expository)	www.kidshealth.org/kid/htbw/eyes.html
RA 2	Alexander and the Wind-Up Mouse	Leo Lionni	Fantasy	Picture Book	appreciating who you are; being happy with what you have; be careful what you wish for; friendship	use of genre characteristics to convey a message; dialogue and events that develop characters and advance the plot	envy, favorite, ordinary, fantasy, transform	letter (expository)	www.asimo.honda.com/asimotv
RA 3	Stand Tall, Molly Lou Melon	Patty Lovell	Humorous Fiction	Picture Book	self-esteem; being unique; respect; the importance of having a mentor	use of exaggeration and humor to entertain readers and convey theme; portrayal of a mentor who guides the main character; portrayal of a bully's character development	glee, somersault, stack, advice, characteristic, exaggerate	extend a letter (narrative)	www.catrow.com/videos
RA 4	Diego	Jeanette and Jonah Winter	Biography	Picture Book	individuality; artistic expression; being proud of one's culture	text and illustrations that work together to tell the facts of an artist's life; portrayal of details from an artist's life that inspired his work	colorful, daydreamed, equality, famous, murals, contribution, inspiration	description (expository)	www.mexicoart.org
RA 5	Looking Like Me	Walter Dean Myers	Poetry	Picture Book	life's many roles; individual talents; celebrating who you are; how others perceive you	rhythm and rhyme of poetry and the actions of characters establish mood; theme and character revealed through first-person point of view and dialogue	bam, celebrating, fist, portraits, proud, role, self-esteem	poetic list (expository)	www.readingrockets.org/books/interviews/
BC 1	Stink: The Incredible Shrinking Kid	Megan McDonald	Humorous Fiction	Chapter Book	self-image; finding strength in differences; friendship	revelation of changes in characters' feelings as the plot unfolds; playful use of language to add humor; story organized into chapters	incredible, measure, shrimp, shrinking, admire, humorous	readers' notebooks	www.stinkmoody.com/images/downloads/stink_create_comic.pdf
BC 2	Marty McGuire	Kate Messner	Humorous Fiction	Chapter Book	being true to yourself; friendship; improvising; making the best of things	use of phrases and thoughts to reveal character; funny scenes that advance the plot; interesting minor characters	disgusted, eardrum, memorize, confidence, improvise, rehearsal, self-esteem	readers' notebooks	http://pbskids.org/arthur/print/playmaker/index.html
BC 3	Giraffes Can't Dance	Giles Andreae	Fantasy	Rhyming Picture Book	doing things your own way; following your own heart; individuality; being different	rhyme and humor are used to show how to face a problem and solve it; problem/solution structure and time-order sequence of plot events; author's message revealed through description, dialogue, and actions	clumsy, crooked, miracle, slim, self-doubt, traditional	readers' notebooks	www.sandiegozoo.org/animalbytes/
BC 4	Goldie	Ellen Miles	Realistic Fiction	Series Book	appreciating differences; respecting diverse viewpoints; taking responsibility	dialogue, humor, and interactions establish realistic characters; plot advanced in tandem with information about dog care; italicized passages that reveal dog's viewpoint	convince, foster, responsible for, socialization, behave, deserve, goal, train	readers' notebooks	http://ellenmiles.net/books.html
Grade 2									
	Strand: Inspired by True Stories								
	Unit: Animal Watch — Unit Focus: What have people discovered by watching and caring for animals?								
RA 1	My Baby Blue Jays	John Berendt	Informational Narrative	Photo Essay	observing nature; people learning from animals; how baby birds grow	use of photos to help tell a story; combination of information and fiction; personification; use of suspense	cautious, enchanted, frantically, inspected, strenuous, mature, newborn, protect	fact book (expository)	www.get-to-know.org/bioblitz
RA 2	Little Pink Pup	Johanna Kerby	Informational Text	Photo Essay	being accepted for who you are; compassion between animals; importance of caring for animals	use of photographs to portray animal bonds across species; repetition of key phrases and concepts	healthy, immediately, piglets, refused, welcomed, different, litter	show details (expository)	www.johannakerby.com
RA 3	The Buzz on Bees	Shelley Rotner & Anne Woodhull	Informational Text	Photo Essay	how animals help people; the importance of nature; conservation	informational text; photographs that explain ideas; anecdotes; questions and answers; suggestions for how to help	decline, mystery, pesticides, pollinate, provoked, transferred, depend, survive	letter (persuasive)	www.gpnc.org/honeybee.htm
RA 4	Two Bobbies	Kirby Larson & Mary Nethery	Informational Text	Picture Book	the will to survive; the bond between animals; the importance of animal shelters	facts woven together to tell a story; vivid sensory details; moments that reveal a friendship between two animals	bobbed, debris, determined, receded, temporary, devastated, mutual	letter (persuasive)	www.kirbylarson.com/books/two-bobbies
RA 5	Boy, Were We Wrong About Dinosaurs!	Kathleen V. Kudlinski	Informational Text	Picture Book	the importance of asking questions; the scientific process; things are not always as they seem; knowledge grows and changes	details and logic that support the main idea; direct and familiar voice; humor	asteroid, clumsily, enormous, fossil, graceful, extinct, theory	cartoon-like drawings (expository)	http://paleobiology.si.edu/dinosaurs
BC 1	Pierre the Penguin: A True Story	Jean Marzollo	Informational Text	Poem	solving problems; helping and caring for animals; the importance of hope and creativity	true story told through rhyme; problem-and-solution text structure; onomatopoeia, personification, and alliteration	aquarium, aquatic, biologist, examined, prescribed, observe, recover, solution	readers' notebooks	www.calacademy.org/webcams/penguins
BC 2	Buddy: The First Seeing Eye Dog	Eva Moore	Informational Text	Chapter Book	the importance of hard work; animals helping people; being independent despite a disability	information provided through specific real-life examples, summarizing, and anecdotes; character shown through actions and dialogue	commands, depended on, frisky, gripped, harness, companions, master	readers' notebooks	www.seeingeye.org/aboutUs/

Code	Title	Author	Genre	Format	Enduring Understandings	Focus	Vocabulary	Writing	Website
BC 3	Panda Kindergarten	Joanne Ryder	Informational Text	Photo Essay	caring for animals; exploring and learning about the world; the importance of protecting and helping wildlife	information about animals in specific, specialized setting; inviting tone that speaks to readers; pandas compared to children	constant, curious, imagine, protected, tenderly, endangered, preserve	readers' notebooks	www.globio.org/glossopedia
BC 4	Ibis: A True Whale Story	John Himmelman	Informational Text	Picture Book	friendship; positive and negative effects of human actions on animals; the value and dangers of curiosity; solving a problem	foreshadowing to signal events; parallel symbolism of starfish and hands; character's feelings revealed through narration	dazzling, drifting, familiar, frightened, struggled, capture, rescue	readers' notebooks	http://kids.nationalgeographic.com

Grade 2

Strand: Genre Study
Unit: Realistic Fiction
Unit Focus: How do authors make the characters and situations they create seem so true to life?

Code	Title	Author	Genre	Format	Enduring Understandings	Focus	Vocabulary	Writing	Website
RA 1	City Green	DyAnne DiSalvo-Ryan	Realistic Fiction	Picture Book	working as a team to effect change; patience and perseverance; every person can make contributions; value of green spaces	character development through description and dialogue; characters revealed through their interactions; illustrations that support details	lease, petition, property, delegate, participate, procedure	describe the garden (expository)	www.growinginthegarden.org/a-special-kind-of-garden.html
RA 2	If the Shoe Fits	Gary Soto	Realistic Fiction	Picture Book	challenging situations can provide learning opportunities; giving can be more satisfying than receiving; close friends and family members support us and help us define our values	challenging situations can provide learning opportunities; giving can be more satisfying than receiving; close friends and family members support us and help us define our values	flecks, glinted, protested, considerate, satisfying	extend the story (narrative)	www.garysoto.com/gallery.html
RA 3	Meet Danitra Brown	Nikki Grimes	Realistic Fiction	Poem	friendship is to be valued; positive thinking is beneficial; individuals have unique characteristics	use of poems to tell a story; first-person point of view that reveals character; colloquial language that reinforces a realistic story	bifocals, culture, hunched, swore, appreciate, characteristic	describe a good friend (expository)	www.readingrockets.org/books/interviews/grimes/
RA 4	Runaway Mittens	Jean Rogers	Realistic Fiction	Picture Book	family support; generosity	use of a pattern and dialogue to tell a story; realistic setting	crackles, radiator, wriggling, climate, culture, environment	letter (expository)	www.alaska.si.edu/browse.asp
RA 5	When Gorilla Goes Walking	Nikki Grimes	Realistic Fiction	Poem	pets can provide comfort; overcoming loneliness	use of a series of poems to tell a story; sensory language; use of rhythm and rhyme in poetry	feline, fierce, flexed, gazes, swipes, companion, relationships	poem (expository)	www.nikkigrimes.com/readings/readings.html
BC 1	Stink and the Great Guinea Pig Express	Megan McDonald	Realistic Fiction	Chapter Book	creativity; commitment and responsibility in pet ownership; resilience; teamwork	humor; factual information woven through a fictional story; characters revealed through dialogue and actions; story organized by chapters	coaxing, peered, toppled, diligent, strategy, volunteer	readers' notebooks	www.aspca.org/pet-care
BC 2	Rich	Nikki Grimes	Realistic Fiction	Chapter Book	friendship; being rich isn't measured in money; people are defined by talent and character rather than life circumstances	storytelling with strong character development, dialogue, poetic descriptions, real-world problem and solution; story organized by chapters	ancient, distracted, grumbled, sponsoring, compassion, encourage	readers' notebooks	www.pbskids.org/arthur/games/poetry/index.html
BC 3	Homework Hassles	Abby Klein	Realistic Fiction	Chapter Book	perseverance; don't try to be the best, just do your best; our friends and family are people we can count on	use of humor, believable dialogue, and first-person narration to develop a story, inform, and entertain; use of chapter headings and endings to create anticipation	hilarious, hysterically, mission, snickered, wincing, consequences, inspiration, optimistic	readers' notebooks	www.batcon.org/index.php/all-about-bats
BC 4	Too Many Tamales	Gary Soto	Realistic Fiction	Picture Book	families and traditions; admitting to mistakes and telling the truth; family members working together to solve problems	use of word choice to reveal character and setting; figurative language, dialogue, and problem/solution structure in narrative text	dusk, husks, interrupt, kneading, participate, sentimental, tradition	readers' notebooks	www.foodnetwork.com/videos/authentic-christmas-tamales

Grade 3

Strand: Community & Relationships
Unit: Brothers & Sisters
Unit Focus: Why do brothers and sisters often clash? How can they get along?

Code	Title	Author	Genre	Format	Enduring Understandings	Focus	Vocabulary	Writing	Website
RA 1	I Will Never NOT EVER Eat a Tomato	Lauren Child	Humorous Fiction	Picture Book	importance of patience and flexibility; value of creativity; cooperation	use of humor and problem/solution; different text styles for food names and paragraphs that represent the characters' imaginary world	fussy, incredibly, rare, tasty, clash, conflict, cooperate, sibling	descriptive narrative (narrative)	www.milkmonitor.com/the_characters/charlie_and_lola/
RA 2	My Rotten Redheaded Older Brother	Patricia Polacco	Memoir	Picture Book	sibling rivalry; sibling loyalty; teasing	description of events from the author's point of view; use of descriptive dialogue; vivid illustrations that support the text	equal, relationship, sneered, brag, competitive, consoled, secure	skit (narrative)	www.readingrockets.org/books/interviews/polacco/
RA 3	Oh, Brother!	Nikki Grimes	Realistic Fiction	Poem	dealing with change; acceptance; considering another's point of view	use of first-person narration in the form of poetry to reveal theme, plot, character, and tone; use of figurative language to reveal emotions	beware, imitation, pact, pondering, confront, resentment, viewpoint	figurative poetry (narrative)	www.nikkigrimes.com/readings/readings.html
RA 4	My Brother Charlie	Holly Robinson Peete & Ryan Elizabeth Peete	Realistic Fiction	Picture Book	love, loyalty, and respect; meeting challenges; value of patience and perseverance	story told from sister's point of view to reveal Charlie's character and the implications of autism for him; afterword that shares facts about autism	collection, snuggled, struggling, autism, disability, loyalty, protective	mini lesson (narrative)	www.child-autism-parent-cafe.com/my-little-brother-emlyn.html
RA 5	Big Red Lollipop	Rukhsana Khan	Realistic Fiction	Picture Book	wishing to fit in with peers; older siblings often look out for younger ones; fairness; adjusting to a new culture isn't easy	first-person narration that reveals theme, character, and realistic plot; transitional sentence that shows passing of time	plead, scurries, skitters, compassion, embarrassment, pity, squabble	character dialogue (persuasive)	www.kidshealth.org/kid/feeling/
BC 1	Rotten Richie and the Ultimate Dare	Patricia Polacco	Memoir	Picture Book	negotiating plays a part in sibling conflicts; value of being open to others' points of view	story told from one character's point of view; first-person narration; vivid illustrations; descriptive dialogue	embarrassment, endure, etiquette, recital, stamina, ultimate, narration, negotiate, triumph, truce	readers' notebooks	www.nhl.com/kids/subpage/learn.html www.abt.org/education/dictionary/index.html
BC 2	Cockroach Cooties	Laurence Yep	Humorous Fiction	Chapter Book	cooperation; justice; empathy; creative problem solving	story events told in sequence from one character's point of view; intertwining subplots; setting used to further the story	notation, obvious, pivoted, slumped, bully, compassion, treaty	readers' notebooks	www.cyh.com

	Title	Author	Genre	Text Type	Themes/Ideas	Author's Craft	Vocabulary	Writing Options	Technology
Grade 3					**Strand: Community & Relationships**				
					Unit: Brothers & Sisters (cont'd.)	**Unit Focus: Why do brothers and sisters often clash? How can they get along?**			
BC 3	*Tales of a Fourth Grade Nothing*	Judy Blume	Humorous Fiction	Chapter Book	jealousy, tolerance, empathy, growth, and change	humor, insight, believable dialogue, and first-person narration used to entertain reader; book organized in chapters	committee, concoction, considered, insult, disgusted, frustrated, mischievous	readers' notebooks	www.pbskids.org/itsmylife/family/sibrivalry/
BC 4	*Trivia Queen, 3rd Grade Supreme*	Derrick Barnes	Realistic Fiction	Chapter Book	the desire to succeed; competition; finding your place in a family; family love and support	first-person narration; realistic dialogue; chapters	positive, pressure, represent, supreme, trivia, determined, encourage, self-confidence, success	readers' notebooks	www.pbskids.org/itsmylife/games/
Grade 3					**Strand: Folklore & Literary Traditions**				
					Unit: Trickster Tales	**Unit Focus: What lessons can you learn from trickster tales?**			
RA 1	*Pretty Salma*	Niki Daly	Folktale	Picture Book	the dangers of talking to strangers; villains and heroes as tricksters; good vs. bad; the wisdom of elders	theme, character, and plot revealed through repetition and humor; use of illustrations to show setting and plot details	appetite, dizzy, fierce, tucked, culture, moral, trickster	chart and book review (expository)	http://mysite.mweb.co.za/residents/njdaly/home.htm
RA 2	*The Hunterman and the Crocodile*	Retold by Baba Wagué Diakité	Folktale	Picture Book	living in harmony with nature; the value of all living things; honesty; trustworthiness	theme, character, and plot revealed through dialogue; illustrations show characters and plot details	barely, guilt, hoisted, wept, justice, oral tradition, trust	poster (expository/persuasive)	www.kids.nationalgeographic.com/kids/animals/creaturefeature
RA 3	*The Gingerbread Girl*	Lisa Campbell Ernst	Folktale	Picture Book	learning from others' mistakes; the value of wisdom; a trickster being tricked	extension of the original folktale to teach new lessons; summary of the original tale in the prologue; use of vivid language and clever dialogue; character and plot revealed through rhyming songs	aroma, dash, gingerly, implore, sly, outwit, revenge	opinion piece (persuasive)	www.kirkusreviews.com
RA 4	*The Tale of Tricky Fox*	Retold by Jim Aylesworth	Folktale	Picture Book	respect for other's property; good vs. bad; a trickster being tricked; the value of wisdom; respect for teachers	rhymes reveal characters, theme, and plot; repetition creates a memorable storyline; the "rule of three" commonly found in folktales develops the plot; use of predictable plot events typical of folktales	bragging, feeble, resist, sassy, suspicious, curiosity, repetition	story map (narrative)	http://ccb.lis.illinois.edu/Projects/storytelling/hempel_403b/index.html
RA 5	*Borreguita and the Coyote*	Retold by Verna Aardema	Folktale	Picture Book	brains vs. brawn; trickster as hero; appearance vs. reality	use of Spanish words to introduce the story's setting and culture to readers; use of onomatopoeia to add interest to the dialogue and narration	grazing, ledge, lush, shattered, predator, prey	summary (expository)	www.acceleratedu.org/assessments/1998EnglishSamplerTest/SenorCoyote.htm
BC 1	*The Seven Chinese Brothers*	Margaret Mahy	Folktale	Picture Book	love of family; compassion for others; good vs. evil; the problem of too much power; heroes as tricksters	theme, character, and plot revealed through foreshadowing; humor supplied in parenthetical descriptions; repetition	emperor, grateful, proclaimed, reunited, sympathy, compassion, justice	readers' notebooks	http://whc.unesco.org/en/list
BC 2	*The Gingerbread Cowboy*	Retold by Janet Squires	Folktale	Picture Book	the importance of caution; friend vs. foe; how a trickster gets tricked	character and plot revealed through rhyme and repetition; a classic tale retold in a new way and in a new setting; distinctive narrator's voice that uses similes to create vivid descriptions	flick, fringe, wriggled, arrogance, deceit	readers' notebooks	www.kidskonnect.com/subject-index/16-history/286-wild-wild-west.html
BC 3	*Zomo the Rabbit*	Retold by Gerald McDermott	Folktale	Picture Book	the importance of courage, good sense, and caution; cleverness vs. size or strength	colorful illustrations that support readers' understanding of the plot; using the "rule of three" commonly found in folktales to develop the plot; using humor to teach the theme, or lesson, of a tale	caution, cleverness, courage, wisdom, challenge, good sense	readers' notebooks	www.geraldmcdermott.com
BC 4	*The Adventures of Spider*	Retold by Joyce Cooper Arkhurst	Folktale	Chapter Book	brains vs. brawn; how a trickster gets tricked	character's traits used to show how things in the real world came to be; plot events and characters' actions reveal themes; storytelling narrator	determined, fare, handle, stalk, greed, traits	readers' notebooks	www.historyforkids.org/learn/africa/literature/anansi.htm
Grade 3					**Strand: Living Things**				
					Unit: Life Depends on Water	**Unit Focus: Why is water so important to all living things?**			
RA 1	*Common Ground*	Molly Bang	Informational Text	Picture Book	interdependence of life on Earth; responsibility; fairness and sharing; conservation	use of repetition and parable; selection and presentation of factual information	commons, fossil fuels, reserves, sustain, conservation, parable, responsibility	poster (persuasive)	www.kids.gov
RA 2	*Life in a Coral Reef*	Wendy Pfeffer	Informational Text	Picture Book	underwater life is dependent on other life for survival; coral reefs support an abundance of underwater life	text that is organized to cover a 24-hour period; presentation of factual information; use of contrast	colonies, habitat, immune, parasites, sturdy, extinct, interdependent, pollute, species	response (persuasive)	www.amnh.org/ology/marinebiology
RA 3	*Manfish: A Story of Jacques Cousteau*	Jennifer Berne	Biography	Picture Book	determination can lead to success; dreams can turn into reality; discoveries can benefit others and the Earth	book organized by revealing Cousteau's traits, talents, and goals; poetic language	expanses, fascinated, shimmering, vast, villain, determination, inspire, inventive, pursue	letter (persuasive)	wwwvideo.nytimes.com/
RA 4	*Dolphins on the Sand*	Jim Arnosky	Informational Fiction	Picture Book	human intervention can help animals in trouble; a respect for nature brings personal reward; one action affects another in a chain of events	use of a true event as the basis for a fictional story; use of problem/solution and fact/opinion; detailed illustrations	agile, ambush, horizon, idealized, pursued, stranded, environment, intervene, tide	journal entry (narrative)	www.dolphins.org/kids_area_funfacts_dolphins.php
RA 5	*Water Hole Waiting*	Jane Kurtz and Christopher Kurtz	Informational Fiction	Picture Book	all animals need water for survival; patience is sometimes needed to survive; water is worth waiting for	use of the rhythm of poetry; use of onomatopoeia; focus on one group of animals; use of a pattern in the text; story is organized from sunrise until sunset	crouches, foraging, reckless, savanna, slinks, ecosystem, natural resource, quench, survival	descriptive narrative (narrative)	www.environmentalgraffiti.com/
BC 1	*Into the A, B, Sea*	Deborah Lee Rose	Informational Text	Poem	sea life depends on clean water to live; all sea animals have a purpose	alphabet format; rhyme; text pattern; large, colorful illustrations	exhale, prey, slumber, soar, thrive, awareness, diversity, marine	readers' notebooks	www.montereybayaquarium.org

	Title	Author(s)	Type	Genre	Topics/Themes	Text Features / Focus	Vocabulary	Writing Genre	Website
BC 2	Winter's Tail	Juliana Hatkoff, Isabella Hatkoff, and Craig Hatkoff	Informational Text	Photo Essay	interdependence of life on Earth; responsibility; resilience; overcoming obstacles; helping others	reporting style; factual evidence and photographs that give the sense of an eyewitness account	blowhole, buoy, peduncle, prosthesis, adapt, challenge, inspiration, resilience	readers' notebooks	www.winterstail.com
BC 3	Ocean Sunlight	Molly Bang	Informational Text	Picture Book	the importance of our sun to underwater life; how underwater life is dependent on other life for survival	factual information presented in a student-friendly manner, the sun as narrator; illustrations reinforce factual information; poetic language	microscope, molecules, nutrients, photosynthesis, phytoplankton, zooplankton, carbon dioxide, food chain, oxygen	readers' notebooks	www.mollybang.com/Pages/osunlight.html
BC 4	The Magic School Bus® On the Ocean Floor	Joanna Cole	Informational Text	Series Book	oceans as habitats; parts of an ecosystem working together; preserving our natural resources; the adventure of learning	fiction/fantasy used to inform and entertain; text features used to inform and support text; wordplay and comments used for humor	appetite, microscopic, mysterious, teeming, observation, phenomenon	readers' notebooks	www.healthyoceans.org/index.html

Grade 3   **Strand: A Sense of Self**

Unit: Courage   **Unit Focus: What does it take to have courage?**

	Title	Author(s)	Type	Genre	Topics/Themes	Text Features / Focus	Vocabulary	Writing Genre	Website
RA 1	Owl Moon	Jane Yolen	Realistic Fiction	Picture Book	going on an adventure; being brave; parent/child relationship; having patience	vivid descriptions that feature sensory details; poetic language that creates strong mood; first-person narration	echo, hooted, pumped, threading, nocturnal, observe	description (persuasive)	www.nationalzoo.si.edu/scbi/migratorybirds/video/video.cfm?id=zplcbPrkmbl
RA 2	Thunder Cake	Patricia Polacco	Memoir	Picture Book	overcoming a common fear; a grandparent/child relationship	first-person narration and an introduction to the story; vivid descriptions that feature sensory details; realistic dialogue and onomatopoeia	ingredients, lightning, recipe, distract, overcome, thunderstorm	advice column (expository)	www.theweatherchannelkids.com/weatherED/
RA 3	The Princess Knight	Cornelia Funke	Humorous Fiction	Picture Book	being determined; overcoming obstacles; working toward a goal; doing things your own way; women's capabilities	traditional character portrayed in a nontraditional way; use of humor to entertain readers; realistic details that portray sibling relationships	determined, honor, knights, struggled, expectations, jousting, tournament	skit (narrative)	www.middle-ages.org.uk/jousting.htm
RA 4	Brave as a Mountain Lion	Ann Herbert Scott	Realistic Fiction	Picture Book	overcoming fears; connection to nature; family values	presentation of a character's conflict and its resolution; use of realistic dialogue; inclusion within the narrative of elements of Shoshone heritage	dreaded, qualified, reservation, anxiety, public speaking	simile (expository)	www.spellingbee.com/about-the-bee
RA 5	The Dot	Peter H. Reynolds	Realistic Fiction	Picture Book	having the courage to try something new; discovering a talent or skill; encouraging others	dialogue and plot that reveal character and theme; description of a process of discovery; story that begins and ends in a similar way; use of illustrations to convey meaning	artist, blank, discovered, experimenting, jab, creative, express, inspire	description (expository)	www.peterhreynolds.com/dot
BC 1	Keep the Lights Burning, Abbie	Peter & Connie Roop	Historical Fiction	Picture Book	showing courage and determination; the power of nature; taking care of your family	historical facts combined with fictional elements, such as dialogue; dialogue to reveal character and add interest; realistic family interactions; suspense	dangerous, lamps, medicine, steered, heroic, isolated	readers' notebooks	www.uscg.mil/History/people/Abbie_Burgess.asp
BC 2	Bobby the Brave (Sometimes)	Lisa Yee	Realistic Fiction	Series Book	facing your fears; parent-child relationships; sibling rivalry; feeling insecure	humor, insight, and believable dialogue that reveal character, entertain readers, and develop themes; story organized in chapters	athlete, confront, embarrass, stress, jealous, self-esteem	readers' notebooks	www.scholastic.com/browse/article.jsp?id=3753197
BC 3	Sophie the Hero	Lara Bergen	Realistic Fiction	Series Book	what it means to be a hero; wanting to feel special and unique; friendship; imagination and creativity	humor and realistic dialogue that reveal character, plot, and theme; story organized in chapters	hero, infraction, plan, prove, saved, backfire, misadventures, status	readers' notebooks	http://larabergen.com/?page_id=31
BC 4	Third Grade Angels	Jerry Spinelli	Realistic Fiction	Series Book	the value of doing good deeds; overcoming problems; getting along with others; showing courage	humor; believable dialogue to reveal character; first-person narration to reveal main character; figurative language	bribed, bunk, disgraceful, halo, predict, principle	readers' notebooks	www.randomactsofkindness.org

Grade 3   **Strand: Inspired by True Stories**

Unit: Sports Stars   **Unit Focus: What makes an athlete great, both on and off the playing field?**

	Title	Author(s)	Type	Genre	Topics/Themes	Text Features / Focus	Vocabulary	Writing Genre	Website
RA 1	Long Shot	Chris Paul	Memoir	Picture Book	determination; family support and encouragement; physical challenges	first-person narration from the author as a young boy; dialogue that reflects real life; emphasis on influential people in the author's youth	deflated, gifts, impressed, sprints, streaking, encouragement, support	scene (narrative)	wwwyoutube.com/user/hrlmglobetrotters
RA 2	Clemente!	Willie Perdomo	Realistic Fiction	Picture Book	persevering despite obstacles; helping those in need; being inspired by others' achievements	combination of fictional elements and facts about Roberto Clemente; Spanish words that reflect Clemente's culture; free-form writing style that features rhythm and rhyme	fans, retired, sacrifice fly, stats, admire, humanitarian, namesake	descriptive poem (expository)	www.robertoclemente.si.edu
RA 3	Girl Wonder	Deborah Hopkinson	Biographical Fiction	Picture Book	persevering despite obstacles; pursuing a dream; overcoming negative attitudes	first-person point of view; language that reflects the time period; division of story into nine innings	bitter, hiss, hurled, jeer, expectations, semipro	article (expository)	www.baseballhall.org/news/personality/game-all
RA 4	Pelé, King of Soccer	Monica Brown	Biography	Picture Book	pursuit of one's passion; making a dream come true; overcoming obstacles through determination	use of chronological order and a story arc that begins and ends with highlights from Pelé's career; bilingual text that appeals to various cultures	chants, national, opponent, shining, obstacle, poverty	opinion piece (persuasive)	www.myhero.com/go/hero.asp?hero=pele
RA 5	Playing to Win	Karen Deans	Biography	Picture Book	persevering despite obstacles; gaining strength from the support and encouragement of others	use of chronological order; transitional phrases that show the passage of time; key events cited; short conclusion provided	barriers, competing, discouraged, tournaments, discrimination, segregation	summary (expository)	www.americaslibrary.gov/jb/modern/jb_modern_gibson_1.html
BC 1	Wilma Unlimited	Kathleen Krull	Biography	Picture Book	a passion for sports; family members supporting each other; overcoming obstacles on the path to success	description of an individual's pain and frustration; suspense; personal traits revealed through actions; facts presented in a narrative context	crippled, fumble, polio, urged, obstacle, unlimited	readers' notebooks	www.olympic.org/wilma-rudolph
BC 2	Family Huddle	Peyton Manning, Eli Manning, and Archie Manning	Memoir	Picture Book	having a passion for sports; family support; doing things as a family	realistic and informal dialogue; football terminology; authentic details from their own lives	huddle, perfect, trivia, jersey, quarterback	readers' notebooks	www.npr.org

	Title	Author	Genre	Text Type	Themes/Ideas	Author's Craft	Vocabulary	Writing Options	Technology
Grade 3			**Strand: Inspired by True Stories**		**Unit: Sports Stars (cont'd.)**	**Unit Focus: What makes an athlete great, both on and off the playing field?**			
BC 3	Play Ball!	Jorge Posada with Robert Burleigh	Biographical Fiction	Picture Book	a passion for sports; importance of support and encouragement; showing perseverance; overcoming obstacles	informal dialogue; third-person voice to reveal character's thoughts and feelings as well as character traits; facts presented as fiction	advantage, awkwardly, lunged, slumped, archival, switch-hitter	readers' notebooks	http://web.clubmlb.com/index.html
BC 4	Mermaid Queen	Shana Corey	Biography	Picture Book	passion for sports; family support and encouragement; overcoming obstacles; changing preconceived ideas	plot presented as a series of problems and solutions; different typefaces used to highlight key words	banned, drastic, invention, scoffed, artistic, controversial	readers' notebooks	www.olympic.org/synchronized-swimming
Grade 3			**Strand: Genre Study**		**Unit: Mystery**	**Unit Focus: What are the elements that make a mystery story work?**			
RA 1	Detective LaRue	Mark Teague	Mystery	Picture Book	following clues; using imagination; interpreting events in different ways	information that is presented in the form of letters and newspaper articles; illustrations that tell more than the text reveals	abducted, apprehended, intrepid, loathsome, rife, speculated, deception, sleuth, theory	letter (persuasive)	www.readingrockets.org/books/interviews
RA 2	The Web Files	Margie Palatini	Mystery	Picture Book	following suspicions; finding evidence; seeking justice	setting that is conveyed with time/location stamps; use of familiar animal characters to add color to a traditional detective story; wordplay	headquarters, luscious, pilfered, quivered, squawking, evidence, wily	narrative (expository)	www.margiepalatini.com/inspiration-2
RA 3	What Really Happened to Humpty?	Jeanie Franz Ransom	Mystery	Picture Book	putting together clues; helping family	use of familiar nursery rhyme characters in a mystery; setting that furthers the plot; combination of traditional elements of nursery rhymes with modern items and technology	commotion, conspiracy, huff, techniques, nursery rhyme, reference	narrative (expository)	http://youtu.be/actpwahPtkk
RA 4	Miss Nelson Is Missing!	Harry Allard	Mystery	Picture Book	learning to appreciate others; taking things for granted; respecting authority figures	contrast of two characters; dialogue that moves the plot; twist ending	discouraged, misbehaving, swarm, wicked, disguise, hoax, scheme	poster (expository)	www.fbi.gov/fun-games/kids
RA 5	Ace Lacewing: Bug Detective	David Biedrzycki	Mystery	Picture Book	following a trail; gathering clues	first-person narration and dialogue that are modeled after classic detective stories; wordplay; humorous illustrations	alibi, larva, molted, pupae, trance, assassin, decoy, rival, suspicious	newspaper article (expository)	www.davidbiedrzycki.com/My_Books.html
BC 1	The Deadly Dungeon (A to Z Mysteries)	Ron Roy	Mystery	Series Book	investigating a mystery; doing the right thing; finding courage	suspense, foreshadowing, and setting that set the mood for a mystery story; details that serve as clues	dungeon, federal, horizon, oozed, buoy, ghoulish, tide	readers' notebooks	www.ronroy.com/atoz/books.php
BC 2	The Mona Mousa Code	Elisabetta Dami, writing as Geronimo Stilton	Mystery	Series Book	seeking adventure; cracking codes; hunting for clues	puns and wordplay used for humorous effect; creative typography used to further humor and to convey emotion and action; first-person narration that reveals character and plot	antique, corridors, disdainfully, manuscript, ancient, curator, esteemed	readers' notebooks	www.scholastic.com/titles/geronimostilton
BC 3	The Talking T. Rex	Ron Roy	Mystery	Series Book	assisting friends; making observations and looking for clues; using strategy	suspense and foreshadowing; details that reveal characters' thoughts, ideas, and strategies	barricade, compartment, donations, mechanical, burglary, tyrannosaurus rex	readers' notebooks	www.ronroy.com/faq/
BC 4	The Case of the Runaway Dog	James Preller	Mystery	Series Book	losing something important; forming strategies to solve problems; being kind to others	dialogue that keeps action moving and reveals character traits; first-person narration to reveal main character's thoughts and emotions; details that serve as clues to the mystery	bellowed, moping, skittish, twinge, jigsaw, journal, suspect	readers' notebooks	www.jamespreller.com/jigsaw
Grade 4			**Strand: Community & Relationships**		**Unit: Boys vs. Girls**	**Unit Focus: What can you learn from the way characters clash and resolve differences?**			
RA 1	Don't Call Me Pruneface!	Janet Reed Ahearn	Realistic Fiction	Picture Book	treating others well; feeling empathy; facing your fears	patterned text; contrast between similar story events and the climax; use of idioms to introduce humor and emphasize the theme	arrested, code, creep, lunatic, surgically, empathy, rude	alternate scene (narrative)	http://pbskids.org/itsmylife/friends/nicknames
RA 2	Angel Child, Dragon Child	Michele Maria Surat	Realistic Fiction	Picture Book	understanding other people; adjusting to a new culture; helping others	use of sensory details to describe how things look and sound; use of symbolism to convey a character's feelings	crinkled, glared, scrawled, trilled, twittered, adjust, prejudge	character letter (expository)	www.timeforkids.com/destination/vietnam
RA 3	Grace for President	Kelly DiPucchio	Realistic Fiction	Picture Book	judging people based on merit; working for change; being open-minded; setting and achieving goals	text structure that makes it easy to compare and contrast different characters; plot twist that highlights the theme	campaign, candidate, constituents, election, nominated, dedication, equality	response (persuasive)	http://kids.usa.gov/president
RA 4	Picnic at Mudsock Meadow	Patricia Polacco	Realistic Fiction	Picture Book	dealing with teasing and rejection; facing your fears; believing in yourself	use of detailed illustrations that support the text and provide information about characters; theme that is revealed through a series of similar events	authority, disqualified, glowered, mortified, swamp, impress, mock	newspaper article (expository)	www.scholastic.com/bookwizard
RA 5	Once Upon a Cool Motorcycle Dude	Kevin O'Malley	Humorous Fiction	Picture Book	working together; creativity; exploring points of view	story within a story; theme within a story; different points of view; different text types that help the reader follow the plot	battled, protect, tremendous, warrior, cooperate, narrate	alternate endings (narrative)	www.build-motorcycle.multitaskdesign.com
BC 1	Oggie Cooder	Sarah Weeks	Realistic Fiction	Chapter Book	staying true to yourself; helping others; appreciating unique talents	changing perspectives used to reveal character and move the plot along; suspense created through use of a third-person narrator	audition, champion, crocheted, fame, talents, self-confident, unconventional	readers' notebooks	www.sarahweeks.com/sweeks-cooder.htm
BC 2	The Broken Bike Boy and the Queen of 33rd Street	Sharon G. Flake	Realistic Fiction	Chapter Book	showing empathy; friendship; kindness; using imagination	character revealed through first-person narration; theme developed through dialogue; setting and character established through detailed descriptions	conduct, humble, insult, manners, punishment, conceited, self-esteem	readers' notebooks	www.our-africa.org
BC 3	Off and Running	Gary Soto	Realistic Fiction	Chapter Book	dedication; importance of hard work; believing in yourself	point of view used to establish and develop the main character; series of realistic events, humor, and a small mystery used to develop the plot and theme and create interest in the story	accomplish, endorse, improve, initiative, strategy, focused, responsible	readers' notebooks	http://teacher.scholastic.com/writewit/speech

Code	Title	Author	Genre	Format	Themes	Essential Elements / Unit Focus	Vocabulary	Writing Response	Website
BC 4	Fudge-a-Mania	Judy Blume	Humorous Fiction	Chapter Book	getting along with others; adapting to new situations; coping in positive ways when things do not go as expected	character established and developed through first-person narration; using humor and realistic dialogue to create interesting situations	century, disaster, disgusting, mania, potential, tolerate, value	readers' notebooks	www.judyblume.com/kids.php
Grade 4	**Strand: Folklore & Literary Traditions**				**Unit: Cinderella Tales**	**Unit Focus: What are the essential elements in a Cinderella tale?**			
RA 1	Cinderella	Barbara McClintock	Fairy Tale	Picture Book	being kind to others; family relationships; rewarding goodness; succeeding despite adversity	inclusion of characters, setting, and plot that reflect the traditional Cinderella story; use of dialogue and narration to reveal character; illustrations that reflect the story's French origins	jealous, luxuries, patient, scold, sneered, selfless, traditional	reader's response (expository)	www.learner.org/interactives/story
RA 2	The Rough-Face Girl	Rafe Martin	Fairy Tale	Picture Book	respect for the natural world; inner vs. outer beauty; rewarding goodness	retelling a Native American version of Cinderella; use of dialogue and plot to reveal character; incorporation of the mystery and beauty of nature into the plot	ashamed, haughtily, invisible, vanished, humble, symbol, transform	compare & contrast (expository)	www.bigorrin.org/algonquin_kids.htm
RA 3	The Irish Cinderlad	Shirley Climo	Fairy Tale	Picture Book	rewarding goodness; using magic; helping others; showing courage	use of dialogue to reveal character; vivid descriptions that feature sensory words; incorporation of elements that are not part of the traditional Cinderella story	coiled, fate, foretold, heaved, pounce, hero, legend	description (expository)	http://animal.discovery.com
RA 4	Mufaro's Beautiful Daughters	John Steptoe	Folktale	Picture Book	rewarding love and goodness while punishing selfishness; showing kindness and generosity to others; sibling relationships	use of dialogue and plot to reveal the character of the sisters; illustrations that reflect the story's African setting and heritage	acknowledges, considerate, destination, pride, servant, advise, folktale, worthiness	alternate endings (expository)	http://pbskids.org/africa/tale/index.html
RA 5	Bigfoot Cinderrrella	Tony Johnston	Fairy Tale	Picture Book	inner vs. outer beauty; rewarding goodness; respect for nature	forest setting; characters that are Bigfoot creatures; simple, humorous dialogue; figurative language	despised, putrid, reek, tantrums, environment, respect	story extension (narrative)	www.cnn.com/HEALTH
BC 1	James Marshall's Cinderella	Barbara Karlin	Fairy Tale	Picture Book	being kind to others; having a wish come true; rewarding goodness; success in the face of adversity; family relationships	characters, setting, and plot that reflect the traditional Cinderella story; dialogue and narrative details that reveal character	enchanting, generous, rejoiced, transformed, vain, familiar, theme	readers' notebooks	http://uconnnclc.wordpress.com
BC 2	Bubba the Cowboy Prince	Helen Ketteman	Fairy Tale	Picture Book	working hard; rewarding goodness; success in the face of adversity; family relationships; cowboy lifestyle	characters, actions, and language that reflect the story's western setting; figurative language that lends Western or cowboy flavor	companionship, disgraceful, exhausted, obliged, raggedy, colloquialism, exaggeration, fractured	readers' notebooks	http://plainshumanities.unl.edu/encyclopedia
BC 3	Cinderella Penguin	Janet Perlman	Fairy Tale	Picture Book	being kind to others; having a wish come true; goodness rewarded; success in the face of adversity; family relationships	characters, setting, and plot that tell the traditional Cinderella tale, with a penguin twist; dialogue and narrative details reveal good and wicked character traits	amazement, curtsies, delicate, shabby, spluttering, portrayal, nontraditional	readers' notebooks	http://www.nfb.ca
BC 4	Cinderellis and the Glass Hill	Gail Carson Levine	Fairy Tale	Series Book	being kind to others; showing determination; family relationships	male Cinderella character; elements of the traditional Cinderella tale presented in a new way; humor; story organized into chapters	bridle, extraordinary, quest, souvenir, weapon, invent, proclamation, rivalry	readers' notebooks	www.rif.org/kids/readingplanet/bookzone
Grade 4	**Strand: Living Things**				**Unit: Amazing Animals**	**Unit Focus: What do authors do to show that animals are amazing?**			
RA 1	The Journey: Stories of Migration	Cynthia Rylant	Informational Text	Chapter Book	animal survival; animal migration; animal instincts; the wonders of nature	short chapters that feature different animals; sequential narration of migration cycles; illustrations that complement the text; introduction and conclusion that connect the chapters	accomplishment, incredible, migrate, survive, instinct, navigate, vegetation	movie pitch (persuasive)	www.spaceplace.nasa.gov/migration
RA 2	Looking for Miza	Juliana Hatkoff, Isabella Hatkoff, Craig Hatkoff, and Dr. Paula Kahumbu	Informational Text	Picture Book	protection of wildlife; families	true story that persuades readers; background information that supports readers' understanding; text features that further explain a problem	diseases, endangered, observe, threat, habitat, illegally, survival	description (persuasive)	www.miza.com
RA 3	Face to Face With Sharks	David Doubilet and Jennifer Hayes	Informational Text	Photo Essay	the wonders of animal diversity; animal survival; wildlife protection	scientific facts combined with personal experience to create voice; photographs and captions that expand readers' understanding; text features that provide added information	extinction, marine, predators, prey, aggressive, diversity, tourism	list & response (persuasive)	www.humanesociety.org/animals/sharks/
RA 4	Almost Gone	Steve Jenkins	Informational Text	Picture Book	animal survival; protection of wildlife; connections between living things	introduction that gives context; headings, descriptions, and illustrations that present information; map included as an overview of content	declined, habitat, species, captivity, development	animal collage (expository)	www.worldwildlife.org/species
RA 5	The Eyes of Gray Wolf	Jonathan London	Realistic Fiction	Picture Book	animal survival; animal behavior; importance of habitat	poetic, figurative language that creates the setting and mood; story told in present tense; facts about wolves woven into a fictional story	inspect, territory, untamed, defend, emotion	alternate endings (expository)	www.wolf.org/wolves/learn/justkids/kids.asp
BC 1	Frogs	Nic Bishop	Informational Text	Photo Essay	wonders of the animal world; animal adaptation	beautifully crafted photographs that capture readers' interests; scientific facts presented in a lively writing style; text features such as captions and end sections support readers' understanding	alert, continent, surroundings, camouflaged, poisonous, rain forest, tadpole	readers' notebooks	www.nicbishop.com
BC 2	Koko's Kitten	Dr. Francine Patterson	Informational Text	Picture Book	human and animal interaction; animal intelligence; animal families	first-person narration reveals point of view; dialogue conveys an animal's thoughts and feelings; text features such as preface and epilogue	abandoned, capable, inspired, communicate, gesture, research	readers' notebooks	www.koko.org

	Title	Author	Genre	Text Type	Themes/Ideas	Author's Craft	Vocabulary	Writing Options	Technology
Grade 4		**Strand: Living Things**							
					Unit: Amazing Animals (cont'd.)	**Unit Focus: What do authors do to show that animals are amazing?**			
BC 3	*Crocodile Safari*	Jim Arnosky	Informational Text	Picture Book	animal survival; protection of wildlife and habitats	catchy headings that help organize text; illustrations and added text features support readers' understanding	ambushed, lunge, preserved, snout, elusive, mangrove, submerge, unpredictable	readers' notebooks	www.pbs.org/wgbh/nova/crocs
BC 4	*Owen and Mzee*	Isabella Hatkoff, Craig Hatkoff, and Dr. Paula Kahumbu	Informational Text	Picture Book	animal survival; animal relationships; friendship	organization that sets up sympathetic story by providing important background; text features that extend readers' understanding	companion, exhausted, grazing, protective, stranded, bond, inseparable, sanctuary	readers' notebooks	www.owenandmzeefoundation.org
Grade 4		**Strand: A Sense of Self**							
					Unit: Taking Responsibility	**Unit Focus: How can you take action to help yourself and others?**			
RA 1	*The Three Questions*	Jon J Muth	Fable	Picture Book	self-contemplation; importance of friendships; thoughtfulness; living in the present	use of Tolstoy's short story to create a fable about what is most important in life; illustrations that further support elements of the genre	injured, peace, uncertain, mentor, moral, quest	book review (expository)	www.kirkusreviews.com/book-reviews/jon-j-muth/the-three-questions/
RA 2	*The Secret Olivia Told Me*	N. Joy	Realistic Fiction	Picture Book	trust; friendship; responsibility; truthfulness	problem/solution story structure to present a story with a message; first-person narration; rhyming verse	accidentally, declared, fretted, overheard, consequence, integrity, responsibility	character's response (narrative)	http://pbskids.org/itsmylife/games/index.html
RA 3	*Alexander, Who Used to Be Rich Last Sunday*	Judith Viorst	Realistic Fiction	Picture Book	sibling and family relationships; saving money; determination and discipline	use of humor and first-person narration to reveal character and themes; use of repetition to organize story events and reinforce themes	absolutely, positively, tokens, vanish, discipline, squander	advice (expository; persuasive)	http://pbskids.org/itsmylife/money/index.html
RA 4	*Wangari's Trees of Peace*	Jeanette Winter	Biography	Picture Book	conviction, determination; conservation, protecting the environment	biography that relates a message; use of poetic language and colorful art; quote and Author's Note that provide additional information	barren, convinces, mission, seedlings, conviction, environment, heroic, protect	summary (expository)	www.nobelprize.org
RA 5	*The Great Kapok Tree*	Lynne Cherry	Informational Fantasy	Picture Book	interdependence of life on Earth; preservation of rain forests; personal responsibility	use of fantasy, graphic elements, and illustrations to organize information that delivers a message; map; diagram; notes	canopy, generations, miracles, pollinate, ruins, deforestation, interdependence, perspective	opinion (persuasive; expository)	www.rainforest-alliance.org/kids/visits
BC 1	*Salsa Stories*	Lulu Delacre	Realistic Fiction	Chapter Book	importance of family and friendships; pride in heritage and cultural traditions; strength of character	use of first-person narration with authentic language and dialogue; text features—a family tree, recipes, Spanish words, links to Latino countries and traditions, glossary; childhood flashbacks (stories within a story)	aroma, processions, recipes, waft, culture, heritage, tradition	readers' notebooks	http://lightbox.time.com/
BC 2	*The Real Slam Dunk*	Charisse K. Richardson	Realistic Fiction	Chapter Book	dreams and ambitions; leadership and responsibility; education creates career options	dialogue, point of view, and a high-interest topic used to convey a message; details about basketball	college, competition, professional, statistics, ambition, leadership, perseverance	readers' notebooks	www.kids.gov/k_5/k_5_careers.shtml
BC 3	*Dexter the Tough*	Margaret Peterson Haddix	Realistic Fiction	Chapter Book	self-awareness; growth and change; dealing with anger/inner conflict; friendship	use of narrative, dialogue, and inner thoughts to develop character; first-person voice used to explore themes of inner conflict and self-awareness	misunderstanding, revise, therapeutic, transplant, anger, chemotherapy, inner conflict, self-awareness	readers' notebooks	www.readingrockets.org/books/interviews
BC 4	*Drita, My Home Girl*	Jenny Lombard	Realistic Fiction	Chapter Book	adjusting to life in a new country; being courageous; negotiating language barriers; dealing with loss and other life changes	two main characters developed through their stories told in alternating first-person chapters; differing perspectives shown through voice, descriptive narrative, and realistic dialogue	challenge, confident, refugee, translate, diversity, immigrate	readers' notebooks	www.dritamyhomegirl.com/p/history.html
Grade 4		**Strand: Inspired by True Stories**							
					Unit: The Artist's Eye	**Unit Focus: How do artists help others experience the world in a new way?**			
RA 1	*An Eye for Color*	Natasha Wing	Biography	Picture Book	how people express creativity; individual accomplishments; how art helps us see things in a new way	demonstration of how life events change a person's perspective; description and examples that show a person's life achievements	abstract, collages, geometrically, optical, observation, perspective, sensory	write about an outcome (expository)	www.albersfoundation.org
RA 2	*Duke Ellington*	Andrea Davis Pinkney	Biography	Picture Book	how people express creativity; what people have in common; individual accomplishments; how art conveys emotions	use of colloquial and figurative language; use of sequence of events	crude, improvise, romp, suite, accomplishments, colloquial, innovative	advertisement (persuasive)	http://archive.org/details/DukeEllington-TakeATrain
RA 3	*Frida*	Jonah Winter	Biography	Picture Book	how people express creativity; how art conveys emotions; how life's events inspire us; how good can come from something bad	simple, lyrical text that tells an overarching story of a person's life; Author's Note	imaginary, microscope, torso, adversity, chronic, folk art	explanation (expository)	www.pbs.org/weta/fridakahlo
RA 4	*Faith Ringgold*	Mike Venezia	Biography	Picture Book	how people express creativity; what people have in common; individual accomplishments; events that change lives	cartoon art; images of famous artwork; sequence of events; captions	appreciated, originated, portraits, prejudice, exploration, interpret, liberated	descriptive time line/story quilt (expository)	http://www.pbs.org/americanquilts/aoq/quiltnational.html
RA 5	*Spiders*	Nic Bishop	Informational Text	Photo Essay	how people express creativity; individual accomplishments; how art conveys information and expresses different perspectives	detailed photographs that support factual information; photograph captions; foldout; author's note	ambush, camouflaged, dribbles, miniature, nozzles, predators, dedication, observant, perception	persuasive paragraph (persuasive)	http://frankphillips.com/beautifulbugs

	Title	Author	Genre	Type	Themes	Description	Vocabulary	Writing	Website
BC 1	Frida Kahlo	Mike Venezia	Biography	Picture Book	events that change lives; how people express creativity; what people have in common; individual accomplishments; how culture influences individuals	photographs, art reproductions, and illustrations used to support text; life story highlighted by chronological sequence of main events	amateur, ancient, easel, adversity, consciousness, controversy	readers' notebooks	www.aaa.si.edu/exhibitions/frida-kahlo
BC 2	Ish	Peter H. Reynolds	Realistic Fiction	Picture Book	using art to express yourself; being different to be creative; giving someone confidence	illustrations that convey emotion; dialogue that shows character traits; artist's perspective used to show the effects of criticism and praise	burst out, crumpled, sneered, appreciation, criticism, discouraged	readers' notebooks	www.peterreynolds.com/art.html
BC 3	Wolfgang Amadeus Mozart	Mike Venezia	Biography	Picture Book	individual accomplishments; how people express creativity; how our circumstances shape our lives; how art conveys emotions	illustrations used to support text; sequence of events and setting promote understanding of life story; humorous cartoons	billiards, classical, masterpieces, antagonize, dominating, prodigy	readers' notebooks	http://archive.org/details/Vocals3
BC 4	Tar Beach	Faith Ringgold	Autobiographical Fiction	Picture Book	how people express creativity; what people have in common; individual accomplishments; how circumstances shape our lives; how art conveys emotions	first-person point of view; artwork as a basis for a story; illustrations that show details	hoisting, possession, skyscraper, inspiration, observations, optimistic	readers' notebooks	www.faithringgold.com/ringgold/collect.htm
Grade 4			**Strand: Genre Study**						
				Unit: Fantasy		**Unit Focus: What makes a fantasy story exciting and fun to read?**			
RA 1	The Night I Followed the Dog	Nina Laden	Fantasy	Picture Book	living with pets; alternate worlds	placement of fantasy elements within a realistic setting; use of handwritten type; artistic treatment of words and phrases	entrance, glamorous, limousine, obedience, neon sign, outlandish, tuxedo	advertisement (persuasive)	www.ninaladen.com/visits/teachers.html
RA 2	Porkenstein	Kathryn Lasky	Fantasy	Picture Book	good vs. evil; friendship	plot elements that are adapted from existing familiar stories; description and dialogue that develop characters; humor	chemicals, incredible, inventor, laboratory, concoction, tremendous	news story (expository)	www.inventnow.org/invent
RA 3	Raising Dragons	Jerdine Nolen	Fantasy	Picture Book	friendship; tolerance; parent-child attitudes	use of first-person narration to tell a story; use of fantasy elements within a realistic setting	fanciful, medicinal, notion, opinions, belief, possibility, tolerance	sequel (narrative)	http://dsc.discovery.com/
RA 4	LaRue Across America	Mark Teague	Fantasy	Picture Book	conflicts with others; handling disappointment	story that is developed through newspaper articles and postcards; animal characters with human traits; text that is contrasted with illustrations to create humor	convinced, persuade, saga, viciously, disappointment, fiasco, ill-tempered	postcard (expository)	www.usa.gov
RA 5	Diary of a Spider	Doreen Cronin	Fantasy	Picture Book	getting to know one another; friendship; tolerance; survival; alternate worlds	portrayal of animals with human traits; inclusion of scientific facts in a fantasy; use of humor to engage readers; theme expressed through the main character's words and actions	drill, molted, vacuum, arachnid, arachnophobia, beneficial	book review (persuasive)	www.kidzone.ws/lw/spiders/facts.htm
BC 1	Knights of the Kitchen Table	Jon Scieszka	Fantasy	Chapter Book	cleverness vs. strength; good vs. evil	a legendary setting used for a modern story; characters developed through dialogue and narration; humor	amusement, relieved, sputtered, vanquish, weird, enchanters, knaves, time travel	readers' notebooks	www.jsworldwide.com/yeah_he_wrote_em.html
BC 2	Felix Takes the Stage	Kathryn Lasky	Fantasy	Chapter Book	being different; tolerance; family values; human and animal interaction; survival; alternate worlds	realistic settings; events and factual details about the natural world that create a fantasy world of animal characters with human qualities	exterminators, infestation, species, toxic, notorious, recluse, settle	readers' notebooks	http://archive.org/details/BrahmsSymphonyNo.3
BC 3	The Capture	Kathryn Lasky	Fantasy	Novel	good vs. evil; survival; hope; heroism; belief in yourself; friendship; family; alternate worlds	animal characters with human traits; realistic dialogue; theme revealed through plot and characters; scientific facts; classic fantasy plot that consists of a journey; foreshadowing	brood, deceptive, fledged, gizzard, soar, freedom, instinct, survival	readers' notebooks	www.kathrynlasky.com/KK/FAQ.html
BC 4	Hewitt Anderson's Great Big Life	Jerdine Nolen	Fantasy	Picture Book	family values; individuality	elements of real life used to develop a world of giants; a well-known folktale extended into a book	generations, mammoth, massive, miniature, gargantuan, resourceful	readers' notebooks	www.pitt.edu/~dash/type028jack.html
Grade 5			**Strand: Community & Relationships**						
				Unit: Better Together		**Unit Focus: How can people work together to reach their goals?**			
RA 1	The Yellow Star	Carmen Agra Deedy	Legend	Picture Book	creativity and working together can solve difficult problems; values are worth fighting for; inner strength can conquer brute force	use of elements of legend to craft a story; foreshadowing; poetic language; imagery; Author's Note	beloved, defense, defiance, resistance, confidence, leadership, loyalty	summary (expository)	www.ushmm.org/maps/
RA 2	Leo the Snow Leopard	Juliana, Isabella, & Craig Hatkoff	Informational Text	Photo Essay	protecting animals; determination; working together	descriptive language that helps convey meaning; photographs and captions that accompany the text; use of authors' letter and notes to provide more information	extraordinary, orphan, treacherous, cooperate, diplomacy, endangered	public service announcement (expository)	www.leothesnowleopard.com
RA 3	March On! The Day My Brother Martin Changed the World	Christine King Farris	Memoir	Picture Book	determination; values; influence	poetic language and imagery; use of bold text that emphasizes certain parts; inclusion of everyday details; Author's Note	conviction, eloquent, influence, nonviolence, civil rights, demonstrate, prejudice	reader's response (expository)	http://mlk-kpp01.stanford.edu
RA 4	Harvesting Hope: The Story of Cesar Chavez	Kathleen Krull	Biography	Picture Book	life changes; fairness; determination; leadership; collaboration	use of chronological order; use of similes and metaphors; Author's Note that provides additional facts	conflicts, contract, justice, rebel, organize, union	character response (narrative)	www.chavezfoundation.org
RA 5	Freedom on the Menu	Carole Boston Weatherford	Historical Fiction	Picture Book	determination; values; nonviolence; unity	first-person perspective that makes the story more realistic; foreshadowing; Author's Note that provides details about actual events	bail, picket, sit-ins, equality, sacrifice, segregation	song/poem (persuasive)	www.npr.org

	Title	Author	Genre	Text Type	Themes/Ideas	Author's Craft	Vocabulary	Writing Options	Technology
Grade 5		**Strand: Community & Relationships**			**Unit: Better Together (cont'd.)**	**Unit Focus: How can people work together to reach their goals?**			
BC 1	Twenty and Ten	Claire Huchet Bishop	Historical Fiction	Chapter Book	compassion; sacrifice; quick thinking; courage; community	symbolism in first chapter that foreshadows events in last chapter; character traits; first-person point of view; dialogue	forbid, guffawed, stealthily, occupied, ration card, refugee	readers' notebooks	www.porcelainunicorn.com
BC 2	Because of Winn-Dixie	Kate DiCamillo	Realistic Fiction	Chapter Book	loneliness; friendship; dealing with loss and grief; having compassion; persuasiveness	short chapters; humor; dialogue; personification of Winn-Dixie; first-person voice; narrator's distinctive voice; character development	distracted, installment, peculiar, chaos, ignorant, melancholy	readers' notebooks	www.scholastic.com/winndixie/
BC 3	One Hen	Katie Smith Milway	Realistic Fiction	Picture Book	taking small steps to make big changes; interdependence; setting goals to make a better future	cause/effect story structure; chronological order; additional information	accounts, coop, loan, interdependence, profit, wages	readers' notebooks	www.onehen.org
BC 4	Tiger Rising	Kate DiCamillo	Realistic Fiction	Chapter Book	self-awareness that leads to growth; showing kindness; having wisdom; releasing strong emotions; friendship	strong development of diverse characters; symbolism; poetic language; realistic dialogue	bitter, contagious, furious, trespassing, desperate, gratitude, soothe	readers' notebooks	www.readingrockets.org/books/
Grade 5		**Strand: Folklore & Literary Traditions**			**Unit: Watch Out!**	**Unit Focus: How do authors use a sense of danger to shape stories?**			
RA 1	Tsunami!	Retold by Kimiko Kajikawa	Folktale	Picture Book	preparing for disaster; making sacrifices for the greater good; man vs. nature	use of folktale elements to tell a story; use of foreshadowing to convey mood; use of a character's actions to express the theme	devoured, tinder, tsunami, typhoon, whirled, catastrophe, sacrifice, selfless	description (persuasive)	www.town.hirogawa. wakayama.jp/inamuranohi/english/sinyo_goryo.html
RA 2	Chicken Big	Keith Graves	Fractured Folktale	Picture Book	truth vs. opinion; using common sense; appreciating satire and humor; story with a moral	retelling of a well-known tale from a different perspective; satire; illustrations and text styles that add humor and engage readers	apparently, poultry, woe, hysterical, preposterous, satire	fractured fairy tale (narrative)	www.keithgravesart.com
RA 3	Lon Po Po	Retold by Ed Young	Fairy Tale	Picture Book	the value of cleverness; protecting family; good vs. evil	use of dialogue to reveal plot details; illustrations that help depict plot, setting, and mood	brittle, disguised, route, imposter, predator	description (expository)	www.pitt.edu/~dash/china.html
RA 4	Rumpelstiltskin	Retold by Paul O. Zelinsky	Fairy Tale	Picture Book	the power of greed; overcoming problems	illustrations that add interest to a familiar story; use of the "rule of three" commonly found in fairy tales to develop the plot	miller, gleaming, inquiries, piteously, spool, plight, predicament	skit (persuasive)	www.ala.org/alsc/awardsgrants/bookmedia
RA 5	The Odious Ogre	Norton Juster	Fairy Tale	Picture Book	the power of kindness; facing disaster; behaving better than your enemies	use of humor to transform a traditionally scary story; narrator with a distinctive attitude, or tone; use of an unlikely story outcome to reveal theme	apprehensively, docile, invincible, reputation, hospitality, odious	newspaper article (expository)	www.npr.org
BC 1	The Rumpelstiltskin Problem	Vivian Vande Velde	Fantasy	Chapter Book	solving a problem; facing challenges	traditional story told with varying plot events, character traits, and motivations; humor	aghast, betrothal, decreed, gnarled, gullible, scenario, scheme	readers' notebooks	www.readwritethink.org/files/resources/interactives/fairytales/
BC 2	Skeleton Man	Joseph Bruchac	Mystery	Chapter Book	coping with loss; finding courage	first-person point of view used to tell a story; suspense built through descriptive plot events and details; cultural context provided through references to Native-American folklore	furtively, heroine, hysterical, loathsome, searing, confide, grief, premonition	readers' notebooks	http://bcove.me/7ky5n341
BC 3	The Monster's Ring	Bruce Coville	Fantasy	Chapter Book	coping with bullying; finding courage; standing up for yourself	fantasy and elements drawn from folklore in an everyday setting; character developed through narration and dialogue; use of simile to add descriptive detail	emboldened, hallucination, petty, rumpus, sullenly, intimidation, metamorphosis	readers' notebooks	www.brucecoville.com/tips.asp
BC 4	Werewolf versus Dragon	David Sinden, Matthew Morgan, Guy Macdonald	Mystery	Chapter Book	good vs. evil; kindness toward living creatures; friendship	descriptive language and context clues that clarify elements of a fantasy world; foreshadowing through clues	aviary, nocturnal, perimeter, quarantine, tranquilizer, archives, cruelty, revolting	readers' notebooks	www.beastlybusiness.com/usa/
Grade 5		**Strand: Living Things**			**Unit: Under the Surface**	**Unit Focus: What tools and techniques help scientists study the human body?**			
RA 1	The Brain: Our Nervous System	Seymour Simon	Informational Text	Picture Book	human body; medical technology; electron microscopy; electrical impulses; memory; parts of the brain and their functions	introduction with a conversational tone; labeled photographs and diagrams; clear organizational structure	regulates, relay, sheath, triggers, microscopic, sensation, techniques	report (expository)	www.traumaticbraininjuryatoz.org
RA 2	You Wouldn't Want to Be an Egyptian Mummy!	David Stewart	Informational Text	Picture Book	ancient Egypt; death; culture; the embalming process; human anatomy	humorous, interesting text; introduction; varied layout with features of informational text; detailed captions	ceremonial, coffin, purification, sensible, eternal, monument, tomb	checklist (expository)	www.salariya.com/web_books/mummy
RA 3	X-Treme X-Ray	Nick Veasey	Informational Text	Picture Book	X-ray history; X-rays as art; the human body; nature; sports; fun facts; part-to-whole relationships	X-ray photographs; question/answer chapter introductions; colorful text boxes; background information and facts about the photos	injury, lethal, portable, straightforward, absorb, dense, exposure, invisible	book review (expository)	www.nickveasey.com
RA 4	Bones	Seymour Simon	Informational Text	Picture Book	learning about the human body; recognizing X-ray photos; high-tech imagery; development and functions of the skeletal system	Photography Note: descriptive language; simple sentence structure, and terms that are defined in context to present information about bones as living parts of the body; photographs, diagrams, and captions	collapse, constantly, inhale, marvelous, flex, framework, tissue, vital	summary (expository)	www.eskeletons.org
RA 5	Charles Drew	Mike Venezia	Biography	Picture Book	values and skills learned in childhood lead to later success; combating prejudice; problem solving; the importance of and improvement in blood transfusions	chronological sequence; context information; historical photographs with captions; cartoons with speech balloons; Glossary	authority, fascinated, insulted, resigned, accomplishment, denied, donate	speech (expository)	www.fi.edu/learn/heart/blood/blood.html

Code	Title	Author	Genre	Type	Theme/Topic	Text Features	Vocabulary	Writing	Website
BC 1	Burp!	Diane Swanson	Informational Text	Series Book	the role of the digestive system in human health; the importance of nutrients; the brain's role in food consumption	organization into chapters, subheads, and sidebars; terms defined in context; pronunciation guides; informal language; humor, trivia, and activities	contract, critical, emotions, variety, appetite, consume, nourish, reaction	readers' notebooks	http://kidshealth.org/kid
BC 2	Skulls and Skeletons	Danielle Denega	Informational Text	Series Book	identifying human bodies; skeletal system facts; history of and tools used in forensic anthropology; current interest in forensic anthropology	three case studies that explain in narrative style how forensic anthropologists identify the dead; information organized into case studies, articles, and text features, supported by photographs and graphics	analyzed, casket, decay, theories, components, profile, reveal	readers' notebooks	http://pbskids.org/dragonflytv
BC 3	Achoo!	Trudee Romanek	Informational Text	Series Book	functions of the immune system; types of germs and how they are spread; ways to fight germs and the illnesses they cause	text organized with informative heads, subheads, text boxes, and sidebars; informal language, accessible similes, and engaging activities that support real-life connection	congestion, dissolved, invade, recover, incredible, symptoms	readers' notebooks	http://pbskids.org/dragonflytv/show
BC 4	Mummies Unwrapped!	N. B. Grace	Informational Text	Series Book	scientists learn about ancient life through the discovery, study, and making of mummies; teams of experts use tools and technology to aid the work of archeologists	variety of narrative styles and formats used to inform about the discovery, study, and making of mummies; information organized into case studies, articles, and text features, supported by photographs and graphics	corpse, fragments, rubble, sacrifice, foreign, textile, theory	readers' notebooks	www.pbs.org/wgbh/nova/ancient

Grade 5

Strand: A Sense of Self

Unit: Dealing With Change — Unit Focus: How do books reflect the kinds of changes people face in real life?

Code	Title	Author	Genre	Type	Theme/Topic	Text Features	Vocabulary	Writing	Website
RA 1	Scaredy Squirrel	Mélanie Watt	Fantasy	Picture Book	fear of the unknown; obsessiveness; self-discovery; change	theme that is introduced on the first page; use of grids and charts to present concepts and events; humorous text and illustrations	consult, distract, panic, regrets, venturing, assured, drastic, environment	graphic story (narrative)	www.kidscanpress.com/
RA 2	Crow Call	Lois Lowry	Memoir	Picture Book	becoming reacquainted; shared memories; father-daughter relationship; the taking of a life; fear	first-person narrative; use of imagery and poetic language to create mood; flashback; serious dialogue; Author's Note and photograph	bulky, decoys, disdain, subsides, flashback, memoir, reacquainted	description (expository)	www.loc.gov
RA 3	Dreaming of America	Eve Bunting	Historical Fiction	Picture Book	bravery; showing confidence; having compassion; trusting others; starting a new life	real photographs with captions; dialogue; culturally specific expressions that help establish genre; Afterword	corridor, parcel, steward, suffocated, wharf, commemorate, immigrant, remarkable	letter (expository)	www.ellisisland.org
RA 4	Grandma's Records	Eric Velasquez	Memoir	Picture Book	immigration; family relationships; emotional responses to music	first-person narration; expressive illustrations; Spanish words; song lyrics	album, percussion, selection, spectacular, appreciate, passion	dialogue (narrative)	www.ericvelasquez.com/index.html
RA 5	Zen Shorts	Jon J Muth	Fantasy	Picture Book	calm; hidden meanings; changing one's response; acceptance; teaching through storytelling	dialogue; description; main story and traditional tales that are distinguished by text and illustrations; surprising and thought-provoking ideas	lamented, rummaging, transported, perspective, preoccupied, traditional	summary (expository)	www.readingrockets.org/books/interviews/muth/
BC 1	The Music of Dolphins	Karen Hesse	Science Fiction	Chapter Book	music as language; trust and compassion; freedom; identity; using the senses; dealing with change	first-person point of view; different fonts and text styles	investment, progress, refugees, territory, adjustment, communication, emotion	readers' notebooks	www.seaworld.org
BC 2	In the Year of the Boar and Jackie Robinson	Bette Bao Lord	Autobiographical Fiction	Chapter Book	cultural differences; showing respect; overcoming misunderstandings; friendship; baseball; determination	chapters organized by months; humor; poetic language: analogy	ambassador, bandit, emperors, formidable, culture, miracle, misunderstanding	readers' notebooks	www.biography.com
BC 3	The Danger Box	Blue Balliett	Mystery	Novel	being different; bonds among family and community; looking at things in a special way; friendship	book introduced with the tale of a mysterious event; unique first-person narrator; similes; other texts interspersed throughout main narrative	desperately, hodgepodge, secretive, specimen, investigate, natural selection, Pathological Myopia	readers' notebooks	www.blueballiettbooks.com/bio.html
BC 4	Anything but Typical	Nora Raleigh Baskin	Realistic Fiction	Chapter Book	challenges of being different; good intentions; acceptance; creative expression	first-person narration; figurative language; self-expression through a story within a story	defective, dilemma, narrator, operation, stubborn, affection, assume, bond, observations	readers' notebooks	www.ted.com

Grade 5

Strand: Inspired by True Stories

Unit: It Takes a Leader — Unit Focus: What makes a great leader, and how do leaders effect change?

Code	Title	Author	Genre	Type	Theme/Topic	Text Features	Vocabulary	Writing	Website
RA 1	Kubla Khan: The Emperor of Everything	Kathleen Krull	Biography	Picture Book	qualities of a leader; influence of nature and nurture	use of chronological order and setting to craft a biography; Author's Note	civilized, empire, nomads, violent, ambitious, barbarians, massacred, realm	essay (expository)	http://history.cultural-china.com/en/46History7949
RA 2	Now & Ben	Gene Barretta	Biography	Picture Book	qualities of a leader; inventiveness; contributing to society	wordplay; structure that shows "now" on one page and "then" on the next; comparison of Ben's inventions with similar items in use today; fun illustrations that support the text	benefits, efficient, gadget, interlude, primitive, ventilation, effective, pivotal, political	essay (expository)	www.fi.edu/franklin
RA 3	Planting the Trees of Kenya	Claire A. Nivola	Biography	Picture Book	qualities of a leader; influence of one person; preserving the environment	narrative that is told in three parts; lyrical prose; detailed illustrations that show the setting; Author's Note	export, nursery, plantations, seedlings, accomplishments, consequences, exposed, movement, sacred	letter to author and illustrator (expository)	www.myhero.com/go/directory
RA 4	John, Paul, George & Ben	Lane Smith	Biography	Picture Book	qualities of a leader; traits that carry over from youth to adulthood; the addition of humorous, made-up details to factual biographies	separate sections that focus on each subject and trait; use of humor and wordplay; illustrations that add humor to the story; True or False section	appreciate, document, pursue, revolution, treasonous, epilogue, liberty, toll	research and write about a character (expository)	www.history.org/kids/games
RA 5	So You Want to Be President?	Judith St. George	Biography	Picture Book	qualities of a leader; comparison of past and present presidents	light-hearted categorization of American leaders; list at the back of the book that includes additional information about each president	Constitution, interview, personalities, priority, adversaries, occupation, spectators	list (expository)	www.whitehouse.gov/about/white-house-101/
BC 1	Rosa	Nikki Giovanni	Biography	Picture Book	qualities of a leader; influence of one person; nonviolent resistance	biography told in a story style using sequence; text reflects the times and the event	anticipation, neutral, provision, segregation, alterations, designated, inherent	readers' notebooks	www.thehenryford.org/exhibits/rosaparks

	Title	Author	Genre	Text Type	Themes/Ideas	Author's Craft	Vocabulary	Writing Options	Technology
Grade 5		**Strand: Inspired by True Stories**			**Unit: It Takes a Leader (cont'd.)**	**Unit Focus: What makes a great leader, and how do leaders effect change?**			
BC 2	Can't You Make Them Behave, King George?	Jean Fritz	Biography	Series Book	stubbornness; ruling as a monarch; how leaders fail; alternate perspective	perspective of King George and the British; king's perception of himself as being a good leader; chronological order	empire, independence, rebellious, repeal, representatives, abdicate, coronation, moral, traitor	readers' notebooks	www.loc.gov
BC 3	Testing the Ice: A True Story About Jackie Robinson	Sharon Robinson	Biography	Picture Book	qualities of a leader; breaking through barriers; taking risks	first-person narration that reveals character; setting integral to metaphor for Robinson's courage; story within a story emphasizing theme of breaking barriers	barrier, historic, insults, reluctantly, determination, pioneer, plaques	readers' notebooks	www.sharonrobinsonink.com
BC 4	Rebel in a Dress: Adventurers	Sylvia Branzei	Biography	Chapter Book	qualities of a leader; breaking through barriers; paving the way for others	twelve chapters, each focusing on a different subject; typeface that highlights a unique quality for each subject; text features such as maps, captions, photos, charts, and newspaper clippings	competitive, gender, prestigious, trek, embodied, gusto, intrepid, tenacity	readers' notebooks	www.makers.com/browse
Grade 5		**Strand: Genre Study**			**Unit: Historical Fiction**	**Unit Focus: How do authors use actual events from history to create memorable fiction?**			
RA 1	The Hatmaker's Sign	Candace Fleming	Historical Fiction	Picture Book	friendship; independent thinking; learning to compromise; stories that deserve retelling	fiction that is based on real characters and events; use of pattern to tell the story; humor added to serious subjects or events	debate, delegate, haughty, magistrate, parchment, quibbled, consensus, parable	make, revise, and compare signs (expository)	www.ushistory.org/declaration/account/index.htm
RA 2	Pink and Say	Patricia Polacco	Historical Fiction	Picture Book	enduring friendship; family love; honoring the memory of loved ones; bravery; cruelty of war	realistic characters and settings; use of colloquial dialogue; rich illustrations that portray depth and emotion	mahogany, marauders, mustered, smote, anxiety, perspective	memorial (expository; persuasive)	www.archives.gov/research/military/civil-war/photos/index.html
RA 3	The Memory Coat	Elvira Woodruff	Historical Fiction	Picture Book	importance of family; reasons for immigration; solving problems in unusual ways; overcoming adversity	believable characters that modern readers can relate to; a sense of place that evokes the past; Author's Note to add information	commotion, epidemic, synagogue, ancestors, heritage	scene (narrative)	www.ellisisland.org
RA 4	Just Like Josh Gibson	Angela Johnson	Historical Fiction	Picture Book	effects of prejudice; following one's dream; recognizing talent	characters that modern readers can relate to; a sense of place that evokes the past; use of historical characters as part of a fictional story	arbitrary, consummate, umpire, accomplishments, legacy, legendary	opinion (persuasive)	www.exploratorium.edu/baseball/
RA 5	Ride Like the Wind	Bernie Fuchs	Historical Fiction	Picture Book	friendship and loyalty; overcoming obstacles; clashing cultures	introduction that establishes historical setting; action and description that appeal to readers' imaginations	descend, doused, treacherous, frontier, terrain	examples and opinion (expository; persuasive)	www.ponyexpress.org/pony-express-historical-timeline
BC 1	Esperanza Rising	Pam Muñoz Ryan	Historical Fiction	Novel	true meaning of wealth; resilience; building empathy for others; value of supportive relationships	circular story pattern; historical context; emotional development of character from privileged girl to compassionate young woman	brooded, listless, monotonous, premonition, renegades, perseverance, symbolic	readers' notebooks	www.pammunozryan.com
BC 2	The Watsons Go to Birmingham—1963	Christopher Paul Curtis	Historical Fiction	Novel	experience of racism; solving problems in unusual ways; family	recurrent theme of near misses; humorous, first-person point of view; historical context of 1960s civil rights struggle	country, hypnotized, juvenile delinquent, reputation, consequences, hilarious, inevitable	readers' notebooks	www.nytimes.com/learning/general/onthisday/big/0915.html#article
BC 3	Elijah of Buxton	Christopher Paul Curtis	Historical Fiction	Novel	learning through experience; the value of freedom; taking on adult responsibilities	authentic characters created through dialogue; boy maturing into a young man; sense of place in the historical past	assumptions, commence, tolerate, charlatan, gullible	readers' notebooks	http://bcove.me/2hfxiipm
BC 4	Riding Freedom	Pam Muñoz Ryan	Historical Fiction	Novel	freedom; being true to oneself; protecting those we love; working toward a goal	unique historical character; sense of history; suspense that draws readers in	intentions, mucking, satchels, disguised, divert, suffrage	readers' notebooks	www.pammunozryan.com/pages/novels/interviewFreedom.pdf

Comprehension Clubs Research Base

Program Feature	Supporting Research

Whole-Class Interactive Read-Aloud

- As teachers read aloud they intentionally embed the teaching of the specific understandings to
  - ❏ demonstrate and involve students in thinking about important aspects related to reading
  - ❏ engage students in discussion, including turn and talk, that lays a foundation for literary analysis
  - ❏ use read-alouds as a starting point for students' own writing
- These embedded lessons are characterized by developmentally friendly language, but the concepts are complex.

The interactive read-aloud, or the read-aloud plus text talk, is based on three understandings; it:
- encourages the child to become an active learner during book reading
- provides feedback that models more sophisticated language
- challenges the child's knowledge and skills by raising the complexity of the conversation

(De Temple & Snow, 2003; Lane & Wright, 2007)

"Because . . . children's listening comprehension likely outpaces reading comprehension until the middle school years, it is particularly important that students in the earliest grades build knowledge through being read to as well as through reading, with the balance gradually shifting to reading independently. By reading a . . . selection aloud, teachers allow children to experience written language without the burden of decoding, granting them access to content that they may not be able to read and understand by themselves. Children are then free to focus their mental energy on the words and ideas presented . . . and they will eventually be better prepared to tackle rich written content on their own" (Common Core, 2010).

The interactive read-aloud results in student gains in vocabulary (Beck & McKeown, 2001; Bennett-Armistead, 2009), comprehension strategies and story schema (Van den Broek, 1997), and concept development (Wasik et al., 2001; Fountas & Pinnell, 2012a).

Simply inviting children to talk during interactive read-alouds doesn't provide the needed learning boost. It's the close reading and textual analysis—deep, intentional conversation about the text (Dickinson & Smith, 1994; Fountas & Pinnell, 2006, 2012a; Serravallo, 2012; and Shanahan, 2012)—that make the difference.

The best way to help our children become readers is to read to them. As young children hear stories read aloud, they learn new words, begin to figure out how letters and sounds are related (phonological awareness), learn how words are conceptually related, and acquire invaluable background knowledge and concepts of print (Clay, 2000; Bernstein, 2010).

Book Clubs

- Within each unit, students choose the book they want to read for book club.
- With the support of streaming audio, students, regardless of independent reading level, access any text they choose.
- The book club is a literature investigation in which students, with guidance from the teacher, try out ideas, analyze text, and search for information to confirm or revise their thinking.
- Students learn from each other as they share ideas and cite textual evidence to support their opinions.

The Chicago schools in which Daniels (2002) implemented book clubs outstripped citywide test score gains by 14% in Grade 3, 9% in Grade 6, and 10% in Grade 8. In writing, the students who participated in book clubs topped citywide gains by 25% in Grade 3, 8% in Grade 6, and 27% in Grade 8.

"When teachers ask students to consider two or more perspectives on a topic or issue, something far beyond surface knowledge is required: students must think critically and deeply, assess the validity of their own thinking, and anticipate counterclaims in opposition to their own assertions" (CCSS, 2010).

In a study of fourth graders by Klinger, Vaughn, and Schumm (1998), students in peer-led groups made greater gains than controls in reading comprehension and equal gains in content knowledge, as measured by standardized tests, after reading and discussing social studies material in peer-led groups; most encouragingly, student small-group talk was 65% academic and content-related, 25% procedural, and 8% feedback, with only 2% off-task.

Various versions of book clubs have increased student enjoyment of and engagement in reading (Fox & Wilkinson, 1997); expanded children's discourse opportunities (Johnston, 2004, 2009; Nichols, 2009); increased multicultural awareness (Hansen-Krening & Mizokawa, 1997; Lehman et al., 2010); promoted a range of perspectives on social issues (Noll, 1998); provided social outlets for students (Alvermann et al., 1996); and encouraged gender equity and an enhanced sense of self (Bettis & Roe, 2008).

"Students read more, understand more, and are more likely to continue reading when they have the opportunity to choose what they read" (Allington & Gabriel, 2012).

Units of Study (Text Sets)

A text set comprises two or more books that are connected in some way—author, theme, topic, illustrator, text structure, genre or a particular aspect of text—that helps students build understanding from book to book.

In *Comprehension Clubs*, each unit of study is a text set consisting of five books to be read aloud by the teacher and four book club choices.

The relationships between the books and supports on the teaching card in the unit provide the structure needed to organize language and content and allow students to build the mental organizing schema that they can use to approach and integrate new ideas and knowledge.

"To understand a text deeply, we need multiple perspectives. To understand a subject, idea, or concept more deeply, we need multiple texts because each text offers another author's perspective on the subject" (Johnston, 2009).

The key to building dialogic conversations around texts and text sets is in the ways we as teachers talk with children. The teachers help children understand what they are doing (not merely reading), who they are, and what to value . . . . "The foundation this instruction provides for children includes building a tolerance for ambiguity and uncertainty, a foundation that will allow them not only to keep a conversation open and treat each other with respect, but to keep their minds open" (Johnston, 2009).

"This normal process of word acquisition occurs up to four times faster for Tier Three words (Beck, McKeown, & Kucan, 2002) when students have become familiar with the domain of the discourse and encounter the word in different contexts (Landauer & Dumais, 1997). Hence, vocabulary development for these words occurs most effectively through a coherent course of study in which subject matters are integrated and coordinated across the curriculum and domains become familiar to the student over several days or weeks" (CCSS, 2010).

". . . Curriculum should be aimed at what Lev Vygotsky called students' zone of proximal development." Vygotsky wrote, "The only good kind of instruction is that which marches ahead of development and leads it." Classroom texts should pose intellectual challenges for readers and invite them to stretch and grow. . . . Reading a broad range of books makes students stronger readers and, over time, stronger people" (Jago, 2011).

"Students need opportunity to stretch their reading abilities but also to experience the satisfaction and pleasure of easy, fluent reading within them, both of which the Standards allow for . . . such factors as students' motivation, knowledge, and experiences must also come into play in text selection. Students deeply interested in a given topic, for example, may engage with texts on that subject across a range of complexity" (CCSS, 2010).

Building Concepts & Acquiring Vocabulary

Comprehension Clubs is a spiraled curriculum developed within the context of a matrix which allows for

- vocabulary and knowledge to build not just within a unit or grade, but from grade to grade as well
- students to conduct grade level appropriate study of six broad areas: Community & Relationships, Folklore & Literary Traditions, Living Things, A Sense of Self, Inspired by True Stories, and Genre Study

A spiral curriculum underlies the Common Core State Standards in fiction and informational reading and in narrative, opinion, and informational writing, revealing the most important ways in which academic expectations change across the years. The spiraled nature of the standards provides learning pathways along which you can move your students (CCSS, 2010; Calkins et al., 2012).

"One of the key requirements of the Common Core State Standards for Reading is that all students must be able to comprehend texts of steadily increasing complexity as they progress through school" (CCSS, 2010).

"Key to students' vocabulary development is building rich and flexible word knowledge. Students need plentiful opportunities to use and respond to the words they learn through playful informal talk, discussion, reading or being read to, and responding to what is read" (CCSS, 2010).

"If topic-related selections are sequenced in order of difficulty and build on each other conceptually and linguistically, students will be better able to tackle increasingly challenging text" (Kinsella, 1994).

Program Feature	Supporting Research

Comprehension & Close Reading

The reading standards focus on students' ability to read closely and grasp information, arguments, ideas and details based on text evidence; they should be able to answer a range of text-dependent questions in which the answers require inferences based on careful attention to the text.

"Close reading requires reading with a pencil . . . the act of making notes helps us pay attention to the text and allows us to return to the text later when we want to provide evidence" (Fisher, Frey, & Lapp, 2012).

"Close reading is entailed in critical reading. It is not an elitist, nose-to-the-text, words-on-the page pedantry, but the way of attending to the interplay of saying and meaning" (Berthoff, 1999).

"Close reading requires a substantial emphasis on readers figuring out a high quality text. This 'figuring out' is accomplished primarily by reading and discussing the text . . . close reading [means] intense emphasis on text, figuring out the text by thinking about the words and ideas in the text, minimization of external explanations, multiple and dynamic rereading, multiple purposes that focus on what a text says, how it says it, and what it means or what its value is" (Shanahan, 2012).

"To grow, our students must read lots, and more specifically they must read lots of 'complex' texts—texts that offer them new language, new knowledge, and new modes of thought" (CCSS, 2010).

Speaking & Listening

In *Comprehension Clubs*, students are invited to speak within two talk structures: 1) the interactive read aloud; and 2) book clubs. Additionally, they may discuss their books with a reading partner or with family members at home.

Every day, as they discuss books and ideas, topics, themes, and genres, they:

- develop a shared language that gradually grows more complex
- learn to use rich and dynamic conversations about text to effectively construct meaning
- learn to ground their talk in the text and cite evidence from the text to back their opinions
- incorporate new vocabulary and text structures into their own language repertoire

Quality talk around books "can promote familiarity with relatively rare vocabulary, understanding the lexical and grammatical strategies for adjusting to a nonpresent audience, identifying the perspective of the listener so as to provide sufficient background information, and knowing the genre-specific rules for various forms of talk such as narrative and explanation" (Snow, 1993, reported in Beck & McKeown, 2001).

"If we wish to help children and adolescents become thoughtfully literate, classroom talk around texts is critical" (Allington, 2012).

"An environment rich in high-quality talk about text should involve both teacher-to-student and student-to-student talk. It should include discussions of text processing at a number of levels, from clarifying basic material stated in the text to drawing interpretations of text material to relating the text to other texts, experiences, and reading goals" (Duke & Pearson, 2002).

"To make discussions interactive, students need to be responsible for articulating their interpretations and ideas to the community of readers, for listening to what other students are saying, and for reconsidering what they are thinking. Members of interactive discussions assume an active role, listening intently to other students' ideas and interpretations and opening lines of communication among students rather than always going through the teacher" (Serafini, 2009).

"Children's oral language competence is strongly predictive of their facility in learning to read and write: listening and speaking vocabulary and even mastery of syntax set boundaries as to what children can read and understand no matter how well they can decode" (CCSS, 2010).

Using a Reader's Notebook & Writing in Response to Texts

In *Comprehension Clubs*, students use their readers' notebooks to:

- organize and collect their thinking about each book they read
- try multiple forms of writing—everything from open-ended thinking about the text to responding to a teacher-assigned prompt to more formal essay-writing perhaps for assessment purposes

Summarizing the Graham-Perin report *Writing Next* (2007), Shanahan (2012) lists key findings that demonstrate the ways in which writing about text provides students with a way into the text that enables them to crack it open and construct meaning and knowledge in more effective and precise ways than would be possible if they were only reading and rereading the text or reading and discussing it. The benefits of writing about text are both abundant and profound; writing about text:

- encourages deeper thinking about ideas
- requires students to draw on their own knowledge and experience
- helps students to consolidate and review information
- inspires the reformulation of thinking
- requires the organization and integration of ideas
- fosters explicitness
- facilitates reflection
- encourages personal involvement
- requires translation into one's own words

- serve as a memory-jogger and place to record the notes students take during the book club discussions
- to use reading, writing, and discussion to support students' thinking

Lesson cards for book club books offer suggested prompts to focus the observations students record in their notebooks.

Write and Respond prompts on the Read-Aloud lesson cards offer suggestions for students to write in response to the read-aloud book and related discussion.

"When people use their literacy skills to think and rethink their understandings of texts, themselves, and the world, it promotes 'personal empowerment.' It gives importance to individuals and the oral and written texts they create and encounter, and calls upon as well as fosters the kinds of language and thought that mark good and sharp thinking" (Langer & Filhan, 2000).

"Structure writing so students can explore what they think they know and transform invalid first reactions to valid interpretations. Permitting students to respond to fiction and informational texts in this way can help students discover the value of using writing to discover what they think, know, and what is valid" (Robb, 2006).

"Arguments are used for many purposes—to change the reader's point of view, to bring about some action on the reader's part, or to ask the reader to accept the writer's explanation or evaluation of a concept, issue, or problem. An argument is a reasoned, logical way of demonstrating that the writer's position, belief, or conclusion is valid. In English language arts, students make claims about the worth or meaning of a literary work or works. They defend their interpretations or judgments with evidence from the text(s) they are writing about. . . . Although young children are not able to produce fully developed logical arguments, they develop a variety of methods to extend and elaborate their work by providing examples, offering reasons for their assertions, and explaining cause and effect. These kinds of expository structures are steps on the road to argument. In grades K–5, the term 'opinion' is used to refer to this developing form of argument" (CCSS, 2010).

Multitiered Support for Struggling Readers

Comprehension Clubs provides Struggling Readers with Tier I & II support; students:

- engage in extended reading every day—in whole group, small group, and independently; they read their way into proficiency
- benefit from scaffolded instruction—precise, differentiated instruction that addresses each student's unique challenges and needs, and includes vocabulary instruction
- draw from multiple strands of support: audio tapes, rich book conversations with teacher and peers, and access to the full support of integrated language arts: reading, writing, talking, and listening.
- participate in collaborative unit projects with peers

"Contrastive studies of classroom experiences consistently indicate that lower-achieving peers simply read less during the school day than their higher-achieving peers, spending more instructional time on other activities" (Allington, 2012).

The National Assessment of Educational Progress collected surveys that suggested the simplest solution for fostering proficient reading is to encourage and challenge children to read (Hoff & Manzo, 1999).

"Students who struggle greatly to read texts within (or even below) their text complexity grade band must be given the support needed to enable them to read at a grade-appropriate level of complexity" (CCSS, 2010).

Guthrie and Humenick (2004), drawing from a meta-analysis of 22 studies, found that four classroom factors were strongly related to student reading growth: 1) ensuring students had easy access to interesting texts; 2) providing choices for students about what to read; 3) allowing student collaboration during reading and writing; and 4) focusing more on student effort than outcomes (Allington, 2012).

"Using books on tape for struggling readers exposes them to literature above their reading levels. Struggling readers . . . . are often reading different books than their classmates, and these books are not on grade level. Sometimes students reading below grade level want to read the same books as their classmates, but they are not able to. Books on tape can help students to feel self-confident and improve reading skills" (Dill, 2010).

"To change low readers into high readers, the amount of time spent reading must increase. The amount of time [spent] reading does not increase when students are avoiding reading" (Guthrie, 2008).

Support for English Language Learners (ELLs)

In *Comprehension Clubs*, ELLs encounter multiple strands of support that help ELLs read with fluency and comprehension—while helping them build the confidence to handle both; ELLs:

- may read along with an audio tape of the book, learning vocabulary, pronunciation, fluency, expression, and reading at an appropriate rate
- benefit from the scaffolded support which enables them to read more challenging text than they could otherwise handle on their own
- are immersed in rich, meaningful talk about books which provides additional language-learning support
- acquire potentially difficult concepts through thematically related curriculum, which features a range of ideas and perspectives
- have multiple ways to demonstrate their competence, such as acting in a dramatic presentation or designing a multimedia project

Fluency and pace affect comprehension (Rasinski, 2010); reading along with a book on tape creates a winning cycle of support for ELLs.

"Texts that make few assumptions about the extent of readers' life experiences and the depth of their cultural/literary and content/discipline knowledge are generally less complex than are texts that make many assumptions in one or more of those areas" (CCSS, 2010).

"Organizing curriculum around themes is beneficial for all students; however, it is especially important that teachers working with English Language Learners organize their curriculum thematically for these reasons:

- Since students are able to see the 'big conceptual picture,' English instruction is more comprehensible.
- Content areas (math, science, social studies, language arts) are interrelated.
- Vocabulary is repeated naturally as it appears in different content area studies.
- Because the curriculum makes sense, ELLs are more fully engaged and experience more success.
- Teachers can use differential instruction to accommodate differences in language proficiency.
- Through themes, teachers can connect curriculum to students' lives and backgrounds."

(Freeman & Freeman, 2007; Cary, 2007)

"[A] focus on oral language is of greatest importance for the children most at risk—children for whom English is a second language and children who have not been exposed at home to the kind of language found in written texts (Dickinson & Smith, 1994). Ensuring that all children in the United States have access to an excellent education requires that issues of oral language come to the fore in elementary classrooms" (CCSS, 2010).

Extending Learning Through Unit Projects

In *Comprehension Clubs*, students are invited to engage in a deeper investigation of texts and the ideas related to a unit of study; they may:

- use unit projects in this guide for deeper inquiry
- shape their own unit project working independently or collaboratively with a group of their peers
- choose from a range of formats to present their project and learning

"Engaging our students in culminating projects challenges us to consider real world applications for the new knowledge our students have developed, creates real outcomes in the world, and promotes deep cross-disciplinary understandings that extend well beyond what a standardized test can measure" (Wilhelm, 2007).

Cognitive research demonstrates that students learn in ways that last when they are able to connect and integrate ideas and wrestle with authentic, real-world questions and challenges (Bransford, Brown, & Cocking, 1999; diSessa, 2000; Linn & Hsi, 2000).

Research on brain-based teaching explains that the brain learns, and recalls learning, through nonlinear patterns that emphasize coherence rather than fragmentation. The more teachers make connecting patterns explicit and accessible for students, the easier it is for the brain to integrate new information (Hart, 1983; Jensen, 2009; Tomlinson & Edison, 2003).

Media & Technology

Comprehension Clubs includes media and technology for each unit of study.

- Each lesson card includes a link to a relevant website to support research.
- Streaming audio versions of book club titles assures that all students can access text and experience fluent reading.
- Optional writing activities and unit projects include opportunities for online research and presentation.

Students who are college and career ready in reading, writing, speaking, listening, and language:

- demonstrate independence
- build strong content knowledge
- respond to the varying demands of audience, task, purpose, and discipline
- comprehend as well as critique
- value evidence
- use technology and digital media strategically and capably
- come to understand other perspectives and cultures (CCSS, 2010)

The Common Core State Standards include basic technology skills to help students learn across the curriculum. The Common Core view technology as part of the overall learning solution rather than as separate competency (Brock, 2012).

Bibliography

ACT, Inc. (2006). Reading between the lines: What the ACT reveals about college readiness in reading. Iowa City, IA: ACT.

Adams, M. J. (1994). *Beginning to read: Thinking and learning about print.* Cambridge, MA: Bradford Books.

Afflerbach, P. (2007). Understanding and using reading assessment, K–12. Newark, DE: International Reading Association.

Allington, R. (2012). *What really matters for struggling readers:* New York, NY: Pearson.

Allington, R., & Gabriel, R. (2012). Every child, every day. *Educational Leadership, 69*(6), 10–15.

Alvermann, D., Young, J. P., Weaver, D., Hinchman, K. A., Moore, D. W., Phelps, S. F., Thrash, E. C., & Zalewski, P. (1996). Middle and high school students' perceptions of how they experience text-based discussions: A multicase study. *Reading Research Quarterly, 31*(3), 244–267.

America's Promise Alliance (2010). Building a grad nation. Annual Report.

Bank Street College of Education (2010). English language learners. Retrieved from: http://bankstreet.edu/literacy-guide/english-language-learners/

Beck, I., McKeown, M., & Kucan, L. (2002). *Bringing words to life.* New York, NY: The Guilford Press.

Beck, I. L., & McKeown, M. G. (2001). Text talk: Capturing the benefits of read-aloud experiences for young children. The Reading Teacher, 55, 10–20.

Bennett-Armistead, S. (2009). Literacy-building play in preschool. New York, NY: Scholastic.

Bernstein, H. (2010). The importance of reading to your child. A Parent's Life. Harvard School of Medicine/InteliHealth. Retrieved from: http://www.intelihealth.com/IH/ihtIH/WSIHW000/35320/35325/375887.html?d=dmtHMSContent

Berthoff, A. E. (1999). Reclaiming the active mind. *College English.* 61.6 (July). 671–680.

Bettis, P., & Roe, M. F. (2008). Reading girls: Living literate and powerful lives. *Research in Middle Level Education Online, 32*(1) 1–18.

Bransford, J., Brown, A., & Cocking, R. (1999). *How people learn: Brain, mind, experience, and school.* National Research Council. National Academy Press. Washington, DC.

Brock, J. (2012). Common Core technology requirements. Arkansas Dept. of Education.

Burke, J. (2002). Reader's handbook: A student's guide for reading and learning. : Steck-Vaughn.

Calkins, L., Ehrenworth, M., & Lehman, C. (2012). *Pathways to the Common Core: Accelerating achievement.* Portsmouth, NH: Heinemann.

Carlo, M. (2007). Best practices for literacy instruction for English language learners. In L. Gambrell, L. Morrow, & M. Pressley, (Eds.), *Best Practices in Literacy Instruction* (pp. 104–126). New York, NY: The Guilford Press.

Cary, S. (2007). *Working with English language learners: Answers to teachers' top ten questions.* Portsmouth, NH: Heinemann.

Clay, M. (2000). *Concepts about print: What have children learned about printed language?* Portsmouth, NH: Heinemann.

Clay, M. (1991). *Becoming literate: The construction of inner control.* Portsmouth, NH: Heinemann.

Common core state standards for English language arts & literacy in history/social studies, science, and technical subjects (2010). Washington, DC: Common Core Standards Initiative.

Daniels, H. (2002). *Literature circles: Voice and choice in book clubs and reading groups.* Portland, ME: Stenhouse.

Day, J., Spiegel, D. L., McLellan, J., & Brown, V. (2002). *Moving forward with literature circles: How to plan, manage, and evaluate literature circles that deepen understanding and foster a love of reading.* New York, NY: Scholastic.

De Temple, J., & Snow, C. E. (2003). Learning words from books. In A. van Kleeck, S. A. Stahl, & E. B. Bauer (Eds.), *On reading books to children: Parents and teachers* (pp. 16–36). Mahwah, NJ: Erlbaum.

Dickinson, D. K., & Smith, M. W. (1994). Long-term effects of preschool teachers' book readings on low-income children's vocabulary and story comprehension. *Reading Research Quarterly, 29*(2), 104–122.

Dill, M. (2010). How to use free audio books for struggling readers: Retrieved from: http://www.brighthub.com/education/special/articles/44946.aspx

diSessa, A. A. (2000). *Changing minds: Computers, learning, and literacy.* Cambridge, MA: MIT Press.

Duke, N., Caughlan, D., Juzwik, M., & Martin, N. (2012). Reading and writing genre with purpose in K–8 classrooms. Portsmouth, NH: Heinemann.

Duke, N. & Bennett-Armistead, S. (2003). Reading and writing informational text in the primary grades: Research-based practices. New York: Scholastic.

Fisher, D., Frey, N., & Lapp, D. (2012). *Text complexity raising rigor in reading.* Newark, DE: IRA.

Fountas, I., & Pinnell, G. S. (2012a). *Genre study: Teaching with fiction and nonfiction books.* Portsmouth, NH: Heinemann.

Fountas, I., & Pinnell, G. S. (2012b). *The Fountas & Pinnell prompting guide 2, for comprehension: Thinking, talking, and writing.* Portsmouth, NH: Heinemann.

Fountas, I., & Pinnell, G. S. (2012c). *Genre prompting guide for fiction (the genre suite).* Portsmouth, NH: Heinemann.

Fountas, I., & Pinnell, G. S. (2012d). *Genre prompting guide for nonfiction, poetry, and test taking.* Portsmouth, NH: Heinemann.

Fountas, I., & Pinnell, G. S. (2006). *Teaching for comprehending and fluency: Thinking, talking, and writing about reading, K–8.* Portsmouth, NH: Heinemann.

Fox, M., & Wilkinson, L. (1997). No longer travelers in a strange country. *Journal of Children's Literature. 23*(1): 6–15.

Freeman, Y., & Freeman, D. (2007). *English language learners: The essential guide.* New York, NY: Scholastic.

Goldenberg, C. (2011). Reading instruction for English language learners. In Kamil, M., Pearson, D., Moje Birr, E., & Afflerbach, P. (Eds.). *Handbook of Reading Research. Volume IV.* New York, NY: Routledge.

Graham, S., & Hebert, M. (2010). Writing to read: A meta-analysis of the impact of writing and writing instruction on reading. *Harvard Educational Review, 81*(4).

Graham, S., & Perin, D. (2007) Writing next: Effective strategies to improve writing of adolescents in middle and high schools. Report to Carnegie Corporation of New York. New York: Carnegie Corporation of New York.

Guthrie, J. (2008). *Engaging adolescents in reading.* Thousand Oaks, CA: Corwin Press.

Guthrie, J. T., & Humenick, N. M. (2004). Motivating students to read: Evidence for classroom practices that increase reading motivation and achievement. In. P. McCardle & V. Chhabra (Eds.), *The voice of evidence in reading research.* Baltimore, MD: Brookes.

Hansen-Krening, N., & Mizokawa, D. T. (1997). Exploring ethnic-specific literature: A unity of parents, families, and educators. *Journal of Adolescent and Adult Literacy, 41*(3), 187–189.

Hargis, C. (2006). Setting standards: An exercise in futility? *Phi Delta Kappan, 87*(5), 393–395.

Hargrave, A. C., & Sénéchal, M. (2000). A book reading intervention with preschool children who have limited vocabularies: The benefits of regular reading and dialogic reading. *Early Childhood Research Quarterly. Special Issue: Evaluating, interpreting, and debating early interventions: The case of the comprehensive child development program, 15,* 75–90.

Harste, J. C., Woodward, V. A., & Burke, C. L. (1984). Language stories and literacy lessons. Portsmouth, NH: Heinemann.

Hart, L. A. (1983). *Human brain and human learning.* New York: Longman Publishing.

Harwayne, S. (2008). *Look who's learning to read: 50 fun ways to instill a love of reading in young children.* New York, NY: Scholastic.

Hillocks, G. (2010). Teaching argument for critical thinking and writing: An introduction. *English Journal,* 99.6, 24–32.

Hoff, D. J., & Manzo, K. K. (1999). States committed to standards reforms reap NAEP gains. *EdWeek.* 10 March. Available: http://www.edweek.org.

Hunter, P. (2012). *It's not complicated: What I know for sure about helping our students of color become successful readers.* New York, NY: Scholastic.

Jago, C. (2011). *With rigor for all: Meeting Common Core Standards for reading literature, Grades 6–12.* Portsmouth, NH: Heinemann.

Jensen, E. (2009). *Teaching with poverty in mind: What being poor does to kids' brains and what schools can do about it.* Alexandria, VA: ASCD.

Johnston, P. (2009). Afterword. In Nichols, M. (2009). *Expanding comprehension with multigenre text sets.* New York, NY: Scholastic.

Johnston, P. (2004). *Choice words: How our language affects children's learning.* Portland, ME: Stenhouse.

Juel, C. (1988). Learning to read and write: A longitudinal study of 54 children from first through fourth grades. *Journal of Educational Psychology, 80*(4), 437–447.

Kinsella, K. (1994). "What is a cowboy?" Preparing English language learners for a culturally based curriculum. *Ideas for Excellence: Newsletter for Bilingual Education.* Spring.

Klinger, J. K., Vaughn, S., & Schumm, J. S. (1998). Collaborative strategic reading during social studies in heterogeneous fourth-grade classrooms. *Elementary School Journal,* 99, 3–22.

Krashen, S. (2004). *The power of reading: Insights from the research.* Portsmouth, NH: Heinemann.

Landauer, T., & Dumais, S. (1997). A solution to Plato's problem: The latent semantic analysis theory of acquisition, induction, and representation of knowledge. *Psychological Review.* Vol. 104(2), April. 211–240. Retrieved from http://psycnet.apa.org/index.cfm?fa=buy.optionToBuy&id=1997-03612-001

Lane, H., & Wright, T. (2007). Maximizing the effectiveness of the read-aloud. *The Reading Teacher. 60*(7) 668–675.

Langer, J. A., & Filhan, S. (2000). Writing and reading relationships: Constructive tasks. In S. R. Copeland & E. B. Keefe, *Effective literacy instruction for students with moderate or severe disabilities.* Newark, DE: International Reading Association.

Lehman, B., Freeman, E., & Scharer, P. (2010). *Reading globally, K–8: Connecting students to the world through literature.* Thousand Oaks, CA: Corwin.

Linn, M. & Hsi, S. (2000). *Computers, teachers, peers.* Mahwah, NJ: Erlbaum.

Neuman, S., & Dickinson, D., Editors. (2001). *The handbook of early literacy research.* New York, NY: The Guilford Press.

Nichols, M. (2009). *Expanding comprehension with multigenre text sets.* New York, NY: Scholastic.

Noll, E. (June, 1998). Experiencing literacy in and out of school: Case studies of two American Indian youths. *Journal of Literacy Research. 30*(2), 205–232.

Pimentel, S. (2012) *What's in and what's out for ELA materials?* [PowerPoint slides]. Retrieved from http://scholasticadministrator.typepad.com/files/120628_publishers-criteria-convening_literacy.pdf

Pinnell, G. S., & Fountas, I. (2009). *When readers struggle: Teaching that works.* Portsmouth, NH: Heinemann.

Pressley, M. (2006). *Reading instruction that really works* (3rd ed.). New York, NY: The Guilford Press.

Purcell-Gates, V., Duke, N., & McIntyre, J. A. (2001). Learning to read and write genre-specific text: Roles of authentic experience and explicit teaching. *Reading Research Quarterly, 42*(1).

Rasinski, T. (2010). *The fluent reader (2nd Edition): Oral & silent reading strategies for building fluency, word recognition & comprehension.* New York, NY: Scholastic.

Robb, L. (2006). *Teaching reading: A complete resource, Grades 4–up.* New York, NY: Scholastic.

Schlick Noe, K. (2004). Literature circles resource center. Retrieved from http://www.litcircles.org/resources.html

Schlick Noe, K., & Johnson, N. (1999). *Getting started with literature circles.* Norwood, MA: Christopher-Gordon Publishers.

Serafini, F. (2009). *Interactive comprehension strategies: Fostering meaningful talk about text.* New York, NY: Scholastic.

Serravallo, J. (2012). *Independent reading assessment.* New York, NY: Scholastic.

Shanahan, T. (2012). What is close reading? *Shanahan on Literacy.* Retrieved from http://www.shanahanonliteracy.com/

Snow, C., Burns, S., & Griffin, P. (Eds). (1998). *Preventing reading difficulties in young children.* Washington, DC: National Academy Press, 314.

Tatum, A. P. (2013). *Fearless voices: Engaging a new generation of African American adolescent writers.* New York, NY: Scholastic.

Tomlinson, C., & Edison, C. (2003). *Differentiation in practice: A resource guide for differentiated curriculum (grades K–5/5–9).* Alexandria, VA: Association for Supervision and Curriculum Development.

Toulmin, S.E. (1958). The uses of argument. Cambridge, UK: Cambridge University Press.

Van den Broek, P. (1997). Discovering the cements of the universe: The development of event comprehension from childhood to adulthood. In P. van den Broek, P. Bauer, & T. Bourg (Eds.), *Developmental spans in event comprehension: Bridging fictional and actual events.* Mahwah, NJ: Erlbaum.

Wasik, B., Bond, M. A., & Hindman, A. (2006). The effects of a language and literacy intervention on Head Start children and teachers. *Journal of Educational Psychology, 98*(1), 63–74.

Whitehurst, G., Falco F. L., Longian, C., Fischel, J. E., DeBarsyshe, B. D., Valdez-Menchaca, M. C., & Caufield, M. B. (1988). Accelerating language development through picture-book reading. *Developmental Psychology, 24*, 552–559.

Wilhelm, J. (2007). Engaging readers & writers with inquiry. New York, NY: Scholastic.